LOVE BY DESIGN

The Art of Dating, Loving Well, and Becoming a Godly Woman!

Aimee Simmons

DEDICATED TO MY "LITTLE SISTERS"—

Lindsay Autrey, Rachel Baker, Rachel Davis, Kathryn Forney, Lindsay Gaskins, Sarah German, Allie Gronewold, Haley Hetrick, Michaela Randolph, Jackie Taylor, and Maggie Webb. It was a privilege to disciple you as young girls. You taught me more about God's love than you'll ever know, and you'll always hold a special place in my heart!

IN LOVING MEMORY OF KAITLIN FOWLER,

another "Little Sister," who showed me the beauty of surrendering to God and living boldly for Him no matter what obstacles stand in the way. After suffering her whole life with Cystic Fibrosis, Kaitlin kissed this world goodbye in 2014 and is now with Jesus, living and breathing freely! Kaitlin shared her story in this book! You'll find her honest and wise words in Reading 38.

A Different Kind of Book...by Design!

Love by Design is for young women who desire to honor God in dating, marriage, and everyday life! It can be used as...

> a devotional book for individuals
> a book with built-in study guide to go through with a mentor or friend
> a small group study or discipleship curriculum

Love by Design is divided into 55 Readings and takes you on an interactive, creative journey through God's Word to discover the art of dating, loving well, and becoming a godly woman!

True Stories!

All of the stories shared in the book are true! It doesn't matter if you have little or no experience in dating because real-life stories create the scenarios for discussion. *Love by Design* is designed for young women in their teens and twenties. If you are age 13-15, you'll benefit most by going through the book with a parent, mentor, or small group.

Discipleship-Focused Questions

You will discover how to apply God's Word in your life. As you journey through the book, you'll design a thoughtful plan for how to approach dating, or to how to reset your dating life, to glorify God.

Written Prayers guide you in how to apply God's Word when you pray.

Creative Challenges provide opportunities to creatively express what you're learning through paintings, drawings, written stories, videos, songs, or dances. When posting your creations on your social media accounts, use hashtags #LovebyDesignBook and #AimforHim, and tag @AimforHimblog.

Suggested Supplies:

For answering application questions:
- PAPERBACK version—colored pens
- KINDLE version—artist's sketchbook or pretty journal; colored pens

For Creative Challenges:
- PAPERBACK and KINDLE—small to medium-sized artist's canvas or sketchbook; colored pens, markers, or paint set/paintbrush

Continue the Conversation!

You'll find Aimee at **AimeeSimmons.com**, home of *Aim for Him* blog.
Follow Aimee @AimforHimblog on Instagram, Facebook, and Pinterest!

Reading Plans

Whether you go through the book individually or as part of a small group, it's important to find a reading schedule that is realistic and allows enough time to read, think, answer application questions, and participate in the Creative Challenges. It's more important to take your time and get the most out of each reading than it is to finish the book quickly. Here are some Reading Plans to choose from:

PLAN A **Complete 2 Readings per week for 27 weeks**	**PLAN B** **Complete 3 Readings per week for 18 weeks**	**PLAN C** **Complete 4 Readings per week for 15 weeks**	**PLAN D** **Complete 6 Readings per week for 10 weeks**
Week 1: Readings 1-2	Week 1: Readings 1-3	*Week 1: Readings 1-2	*Week 1: Readings 1-4
Wk 2: Readings 3-4	Wk 2: Readings 4-6	Wk 2: Readings 3-6	Wk 2: Readings 5-10
Wk 3: Readings 5-6	Wk 3: Readings 7-9	Wk 3: Readings 7-10	Wk 3: Readings 11-16
Wk 4: Readings 7-8	Wk 4: Readings 10-12	Wk 4: Readings 11-14	Wk 4: Readings 17-22
Wk 5: Readings 9-10	Wk 5: Readings 13-15	Wk 5: Readings 15-18	Wk 5: Readings 23-28
Wk 6: Readings 11-12	Wk 6: Readings 16-18	Wk 6: Readings 19-22	Wk 6: Readings 29-34
Wk 7: Readings 13-14	Wk 7: Readings 19-21	Wk 7: Readings 23-26	*Wk 7: Readings 35-39
Wk 8: Readings 15-16	Wk 8: Readings 22-24	Wk 8: Readings 27-30	Wk 8: Readings 40-45
Wk 9: Readings 17-18	Wk 9: Readings 25-27	Wk 9: Readings 31-34	*Wk 9: Readings 46-49
Wk 10: Readings 19-20	Wk 10: Readings 28-30	Wk 10: Readings 35-38	Wk 10: Readings 50-55
Wk 11: Readings 21-22	Wk 11: Readings 31-33	Wk 11: Readings 39-42	
Wk 12: Readings 23-24	*Wk 12: Readings 34-37	*Wk 12: Readings 43-45	
Wk 13: Readings 25-26	Wk 13: Readings 38-40	*Wk 13: Readings 46-48	
Wk 14: Readings 27-28	Wk 14: Readings 41-43	Wk 14: Readings 49-52	
Wk 15: Readings 29-30	Wk 15: Readings 44-46	*Wk 15: Readings 53-55	
Wk 16: Readings 31-32	Wk 16: Readings 47-49		
Wk 17: Readings 33-34	Wk 17: Readings 50-52		
*Wk 18: Readings 35-37	Wk 18: Readings 53-55		
Wk 19: Readings 38-39			
Wk 20: Readings 40-41			
Wk 21: Readings 42-43			
Wk 22: Readings 44-45			
Wk 23: Readings 46-47			
Wk 24: Readings 48-49			
Wk 25: Readings 50-51			
Wk 26: Readings 52-53			
Wk 27: Readings 54-55			

*May contain more or less readings than the standard due to topic.

Introduction

As I led a group of young women through *Love by Design,* one of them jokingly commented, "Wow, Aimee! We're learning a LOT about you." Then, she added, "Thanks for being so honest."

I'm pretty much an open book in this context! I'll share some things about my journey in dating and singleness that will make you laugh. I'll share things that will stir up some sadness. I'll share things that will make you think. I'll share things that will encourage you to dream! I'll share things that may surprise you. I'll share things that will inspire you! I'll share some embarrassing and unwise things I did because I want you to be better than me! Do I enjoy sharing my mistakes? Um, no, but the way I see it, sharing my mistakes may help you make better choices. I'll share things God helped me get right. Some of my friends will share their redemptive stories, too! I'll share a lot from the Bible, which will guide us and reveal God's heart for us every step of the way!

It's going to be an incredible journey—a journey with Jesus, me, my friends, and the friends in your small group who go through the book with you!

It only seems fitting to start this journey with a confession: I played with Barbie dolls until I was 13. I used to feel embarrassed about that because I gave up Barbies long after my friends did.

Barbies were my favorite toy growing up. My final count was nine Barbies, three Kens, one Skipper, and one whatever Skipper's boyfriend was named. I created Barbie storylines that took hours to play out. There were swim parties at the Barbie pool, birthday parties at her mansion, fashion shows, and Barbie concerts. The biggest storyline was the triple wedding where three Barbie-Ken couples got married! I thought of every detail, from live music to a "Just Married" sign and dangling toy cans on the back of Barbie's pink Corvette. Trust me, it was a fairytale wedding. I even took pictures of it.

I gave up playing with Barbies because my friends started playing with boys. My friends talked about boys. ALL THE TIME. They started wearing makeup, dressing in shorter skirts, and confessing crushes in notes passed back and forth between classes. Some had boyfriends and bragged about kissing them and sneaking out at night to meet them. This drastic change in my friends seemed to happen overnight.

If I didn't start talking and acting like my friends, I feared I wouldn't have any friends. I also figured it might be time to grow up, and giving up Barbie dolls seemed like a good first step toward adulthood!

I began playing the game and acting like I was crushing on guys like everyone else. Sure, I thought some guys were cute, but I would have been happier playing with Barbie dolls.

I started dating when I was 16 and quickly learned that it's not as easy as it seems. All the conversations with my friends and the few lessons about anatomy and sex in middle school health class didn't help me one bit with the basic emotional, spiritual, and physical aspects of guy-girl relationships. I entered dating with all of its adult-sized scenarios and put-your-heart-and-life-on-the-line decisions and stumbled my way through it. Event planning for Barbie dolls was WAY easier.

I basically went from playing Barbies to dating boys. Think about that.

Later when I worked on staff in Student Ministry at my church, I discipled and counseled many young women whose moms made great efforts to prepare them for dating. The moms planned mother-daughter weekends away and led their daughters through a curriculum. The majority of the young women walked away with a good understanding of God's plan for marriage, but they didn't know how to practically maneuver basic dating decisions and situations.

They desired to obey God and not have sex until marriage, but most couldn't articulate why they believed in waiting until marriage and had little to no real conviction about their decisions. Many believed that as long as they dated a boy who was a Christian, they would always be treated well and wouldn't have to guard their purity. When it comes to dating, that is dangerous thinking that will lead you to learn lessons the hard way.

If dating leads to marriage, which God designed to be a lifelong commitment, have you ever wondered why we don't spend more time preparing for dating?

Think about the things in life we prepare for:

We prepare for the first day of school or work.
We study for tests.
We practice for dance performances.
We practice for musical performances.
We practice for sports games.
We practice for plays.
We practice driving before we get our driver's license.
We prepare for college and careers.
We practice for graduation ceremonies.
We schedule premarital counseling to prepare for marriage.
We even practice walking down the aisle for the wedding.

That's just off the top of my head.

Do you want to know more about love, dating, and marriage, but you don't know what questions to ask?

Are there questions you have about love, dating, and marriage, but you wish someone else would start the conversation?

Do you desire to understand how to apply God's Word in dating decisions and situations?

Have you made mistakes in dating relationships and long to find forgiveness and move forward?

Do you desire to grow as a godly woman and enjoy the benefits of singleness?

This journey will help you discover answers to your questions and to the questions you didn't know you needed to ask. If you have little or no experience in dating, you can get just as much out of the book as someone who has dated a lot. True stories shared throughout the book create the scenarios for discussion. God's Word creates our path.

Along the way, you'll discover the intentionality of how God designed man, woman, love, marriage, sex, and the Bible. You'll discover how He wove you together with Powerful PURPOSE, Beautiful DESIGN, and World-Changing POTENTIAL. You'll also learn about grace, fellowship with Jesus, leadership, good communication in relationships, guarding your heart and mind, boundaries, and making wise decisions.

By the end of the journey, you will have a thoughtful plan for how to approach dating, or how to reset your dating life, to glorify God more. No matter how "good" or how "bad" your story may seem, Jesus can bless your story. He said, "I came that they may have life and have it abundantly" (John 10:10). Your story can unfold into abundant life!

I lived out many storylines in dating, many of which I would have never written for myself. My mentor, Carolyn, and my good friend, Cheryl, stuck with me through the dramas and traumas of dating in my 20s. They seriously deserve medals. I remember one particular lunch with them when Carolyn made a surprising suggestion, "You should write a book. You've been through so much in dating, and you have unique insights that could help others."

Lunch with Carolyn and Cheryl was the first time the idea of writing a book came up, and God eventually grew the idea into a heart desire. In the early days of writing the book, I sensed God whispering, *This book is for your healing.* As I wrote the book, I would often cry. You see, my story has some sad chapters. Allowing the stories to pour out of my heart and onto the Word document caused pain and sadness within me to surface.

After a few years of writing, I pushed the book aside for almost a decade! During that time, God brought healing to my heart's hurts and took my relationship with Jesus to a whole new level. He began using what I had been through to help other women, and I experienced His redemption in a new light. He taught me that our experiences don't define who we are, but they serve a redemptive purpose—to teach us how to glorify God and help others know Him.

I tried to forget the book, but God wouldn't allow me to let it go. When I returned to the book, I rewrote almost all of it. I shared with new boldness. I shared the things I wish someone had shared with me. I would often cry at the end of writing sessions. This time as I recalled the painful things I've been through, I remembered how God helped me through it all. His love conquers ALL. I know with all my heart it does.

God has met me in these pages over and over again. Literally. I don't believe God led you to this book by chance. Everything God does is by design. Seek Him with all of your heart, mind, and soul, and I have no doubt that you'll find Him! This journey is really your journey with God. It's a journey filled with grace. A journey of redemption. True love. New beginnings. Hope. Freedom. Peace. Joy. A journey I can't wait for you to experience!

I hope you'll stay in touch! I'd love to know where your travels with God take you!

Much love! Keep aiming for Him!
Aimee

www.AimeeSimmons.com
Follow @aimforhimblog on Instagram, Facebook, and Pinterest

Writer's Note: Many years ago, I read a book in which the author named satan with a lowercase "s" as a reminder that God is greater than His enemy. Because that had a big impact on me as I read the book, I decided to adopt it in this book.

Contents

1 – What is Your Plan? 3

2 – What is Your Story? 7

3 - Not Matching Up 11

4 - A Higher Vision 13

5 - Devastated 17

6 - Surrender 21

7 - First Brushstroke 24

8 - Perspective 27

9 - Very Good 30

10 - Defined by God 33

11 - United as One 37

12 - Love, Respect, Honor 40

13 - Say Goodbye 44

14 - Wounded 48

15 - Bitter Aftertaste 52

16 - Rotten Apple 55

17 - Eve's Footsteps 59

18 - Life Lessons 62

19 - Our Perfect Path 66

20 - His Resurrection Power...69

21 - Heavenly Husband 73

22 - Sharing His Life...76

23 - Godly Husband..80

24 - Godly Wife 84

25 - Help or Hinder? 88

26 - Read My Lips 91

27 - This Thing Called Love 95

28 - What's Next?...99

29 - God's View of Sex..102

30 - Good and Perfect Gift....................................105

32 - Step into Their Shoes.....................................113

33 - Rebecca's Story...117

34 - Katie's Story...120

35 - Lynne's Story..123

36 - Sarah's Story...126

37 - Sarah's Story, Part 2.......................................129

38 - God's Children..132

39 - Pure Potential...136

40 - Think Purity...140

42 - Started with A Kiss..148

43 - Becoming A Blessing......................................152

44 - Just Friends..156

45 - Emotionally Healthy.......................................160

46 - Heart-Attack Relationship................................164

47 - The List...168

48 - Boundaries...172

49 - Communicating Boundaries..............................176

50 - Social Share or Strike?....................................180

51 - Your Heart's Song..185

53 - Butterflies..193

54 - I Belong to Him!...197

55 - Heart Treasures...201

1 – What is Your Plan?

As a 15-year-old girl, dating was a new, white canvas ready for me to record on it the multi-colored pursuits of life, love, and happiness. I anxiously awaited an opportunity to dab my paintbrush in the palette of many colors and begin filling that canvas. What vibrant, joyfully intricate designs would find a place on my canvas? What sorrowful brushstrokes would fill pure, white spaces with darkness?

I could have never anticipated the joys and sorrows that would fill my canvas. I could have never envisioned that God would one day lead me to share my experiences—the good and the bad—in a book for others to read. I didn't even know God at age 15! Sharing my canvas with others was NOT part of *My Plan*. You know—THE PLAN. Every girl has one.

My Plan included being happily married by age 26. When I turned 26 and wasn't married, I decided 27 would be a fine age to marry. When my 27th birthday came and a husband was not one of my birthday presents, I decided that I just wanted to get married before my hair turned gray, I lost my figure, and got bags under my eyes!

I waited for a husband to come along…and waited…and waited…and waited some more. It felt like I spent the first decade of my adulthood celebrating *everyone else's plans* coming true. One year I was invited to 12 weddings. Do the math. That's an average of one wedding every month for a year, plus wedding showers, bridesmaids' luncheons, and bachelorette parties. I've always enjoyed a good party, but after hearing the same songs, seeing the same decorations, and tasting the same hors d'oeuvres at wedding after wedding, month after month, year after year, those truly joyous events evolved into sobering reminders that I was still waiting. My canvas was still a work in progress.

I was sincerely happy my friends had found love, yet the unfulfilled longing in my heart to know love made every wedding feel bittersweet. I would have been fine if I could have attended weddings and simply celebrated my friends' happiness. Yet, the traditional wedding celebration includes an element that always forced me to look at myself and remember I was still waiting for my canvas to be completed. What is that element?

It's the bouquet toss.

It was fun to participate in bouquet tosses during my teenage years and into my early 20s when my chances of falling in love were optimal and my hopes were high. In my mid-20s, I noticed something different about the bouquet toss. Because most of my friends had gotten married, participating in this wedding tradition meant that my 25-year-old-self stood in a group primarily made up of teenage girls! Even worse, the brides throwing the bouquets were usually younger than me! So much for staying focused on my friends' happiness; all I could think about was how awkward I felt!

I knew the brides who tossed their flowers were doing it for the sake of tradition or simply for fun. I questioned why bouquet tosses no longer seemed fun to me. Though I was probably over-analyzing it, stick with me! I realized that I was in a season where I was learning about what it meant to be a woman after God's heart. I had participated in several Bible studies, all of which explored the *Proverbs 31 Woman,* the Bible's best description of a godly woman.

Check out how a godly woman is described in Proverbs 31:
(v. 10) "She is far more precious than jewels."
(v. 20) "She opens her hand to the poor and reaches out her hands to the needy."
(v. 25) "Strength and dignity are her clothing, and she laughs at the days to come."
(v. 30) "Charm is deceitful, and beauty is vain, but a woman who fears the Lord is to be praised."

Good stuff, right? The image of the *Proverbs 31 Woman* doesn't match up with the image of ladies at a bouquet toss. Think about it. All the single ladies, who show up for an elegant wedding celebration in their prettiest dresses and showing off their best manners, are led to gather like a bunch of groupies at a rock concert. Why do they gather? They jump, leap, grab, snatch—whatever it takes—to catch the destiny of being the next to marry. It all seemed more desperate than dignified.

I remember weddings where I tried to blend into the crowd unseen during the bouquet toss. Then, a so-called friend would yell out, "Where's Aimee? She's single!" I would attempt to escape the embarrassment only to have someone drag me by the arm to the very front of the group of single ladies, who had been in position for minutes. Not only did I get a good "spot," but I also became the center of attention as ALL the wedding guests (including cute, single guys) witnessed my public humiliation.

Why did my friends do this to me? Some did it for their own entertainment. Most did it so I could have the "wonderful" opportunity to catch some beautiful flowers that would inevitably wilt and die and contribute nothing to my getting married. I actually caught the bouquet once. The next guy I dated turned out to be the worst boyfriend I ever had, and I'm sure many of the single ladies who participated in that particular bouquet toss married long before I even had a prospect. To me, bouquet tosses seemed demeaning and unnecessary. After all, I bought nice presents for the brides. The least they could have done was let me enjoy their celebrations, and let me keep my dignity intact!

After enduring years of miserable bouquet toss experiences, I began to question, "God, have you forgotten *My* Plan?" I didn't think I was expecting too much by desiring to be married by 26. After all, most girls are dying to get married much earlier. Some say that in college, the cards are stacked in one's favor to find a spouse more than any other time in life. During college, I was involved in the Wesley Foundation, a campus ministry through which I came to know Jesus. During my time at Wesley, I dated two godly men, but neither relationship led to marriage. There were only a handful of Wesleyans who didn't meet a life partner through the campus ministry, and I was dealt the losing hand.

At 25, I grew a little antsy about being single. At the time, I was attending a church Sunday School class for young singles. Only a few people in the class were dating until Cupid suddenly appeared out of nowhere with a bag full of arrows ready to devastate the singles' group with weapons of mass matchmaking destruction. There were many casualties from Cupid's lovefare. Over the course of a year, over a dozen couples dated and announced their engagements. While Cupid's arrows were flying around, I began dating a guy in the group. Apparently, we were not on Cupid's Hit List; we broke up! I later changed churches, and before long, Cupid appeared again. Several of my friends married, while I dated and lived through one breakup after another. I saw the effects of Cupid's work many times, but in all those years, somehow missed his heart-gripping arrows.

When it comes to dating, that's my story in a nutshell. Year after year, I watched my friends fall in love, marry, leave the singles' group to join the newlyweds' group, and have babies. My friends' lives changed while I continued dating and wondering if I'd ever fall in love.

One day I did fall in love—deeply in love. It was quite an amazing journey that I look forward to sharing with you in the days to come. What transpired in my life did not go as I planned. "The heart of man plans his way, but the LORD establishes his steps" (Proverbs 16:9). My life followed *God's Plan.* My canvas was hand-painted by God, and it turned out to be more beautiful than I ever could have imagined.

Your canvas was meant to be a breathtaking work of art, painted by a God who loves and delights in you. "But, as it is written, 'What no eye has seen, nor ear heard, nor the heart of man imagined, what God has prepared for those who love him'" (1 Corinthians 2:9).

Think about it!

What is *Your Plan?* You may be a young lady excitedly awaiting your first date or a lady who has dated many years. Whether your canvas has many brushstrokes, just a few, or none yet, you have a plan. You may have this "love thing" all planned out, or you may have just begun to think about it. Take some time to explore the hopes and dreams bouncing around in your heart.

Draw *Your Plan,* or put it into words. Bring to life only the hopes, dreams, and expectations that already exist in your heart. There's no need to develop *Your Plan* for the sake of this activity. If you have only a few hopes and dreams in your mind, that is perfectly fine. It is *Your Plan,* so enjoy illustrating and writing where you are today in your pursuit of life, love, and happiness! Some questions are included to help guide you as you put *Your Plan* into drawings and words:

Master Plan
This is your master plan for the future. What age do you see yourself getting married? How long will you date before getting engaged? How many children do you want?

Plan for a Man

What character traits do you want in the man you marry? What will his personality be like? What will he look like in appearance? Will your groom be older or younger than you?

Wedding Plans

Where do you want to get married? What time of year do you want to get married? What will your dress look like? What colors would you like to use in your wedding? Which friends will you choose as bridesmaids? What will your wedding ceremony be like? What will your reception be like?

Pray about it!

Dear God,
I have no idea what you have prepared for me when it comes to love and marriage, but I sure want to know!

God, let this book be more than just a book I read or rush to complete. When I open these pages, open my heart and mind, as well. Help me to break away from the distractions of each day, settle any anxious thoughts bouncing around in my head, quiet my heart, and let me experience peace in Your presence. Reveal Yourself to me! I pray that You would use this book in my life to…(insert your hopes). In Jesus' Name I pray, Amen.

2 – What is Your Story?

The pursuit of life, love, and happiness is filled with ups and downs, twists and turns. No matter what her age, and no matter how much or little she has dated, every lady has a story. The following are true stories of ladies, ranging in age from 13 to 30. While their names have been changed, they are real people with real thoughts, feelings, and desires. As you read about them, see if their stories have any similarities to Your Story.

Ashlyn anxiously awaited the day her parents would allow her to start dating. When asked why she was looking forward to dating, she replied, "I don't know–I just think it will be fun." She asked me a lot of questions such as, "What is it like to kiss a boy?" and "How far is too far (to go physically)?"

Jen was a strong Christian who was always sharing her faith and could be counted on as a prayer warrior. She was a beautiful lady—inside and out—yet she had only been on a handful of dates. I was never a big fan of matchmaking, but I wanted Jen to meet one of my guy friends. They had a lot in common and were both great people, so I thought they would enjoy getting to know each other. I asked Jen if she preferred meeting my friend in a casual, no-pressure setting or on a double date with my boyfriend and me. In her boisterous voice she answered excitedly, "He might not notice me in a group. I want a date!"

Christy was flattered and taken a little off guard when Andy, a friend of hers at school, asked if she would be his girlfriend. Christy thought Andy was sort of cute and really enjoyed being around him. It seemed like a no-brainer to tell Andy, "Yes." That evening, she felt confused and questioned what her decision meant.

Kimmie had a lot of close guy friends. She spent more time with the guys than she did with the girls. She enjoyed the company of her guy pals and stated, "We're just good friends." Kimmie talked about personal things with her guy friends. For example, Mitch shared with Kimmie that he was interested in a "girl who was pretty and lots of fun to be around" and asked if she thought he should ask the girl out. Kimmie encouraged him to ask out the anonymous girl. When Mitch asked out Kimmie's friend, Dayna, Kimmie felt shocked, disappointed, and hurt.

Rachel felt extremely discouraged when her last dating relationship ended. "I don't care anything about dating right now," she remarked. A few weeks later, a guy from church took her out on several dates. When Rachel and I talked, she expressed many fears and hesitations about getting involved in a serious relationship, and she questioned whether she was ready to begin dating again. Two weeks later, the guy from church told Rachel that he wanted to date her seriously. The rest was history. Rachel and her boyfriend texted each other sappy, sweet messages, talked on their cell phones numerous times a day, and spent several evenings a week together…until three months later when they broke up.

Mackenzie went to a party and struck up a conversation with a girl from another school. They had a lot in common and spent a long time talking. Mackenzie was taken off guard when her new friend leaned in to kiss her, but she kissed back. It felt kind of wrong and kind of nice all at the same time. It also felt confusing. She wondered if she should kiss a girl again.

Susan had a happily married friend who met her husband through an online dating service. Inspired by her friend's story, Susan took the leap and signed up with the same service. After completing the preliminary questionnaires, the result was one compatible match. Over time, Susan and her "match" began a relationship, spending time together every weekend. Though very cautious, she felt hopeful because Dan displayed strong character, he treated her respectfully, and they had many common interests.

Becky dated a guy who constantly found fault with things she said and did. Her parents and her friends noticed a drastic change in her shortly after she started dating him and became very concerned about her. They commented that she wasn't the same "happy Becky" they knew. Becky admitted that she was not happy in the relationship but held on to the hope that things would get better one day.

Robin had been on lots of dates and involved in several serious dating relationships. She dated one guy for four years. When the relationship ended, she felt weary and discouraged. Robin invested so much in the relationship and couldn't imagine what it would be like to start all over in building a relationship with a new guy. Even as she shed tears over the pain and loss of her last relationship, she told friends, "I find myself drawn to Mark (a new guy who was showing interest in her). My heart comes alive every time I see him, and I can't control the bigness of my smile to save my life."

Emma and Will had been flirting with each other for a while. Flirty glances across the classroom turned into text messages. Emma could barely carry on a face-to-face conversation with Will without being overwhelmed with shyness and tongue-tied. She felt rare confidence with her cell phone in hand. Emma could type a text in seconds without all the awkwardness. Their flirtatious texting grew into seductive proposals, and she interpreted Will's sexting with hopeful anticipation. She texted Will a picture of herself undressed and checked her cell phone every minute to see if Will had texted back a response.

Summer wanted to save herself for her husband. She and Ryan had been girlfriend and boyfriend a couple of months when he hinted that he would like oral sex. She fulfilled his request, thinking it was a win-win for both of them. She knew guys had needs. She also believed that oral sex was not "real" sex and that she could meet Ryan's needs without compromising her standards or endangering her health.

Shay frequented a popular teen hangout on the weekends. She met a guy there that she liked. Because he was four years older, she lied and told him she was 19. She did some sneaky things to spend time with him alone. She explored the physical side of being in a relationship. Ten years later, at age 25, Shay has had lots of relationships and has had sex with almost every guy she's dated.

Lori graduated from college and began attending a church singles' group. She stayed involved in that singles' group for many years. During that time, her closest friends married. She eventually became one of the oldest members of the singles' group. Not only was she an inspiration to me, women and men of all ages in our church had tremendous respect for her and viewed as a leader. During her time in the singles' group, she discipled numerous young ladies and was a bridesmaid in most of their weddings. She saw many women come and go while her wait for God's best continued.

Think about it!

1—Can you relate to any of the girls above? Who are you like, and what do you have in common with her?

2—In a few sentences, summarize *Your Story* up to this chapter in your life.

3—As you put *Your Story* into words, what emotions stirred within your heart?

Pray about it!

"I came that they may have life and have it abundantly." –John 10:10b

"No, in all these things we are more than conquerors through him who loved us. For I am sure that neither death nor life, nor angels nor rulers, nor things present nor things to come, nor powers, nor height nor depth, nor anything else in all creation, will be able to separate us from the love of God in Christ Jesus our Lord." –Romans 8:37-39

Dear God,

Help me to believe and receive Your promise of abundant life. You have promised that nothing will separate me from Your Love–not death nor life, not angels nor rulers, not things present nor things to come, not powers, not height nor depth, not anything in all creation. God, I fear that the following might separate me from Your Love: (insert your fears)

Replace that fear with faith in You and Your promise. Make me more than a conqueror through Jesus. Thank You for sending Jesus! In Jesus' Name, Amen.

3 - Not Matching Up

Over the past two days, you have spent time describing Your Plan and Your Story. Your Plan reflects your desires and expectations. Your Plan is what you hope will happen, while Your Story is what has actually happened up to this point in your life. How has Your Story matched up to Your Plan so far?

Every lady will experience chapters in her story that are pivotal, shaping who she is and marking a turning point in her life. The following was a pivotal chapter in *My Story*:

A small group of friends from my singles' group met weekly to go through the Bible study, *Becoming a Woman of Excellence* by Cynthia Heald. The focus of the study was to discover God's perspective on our lives and relationships. My friend, Liz, led the group. Liz became a Christian at an early age. She came from a well-respected Christian family, had an established career, and was outgoing, smart, pretty, and sweet. She had lots of friends and was actively involved in ministry to others. Successful and confident, Liz seemed to have her life together while the rest of us were seeking to understand how all of the pieces of our lives fit together.

Liz was very knowledgeable about the Bible and was a great teacher. I had only been a Christian for a few years, and I learned a lot from her. The time I spent in that Bible study group was extremely impactful. There was one meeting I will never forget.

As the group meeting was drawing to a close, we began sharing our prayer requests. When it was Liz's turn to share, she broke down crying. It wasn't unusual for the rest of us to get teary-eyed or cry as we shared things close to our hearts, but it was out of character for Liz. We were all taken by surprise by her tears. You could have heard a pin drop in the room as we focused all of our attention on her.

She told us her 29th birthday was approaching. She shared that she greatly desired to get married and have children but feared she would turn 30 and still be single or never marry. Then she began weeping. *WHOA! Her Plan* was NOT matching up with God's Plan. *Uh-oh.*

I had always heard that as many single ladies approach their thirties, they worry that they have lost their chance to marry. Anxiousness can set in as they realize they are growing older and their biological clocks are ticking—with no prospects of marriage in sight. Many ladies fear they will never realize their dreams of becoming wives, mothers, and grandmothers.

My friend's tearful honesty gave me a lot to ponder. Although I was only 24 at the time and my 30th birthday seemed a long way off, I realized I might end up in Liz's shoes one day. I asked myself, "What if God's Plan is for me to be single when I turn 30?" If that was His Plan for me, then I decided that I didn't want to cry on my 30th birthday over being single nor on any other birthdays for that matter. As I prayed for Liz to find comfort and satisfaction in Jesus, I asked the Lord to help me do the same.

Think about it!

1—What if God's Plan is for you to be single on your 30th birthday? Would you be okay with that? Why or why not?

2—Look up Jeremiah 29:11, and seek to better understand this verse by using a dictionary like dictionary.com to define the following words:

Plans -

Welfare -

Evil -

Future -

Hope -

3—Jeremiah 29:11 is God's promise to you. What does this promise reveal about God?

Pray about it!

Dear God,
Thank You for thinking of me. Your promise in Jeremiah 29:11 reveals that I am not forgotten nor abandoned. I am on Your mind. My Plans may not match Your Plans for my life. Yet, I know that You have a prosperous, hope-filled future planned out for me. Prepare my heart to embrace Your Plans and to fully experience and enjoy the blessing of my future when it comes to fruition. In Jesus' Name, Amen.

4 - A Higher Vision

A s a 24-year-old woman, there were a few things I knew for certain. I didn't want to be single on my 30th birthday. If I was single on my 30th birthday, I didn't want to cry about it. Whether I was single or not on my 30th birthday rested in God's hands. God had a Plan for me; I just didn't know all the details of His Plan. I was single at that very moment because that was God's Plan for me. Was I happy with that Plan? Uh—not so much. If I wasn't happy about being single at 24, then I wouldn't be happy being single at 30. Whatever the day, whatever my circumstances, I knew I must learn to be...(drum roll please)...content.

Content—adj. satisfied with what one is or has; not wanting more or anything else.[1]

On a scale of 1-10, how content would you say you are with God's Plan for your love life?
1 = Am I content? That would be a BIG, fat, "NO!"
5 = I've got one foot in God's Plan and the other foot in My Plan.
10 = I'm so content I could teach a class about it! (In other words, you are embracing and rejoicing in God's Plan!)

Being content is a concept that can radically impact every person, single or married, young or old. It is a concept that opens our eyes to a whole new way of looking at the world, empowers us to face trials victoriously, and escorts us into deep enjoyment of God. The Apostle Paul talked about being content in the Bible book of Philippians.

About Paul

If you are not familiar with Paul, he was an intriguing man. Originally named Saul, he was a prominent and fierce persecutor of Christians. Saul was about to thwart the efforts of missionaries to spread the gospel of Christ when the biggest shock of his life occurred: He saw a brilliant light all around and fell to the ground terrified. Next, Jesus appeared and spoke to him! Saul believed in Jesus as his Lord and Savior and was baptized. God changed his name from Saul to Paul, symbolizing that the old man and old beliefs were gone. Paul became a new man in Christ with new beliefs. After years of devout study, he eventually became one of the most passionate, boldest preachers of the gospel. He traveled on several missionary journeys and planted many churches, including one in Philippi. Paul cared deeply for the people in the church in Philippi and wrote a letter to encourage them to look to Jesus as they faced trials. Here is an excerpt from his letter:

"Not that I am speaking of being in need, for I have learned in whatever situation I am to be content. I know how to be brought low, and I know how to abound. In any and every circumstance, I have learned the secret of facing plenty and hunger, abundance and need. I can do all things through him who strengthens me." –Philippians 4:11-13

Did you catch that?

Contentment is found in Christ.

When Paul wrote those words, he wasn't sitting on a comfy chair in a Starbucks sipping a delicious mocha frappuccino topped with whip cream and drizzled with chocolate syrup. *I know, I know—there weren't any Starbucks in Paul's day or frappuccinos. Very sad!* My point is that he was writing about being content in a very unlikely place—prison! Paul was imprisoned for standing firm in his faith and was guarded around the clock. Imagine how Paul, who devoted his life to missionary work to share the gospel, must have felt when he was thrown in jail. He could no longer travel from city to city preaching. It seemed doubtful that he could fulfill his purpose. His situation seemed meaningless, yet Paul did not throw himself a pity party. He chose to view his circumstances with Jesus in mind. He chose to look beyond the prison bars and past his circumstances with the hope of seeing God in some way.

In an earlier part of Paul's letter, he says, "I want you to know, brothers, that what has happened to me has really served to advance the gospel, so that it has become known throughout the whole imperial guard and to all the rest that my imprisonment is for Christ. And most of the brothers, having become confident in the Lord by my imprisonment, are much more bold to speak the word without fear.

Some indeed preach Christ from envy and rivalry, but others from good will. The latter do it out of love, knowing that I am put here for the defense of the gospel. The former proclaim Christ out of selfish ambition, not sincerely but thinking to afflict me in my imprisonment. What then? Only that in every way, whether in pretense or in truth, Christ is proclaimed, and in that I rejoice." -Philippians 1:12-18

When Paul chose to view his circumstances with Jesus in mind, Paul saw evidence that God was doing something unbelievable! He discovered his life still had purpose. God was doing something with his situation. Paul's life was being used by God to share the gospel. Christ was being proclaimed through Paul's life not in the way Paul envisioned but according to God's Plan. Being content meant that he had to let go of his plan and embrace God's Plan: "I am an ambassador in chains" (Ephesians 6:20). Paul may have been confined physically by the prison cell, but he was not confined spiritually or emotionally. In God's Plan, he found purpose and reasons to rejoice!

When Paul embraced God's Plan, he also embraced a much BIGGER perspective and a HIGHER VISION. He was an active, willing participant in God's Plan. God empowered Paul to encourage believers at Philippi (and many other churches) through letters he wrote from prison. He also told his guards and fellow prisoners about Jesus. Though Paul is no longer living, his words and life continue to inspire believers and countless others around the world to focus on Jesus, even in seemingly hopeless and meaningless circumstances.

Think about it!

1—Have you taken the time to look past your current circumstances (whether good or bad) with the hope of seeing God, of seeing His Higher Vision? If yes, how have you seen God? If no, there is no better time than now to look for God; the following exercise will help you find Him!

"Take Time"—APPLICATION ACTIVITY

Take time to look inside your heart.

"I love those who love me, and those who seek me diligently find me." –Proverbs 8:17

Take time to express to God how you feel about your circumstances.

You can be honest with Him—completely honest. Admitting that you don't understand or are struggling does not make you any less godly or weak. In fact, it draws you closer to God, who will strengthen you. "Humble yourselves before the Lord, and he will lift you up" (James 4:10).

Take time to *Pray about it!*

Ask God to teach and empower you to experience contentment with His Plan for your life. Taking scripture and turning it into a prayer—essentially speaking God's Word back to Him—can be a powerful way to ask God to reveal Himself in your life. Below, Philippians 4:11-13 has been turned into a prayer for you.

Dear God,
"Teach me to be content in whatever the circumstances. Teach me what it is to be in need, and teach me what it is to have plenty. Teach me the secret of being content in any and every situation, whether well-fed or hungry, whether living in plenty or in want. I can do everything through Christ who gives me strength." In Jesus' Name, Amen.

Take time to receive the promise found in Philippians 4:13.

"I can do all things through him who strengthens me." Christ will strengthen you!

What happened to my friend, Liz?

Remember my friend, Liz, who was concerned that she might be single on her 30th birthday? Though I don't know what happened behind closed doors when Liz spent time with God, I do know Jesus was faithful to strengthen her. She saw purpose in being single, embraced God's Plan, and continued to make the most of every opportunity to enjoy her relationship with Jesus, serve Him, and share the gospel.

When Liz turned 30, she was still single. Shortly after her 30th birthday, God brought her together with the man she would marry. That man had been a member of the singles' group during the time Liz was leading my Bible study group! Liz and Aaron were friends first. They dated and married within a year's time. They now have three beautiful children. When Liz fell in love, she didn't forget God's goodness and boldly and excitedly told others what He had done for her. God continues to use her and her story to inspire others.

5 - Devastated

After work, I returned to my apartment, ate a frozen dinner, and retreated to my bedroom for the rest of the evening. I closed the bedroom door, shutting myself off from the rest of the world. I sighed with great relief. Another day of having to be "strong" and "professional" in the presence of others was over. Finally, I could acknowledge the pain hidden behind my forced smile.

I climbed into the comfort of my bed, assuming a sitting position with my back propped with pillows and covers pulled up under my arms. Wrapped in the warm covers, I felt like God was hugging me. My bed was the altar where I laid my heart before the Lord. My bedroom had become a refuge for me. It was the only place I felt completely accepted, safe, understood, and loved. I would journal for a while, just long enough to draw out the pain and invite it to show its face.

The tears always came, sometimes falling in gentle streams down my cheeks and other times, soaking my face like rain in a thunderstorm. Each tear diluted the pain in my heart, bringing great release. I found comfort and encouragement in praying and reading my Bible as the tears flowed into the late hours of the night. I cried like that for almost six months— no kidding.

I have never cried that long or hard in my whole life. Psalm 56:8 tells us that God cares about us so deeply that He places our tears in His bottle and keeps record of them. I either filled hundreds of God's bottles, or He has one GIGANTIC bottle!

That was one of the most painful times in my life. It didn't take long for me to get to that place of deep suffering. One day I was growing strong in my relationship with Jesus and flying high. Just eight months later, I crashed into a deep valley.

I was 25 when I began dating John. I met him in a singles' group at church. He treated me well in the beginning stages of our relationship, was a nice guy, and encouraged me with compliments. Our relationship progressed quickly. We eventually stopped hanging out with friends from the singles' group, and those friendships grew distant. We spent every hour we could together, and my devotional times with God quickly became nonexistent.

Gradually and subtly over time, I began to see a different side of John. In public, he continued to treat me well. What happened behind closed doors was a different story. He found fault in almost everything I did. Anger raged inside of him and unleashed itself through verbal teardowns directed at me and emotional roller coasters. John never hit me physically, but his criticizing words pierced my heart like arrows. His inconsistent behavior confused me and scared me. After seven months in this dating relationship, I felt exhausted mentally, emotionally, and physically.

In the eighth month of our relationship, I experienced what I call a personal breakthrough. One morning as I was putting on my makeup, I looked in the bathroom mirror and kept peering into it for several minutes. I saw an unhappy, lost, scared girl who felt distant from God. I didn't recognize the person in the mirror. *What happened to the Aimee who was growing in relationship to God, who felt so close to Him, and who was passionate about the things of God?*

I missed God. My heart was longing for Him.

That evening after work, I decided not to go to John's place, which was my usual habit. I went home to my apartment and spent the evening reading the Bible and praying. Being with God again was so peaceful…loving…safe. I wanted more of God.

In the days to follow, I began pulling away from John in order to spend time with God. As I spent more time in God's Word and in prayer, I realized something wasn't right in my relationship with John. At that point, I didn't understand what was wrong, yet that quiet voice deep inside of me, in my gut, was whispering that the relationship wasn't good for me (or for John).

Several weeks later, God strengthened me enough to end the relationship. I ended it by phone, afraid I would change my mind if I did it in person. I also felt afraid of John and feared how he would respond. After our short conversation ended, John called me over and over and over again that night. I had to silence my phone to get some peace.

At 2:00 a.m., I awoke to someone pounding on my door. A glimpse through the peephole revealed it was John. I felt intense fear. My heart pounded just as hard as he pounded on my door. I don't know what I was thinking, but I foolishly opened the door. When I opened the door, John looked angry and was sweating profusely. He started to speak, and his hand reached for me. Suddenly, he moved his hand to his stomach and hunched over, too sick to speak. A few minutes later, he uttered the words, "I'm going home." I watched him get in his car and drive away.

I'm convinced God intervened that night, sparing and protecting both John and myself from *something* that remains unknown to this day. "For I know the plans I have for you," declares the LORD, "plans for welfare and not for evil, to give you a future and a hope" (Jeremiah 29:11).

By the time the relationship ended, I was an absolute mess. I chose to retreat away from the singles' group and from that particular church for an indefinite amount of time to spend every free moment I had with God. I was desperate for God, and He was all I wanted.

My times with Him were sweet. I was like the lost son in *The Parable of the Lost Son* found in Luke 15:11-31. Like the lost son, I had wandered off to a distant land, far from my (Heavenly) Father. Seeing my folly and feeling unworthy of my Father's love, I returned to my Father to ask forgiveness. "And he arose and came to his father. But while he was still a long way off, his father saw him and felt compassion, and ran and embraced him and kissed him" (Luke 15:20). Like the Lost Son who returned home, my Heavenly Father celebrated my homecoming. Each day, God loved me like I had never left His side, and He strengthened me. The love I had for Him grew deeper.

The breakup of my relationship with John was a big event in my life. Unfortunately, it also turned out to be a big event in the singles' group. As I retreated away from the singles' group and the church, John did the opposite. He began to hang out with friends in the group from whom we had distanced ourselves when we were dating. I know this because a few friends from the group had heard about the breakup from John, had not seen me around, and called to see if I was okay. They also wanted to give me a heads-up that John was acting strange. According to them, John had approached almost every guy in the group, asking the guys to meet with him for breakfast or dinner. Those who met with him got an earful about our relationship and about me. As you can imagine, I was not portrayed in a positive light. I was told that two of the ladies in the group had commented that they thought I was wrong to break up with John.

I felt a mix of emotions about the relationship and breakup becoming the hot gossip of the day. It was extremely hurtful to learn my character was being questioned and attacked. My pride welled up inside of me, and at times, I wanted to defend myself. When a couple of friends asked me what happened, I shared details with them. As much as they wanted to understand, neither of them could fully grasp it. Seeking to be understood by other humans was a futile effort. Additionally, I felt tremendous remorse. God had recently blessed the singles' group with a mountaintop experience that had changed the lives of many people in the group. I felt horrible that my breakup was taking attention away from the incredible things God was doing in the hearts of His people.

I also felt incredibly fearful. The thought that I had allowed the relationship with John to dramatically change me in a matter of months scared me and made me feel helpless. I also felt a great sense of responsibility. I knew that I had made my own choices, and I would have to reap the consequences of those bad choices.

The most heartbreaking part of the breakup came when I met with my singles' pastor. When John and I were dating, I borrowed a tv and some other items from him that needed to be returned. After a failed attempt to have a friend return the items to John, I ended up dropping off those things at church to my singles' pastor. He invited me into his office to talk.

Believing my singles' pastor was a safe person in whom I could confide, I began sharing the details of the relationship and began sobbing. My singles' pastor had no compassion for me. He had already heard the story from John's perspective, so his opinion of me was skewed. His analysis of the relationship was that I had seemed happy with John in public and had ended the relationship for no apparent reason. In his eyes, it looked bad that I had stopped attending the singles' group and going to that church. My sobbing and desperation to be understood and defend my character did not help matters. What happened next was devastating.

My singles' pastor silenced me from speaking and harshly rebuked me for treating John poorly.

When I walked out of his office, I knew I had lost a LOT. I lost a dating relationship. I lost Aimee. I lost my reputation. I lost my church. I lost my singles' group. I lost friendships. I even lost my apartment (as it no longer seemed wise to live alone and so close to my ex-boyfriend). I lost my ability to trust. I lost my sense of safety. I lost confidence. I lost innocence, for I had seen the evil in my heart…and in others' hearts. I lost heart. The worst part was that I wasted eight months of my life—EIGHT MONTHS that I could have been enjoying relationship with God. I LOST IT ALL.

When I think of that chapter in my life, I visualize my life as a city devastated by war. Once thriving with great potential, all that remained were broken pieces, rocks and rubble, and shattered memories of what could have been. There were remnants of beautifully sculpted architecture, but you had to dig to find it.

Think about it!

1—What are your reactions to today's story?

2—Have you lost anything in dating relationships? If so, what?

3—How do you need God to strengthen your heart?

Pray about it!

Heavenly Father,
You are a loving refuge. My weary heart rests in Your hands. Father, my heart feels weak when it comes to…

Father, strengthen my heart, and cause it to beat strong for You! In Jesus's Name, Amen.

6 - Surrender

There I was, 25 years old, sitting in the ruins of what used to be my life. I needed to find a new apartment. I needed to find a new church. I needed to make new friends. I needed to figure out who Aimee was and learn how to stay close to God. I needed to learn how to trust again and learn who could be trusted. I needed to learn discernment and how to not be so naïve. I needed to learn to forgive myself. I needed to learn to forgive others. I needed to learn how to walk with faith and not with fear. I needed to learn what it meant to be emotionally healthy and learn what it meant to have a healthy relationship.

Most of my close friends were married by this time, and there I was with my life in shambles. I needed to learn how to see my circumstances through God's eyes like the Apostle Paul did when he was in prison. Needless to say, I was incredibly needy and feeling very overwhelmed!

During this time of soul searching, I was deeply encouraged by God's Word, specifically the book of Philippians written by the Apostle Paul. Some verses that were especially meaningful, included:

Philippians 3:7-8
"But whatever gain I had, I counted as loss for the sake of Christ. Indeed, I count everything as loss because of the surpassing worth of knowing Christ Jesus my Lord. For his sake I have suffered the loss of all things and count them as rubbish, in order that I may gain Christ."

Philippians 3:12-14
"Not that I have already obtained this or am already perfect, but I press on to make it my own, because Christ Jesus has made me his own. Brothers, I do not consider that I have made it my own. But one thing I do: forgetting what lies behind and straining forward to what lies ahead, I press on toward the goal for the prize of the upward call of God in Christ Jesus."

As I surveyed my life and all of its broken pieces, I knew God could repair all that was broken and put my life back together. But I didn't want Him to rebuild my life to what it used to be prior to the dating relationship. I desired to let it ALL go—"forgetting what is behind and straining toward what is ahead." I desired for God to start over and build my life from scratch. I yearned for Him to mold and shape my life into something *better*. God gave me that desire—that HIGHER VISION—and that became the prayer of my heart.

When an unhealthy dating relationship comes to an end and all that remains are broken dreams, broken hearts, and hurt feelings, it's easy to think the person you once cherished is now your enemy. Ephesians 6:12 (also written by the Apostle Paul) says: "For we do not wrestle against flesh and blood, but against the rulers, against the authorities, against the cosmic powers over this present darkness, against the spiritual forces of evil in the heavenly places."

How did that truth apply to me when my unhealthy relationship with John ended? I had to realize John was not my enemy. The singles' pastor was not my enemy. No one in the singles' group was my enemy. They were my brothers and sisters in Christ. My adversary was the devil. If I had held onto hatred towards my brother and had been focused on seeking revenge or the praises of men, then satan would have won the battle in my life. Surrendering to God was definitely the right choice. I clung to these truths:

Exodus 14:14
"The Lord will fight for you; you need only to be still."

Psalm 46:10
"Be still, and know that I am God; I will be exalted among the nations, I will be exalted in the earth."

In the months that followed, my God fought for me. He understood me when others couldn't comprehend. He had compassion for me when others judged me. He collected my tears in a bottle when another rebuked me. He strengthened me when another tore me down. He was trustworthy and more than able to help when I needed help. He loved me— even though I had abandoned Him. I lost a lot, but the one thing I got to keep was relationship with God. At the end of the day, that was the only thing that really mattered.

In her book *Passion and Purity*, Elisabeth Elliot says, "If there is an Enemy of Souls (and I have not the slightest doubt there is), one thing he cannot abide is the desire for purity. Hence a man or woman's passions become his battleground."[2] I believe there is a lot of truth in her statement. My relationship with John revealed that God was not the greatest passion in my life. For eight months, I chased after the love and acceptance of a guy while my pursuit of God diminished. For me, dating was a battleground on which it would be determined: Who was the god of my life—God or satan?

Could it be that dating is a battleground for you? Could it be that dating will become a battleground for you?

Dating relationships are one of the places where you will choose whether or not to open your heart and invest your heart. When your heart is engaged in these ways, it is vulnerable. In a dating relationship, you will explore what it means to build a relationship with a person who has his own beliefs, values, standards, and goals. In finding common ground for the relationship, your purity will be tested. Purity is a critical element in your emotional, physical, and spiritual health.

Purity—n. the condition or quality of being pure; freedom from anything that debases; freedom from guilt or evil; innocence; also physical chastity; virginity.[3]

Think about it!

1—Is the pursuit of God your #1 passion?

2—When it comes to dating, who is the god of your life—God or satan?

3—Do you need God to fight for you? Your Heavenly Father is waiting for you with open arms and ears.

Pray about it!

Heavenly Father,
You are my God. You are the God above all gods, the God of all nations, and God in all the earth. (Be still, and ponder God's position.)

I desire for You to be the God of my dating life. Teach me to fill the longings of my heart with Your love.

Fight for me when I am tempted to shower my heart's affections on the wrong people and things. Protect me from the evil one. I also need You to fight for me in this way…(add your personal plea).

Be exalted in my heart! In Jesus' Name, Amen.

7 - First Brushstroke

In the process of healing and making me new, God led me to my canvas of dating experiences. That canvas was no longer completely white; it had some design and texture, splashes of color, as well as dark spots. There were still many empty spaces yet to be filled.

Together, we observed my canvas as if it were a work of art displayed on a museum wall. At times, looking at my canvas was like struggling to interpret an abstract painting. Other times, looking at my canvas was like trying to find the beauty in an ugly painting. I'm thankful God was there because He acted as a museum curator by describing the heart of the artist, pointing out themes and teaching me to find beauty in every brushstroke. Every brushstroke embodied something to be learned, and we spent much time on the very first brushstroke to touch the canvas: my first date.

Most girls and guys I know have wonderful memories of their first dates. They talk about that infamous "first date" as if it was a landmark in their memory books of all-time greatest events in history. Unfortunately, I can't relate. My first date, which was *supposed* to be magical, turned out to be a miserable experience!

I was 16, and it was the evening of my first date. I was excited and nervous. I must have spent at least two hours getting ready. Everything had to be *perfect*—my outfit, my hair, and my nails. You would have thought I was a movie star. The bathroom became my personal dressing room. All it needed was a gold star on the door imprinted with my name. A hair stylist, makeup artist, and manicurist would have been nice additions, too! When every strand of hair was in place, eyelashes curled, and fingernails colored pink, I was confident enough to swing open the bathroom door. After the cloud of hair spray settled, I emerged triumphantly with a huge smile framed with pretty pink lipstick. My parents even snapped a picture of me.

The details of getting ready for my date are about the only pleasant things I recall about the evening. I guess it's a good thing I spent two hours getting ready so that I could remember something fondly! I remember eating dinner with my date, feeling terribly nervous and uncomfortable. I could hardly eat. As far as the conversation went, I agreed with everything he said and said whatever I thought he wanted to hear.

It was a relief when dinner ended, and we headed to the movie theater; I no longer had to worry about what to say or if I had a piece of lettuce stuck in my teeth. Dirty teeth turned out to be the least of my worries. During the movie, my date turned my face toward his and aggressively kissed me for what felt like an eternity. I was extremely embarrassed, especially since another moviegoer was sitting on my other side.

On the drive home, I was relieved to finally pull into my neighborhood. I was almost home, and this date was about to end...and not a moment too soon. Just seconds from my house, my date slowed the car and parked it on the side of the street. His hand brushed my leg and began moving up my skirt. I sat in paralyzing shock, too scared to move or speak.

Thankfully, as soon as he realized I was wearing pantyhose, he stopped and proceeded to drive me home. Words cannot express how relieved I felt when he stopped touching me. Thank God that pantyhose was a popular item to wear at that time! That's right, God can use anything, even pantyhose, to turn around a bad situation! I truly believe God was protecting me, even though I had no clue who God was at 15.

Once I *finally* made it home, I walked in the door, plopped myself on the floor, and leaned against the couch in the den where my parents were watching tv. Mom and Dad asked me how the evening went. I replied, "I never want to go on a date again." They chuckled, probably relieved and secretly hoping I was serious.

That was my first date—the big event most teenage girls can't wait to experience. I had looked forward to my first date. I didn't know what it would be like, but I never imagined I wouldn't get to watch a movie because a tongue was shoved down my throat. I never dreamed I would feel so scared in the car on the ride home. So much for the fairytale portrayed in the movies.

Thankfully, some young women never experience what I did. Unfortunately, many young women do. If you have experienced anything like that, you can trust God is grieved that you were treated with disrespect and violated (emotionally or physically). The God who gave His One and Only Son to die to rescue those He loves from sin and to one day usher them into paradise is deeply grieved. He has a much HIGHER VISION for your life. "For I know the plans I have for you,' declares the LORD, 'plans for welfare and not for evil, to give you a future and a hope" (Jeremiah 29:11).

The biggest tragedy of my first date is that as a young woman, I didn't realize I had choices. I didn't have to kiss my date. I could have told him, "No." He bought me dinner and a movie ticket, but that didn't obligate me to finish a date during which I felt incredibly uncomfortable and invaded. I had the choice to ask him to take me home early or to call someone to pick me up. I could have chosen to get to know him in the context of a group date with my friends there. I also didn't have to agree with everything he said. I could have paid for my own dinner. When it comes to dating and going on dates, do you know that you have choices?

Needless to say, my date displayed little character. Though I didn't ask to be treated poorly, let me suggest that I contributed to some of the misery of the evening. Let me explain.

I was most actively engaged and enjoying myself during the prep time preceding the date. No one has ever used the term "tomboy" to describe me. I've always been a girly girl who enjoys getting dressed up and wearing makeup. There's nothing wrong with wanting to look nice, but I think you'll agree that spending two hours primping for a date is pretty obsessive. The activities to which you devote the most time are a good indication of what's important to you. "For where your treasure is, there your heart be also" (Luke 12:34). There was more to those two hours than my wanting to look nice; there was a strong driving force behind my behavior.

My contribution to our dinner conversation was minimal. A date can be a wonderful opportunity to get to know someone. I didn't make the most of the opportunity to learn about the guy sitting across the table from me because I was too consumed with myself. I was worried about food in my teeth. I don't remember asking many questions about him or his life. I didn't share my own thoughts and opinions because I was too busy crafting my words to please him.

Why did I behave like that? I believe my actions and words were a desperate attempt to earn my date's *attention, acceptance,* and *adoration*—the *Triple A's.*

Think about it!

1—What have you done or said to attempt to earn any or all of the *Triple A's?*

Attention—n. notice or awareness.[4]

Acceptance—n. favorable reception; approval; favor.[5]

Adoration—n. the act of paying honor, as to a divine being; worship; fervent and devoted love.[6]

Pray about it!

"O LORD,
You have searched me and known me! You know when I sit down and when I rise up; you discern my thoughts from afar. You search out my path and my lying down and are acquainted with all my ways. For you formed my inward parts; you knitted me together in my mother's womb. I praise you, for I am fearfully and wonderfully made. Wonderful are your works; my soul knows it very well. {Help me to become the woman you had in mind when you created me.} My frame was not hidden from you, when I was being made in secret, intricately woven in the depths of the earth. Your eyes saw my unformed substance; in your book were written, every one of them, the days that were formed for me, when as yet there was none of them. Search me, O God, and know my heart!

{Reveal to me the desires and motives that birthed my thoughts.} And see if there be any grievous way in me, and lead me in the way everlasting!" In Jesus' Name, Amen.

8 - Perspective

Perspective—n. a way of regarding situations, facts, etc., and judging their relative importance.[7]

Together, God and I continued to look at the canvas of my dating experiences. With the first brushstroke touching the canvas when I was 16 and the latest brushstroke at 25, there were a lot of brushstrokes to ponder. The brushstrokes reflected a spectrum of dating experiences, ranging from wonderful to horrible with a few mediocre experiences painted along the way.

We didn't stop to interpret every dating experience; there was no need. You see, there were certain brushstrokes that seemed to leap off the canvas, triggering specific memories and feelings to surface from the depths of my heart. Those captivating brushstrokes looked like dots in a connect-the-dots activity. *Was it possible that all of those varied experiences had something in common?*

With paintbrush in hand, God gently touched the brush's tip to the canvas. Slowly and carefully, He painted a line that connected EVERY single dot without ever taking the paintbrush off the canvas! He helped me see there was a common theme connecting my dating experiences:

At 16, when the first brushstroke touched my canvas, I didn't know who I was.

At 25, when the latest brushstroke hit my canvas, I still didn't seem to know who I was.

God led me to take a few steps back from my canvas so that I could see more clearly the picture formed through this connect-the-dating-dots-activity. What I saw was a bigger revelation:

When I accepted Jesus as my Lord and Savior, every part of my life changed *except* the way I dated.

I came to know Jesus at age 20 and continued to date in the same way I dated before

27

knowing Jesus. Somehow knowing Jesus had transformed every part of my life that I could think of…except my dating relationships. *How in the world did that happen?*

Though I was thankful for the revelation God showed me, I felt confused. I had truly wanted to honor God in my dating relationships, and I sincerely thought I *was* growing and succeeding in that area…until this last relationship. In my five years of knowing Jesus, I had three dating relationships, all with Christian guys. With the exception of the relationship with John, the other two relationships were the best relationships I had ever experienced. I questioned, *How could two of the three relationships be so wonderful and the other one so awful?* Because the good relationships were with fantastic guys who had known Jesus since they were children and were strong in their faith, I wondered if the strength of their faith carried the relationships. After all, I was still a young believer, a baby in the faith, learning how to walk, extremely clumsy, and prone to fall.

Throughout the nine years of dating experiences on my canvas, I had been pretty moral. I knew the rules: Don't date someone of the same sex. Don't call the guy; wait for him to call you. Don't ask a guy out. Don't kiss a guy on the first date. Don't have sex before marriage. Don't cheat on your boyfriend. I had always tried to uphold all of those "Don'ts." Looking at my canvas made me realize that I didn't have a clue how all those rules connected to Jesus. I didn't even understand why I had those standards!

Questions flooded my mind: *How was Jesus supposed to be a part of my dating relationships? What would it mean to honor God in my dating relationships?* I wondered, *Will I EVER get this "following Christ" thing down?*

Have you ever felt that way?

I prayed, specifically surrendering my dating life and relationships with guys to God. I asked Him to help me date and relate to guys in ways that would honor Him. That was the beginning of a journey with God that would transform my life—ALL of it—into a more God-honoring life marked by true and everlasting love. You can have that, too! Jesus said, "I came that they may have life and have it abundantly" (John 10:10).

Think about it!

1—What standards in dating/relationships with guys do you have? Why do you have each of those standards?

2—In what areas of your life do you need wisdom?

3—Whom better to teach us how to live our lives than the God who created our lives! Read Proverbs 3:1-27 to discover the countless rewards that come from applying His wisdom, His Word, in our lives. What rewards are especially meaningful to you?

Pray about it!

James 1:5 says, "If any of you lacks wisdom, he should ask God, who gives generously to all without finding fault, and it will be given to him."

Wise Father,
You possess all the wisdom of the universe, and I need Your counsel. Thank You for inviting me to come to You and for being a safe place to admit that I don't know what I'm doing when it comes to…

Please give me wisdom to know what to do and say to honor You. Empower me, through the Holy Spirit, to apply Your wisdom in my life. In Your Son's Name, Amen.

9 - Very Good

This book is inspired by my journey with God to learn how to honor Him in all areas of my life, especially in dating relationships. It is my prayer that the devotional readings will guide you on a beautiful journey—a journey unique to you and God. May He bless you beyond belief!

The journey with God begins in the first chapter of the first book of the Bible, *Genesis,* which means "beginning." How fitting! It was the sixth day of creation. The land, seas, vegetation, sun, moon, stars, day, night, and animals of all kinds had been created. The Creator continued crafting the world.

Genesis 1:26-31
"Then God said, 'Let us make man in our image, after our likeness. And let them have dominion over the fish of the sea and over the birds of the heavens and over the livestock and over all the earth and over every creeping thing that creeps on the earth.'

So God created man in his own image,
in the image of God he created him;
Male and female he created them.

And God blessed them. And God said to them, 'Be fruitful and multiply and fill the earth and subdue it and have dominion over the fish of the sea and over the birds of the heavens and over every living thing that moves on the earth.' And God said, 'Behold, I have given you every plant yielding seed that is on the face of all the earth, and every tree with seed in its fruit. You shall have them for food. And to every beast of the earth and to every bird of the heavens and to everything that creeps on the earth, everything that has the breath of life, I have given every green plant for food.' And it was so. And God saw everything that he had made, and behold, it was very good. And there was evening and there was morning, the sixth day."

God poured much attention and care into creating people. He made them unique and full of purpose. For five days, God spoke creation into being by saying,

"**Let** there be light." (Genesis 1:3)

"**Let** there be an expanse between the waters to separate water from water." (Genesis 1:6)

"**Let** there be…**Let**…**Let**…**Let**…**Let**…" (Genesis 1:9, 11, 14, 20, 24)

God spoke, "**Let** there be, and POOF! It appeared! God's Word is that POWERFUL!

It was the sixth day when God created Man (referring to all people, male and female). When it came to creating Man, God took a different approach. "Then God said, 'Let us make man in our image, after our likeness'" (Genesis 1:26). The "us" in the verse refers to God the Father, God the Son, and God the Spirit—the Trinity. All three persons of the Trinity were present at creation. God deemed Man to be such a special creation that His Word points out the presence and unity of the Trinity at man's formation.

God the Father, Son, and Spirit collaborated together to bring their creative vision of Man into being. They designed Man to be unique of all the creations. He was made in the image of God, in the likeness of the Creator. Man looked like his God in that he had a spiritual self, an inner being. Man was given the ability to exemplify God in knowledge, righteousness, and holiness.

With this last human creation, God was much more intentional about what He was doing. Instead of speaking Man into being with a few command-like words and moving on, God spent some quality time building worth and purpose into Man. He did this by…

blessing Man,

giving him instruction,

entrusting creation to him,

empowering him to rule over creation,

and verbally expressing His approval of Man.

God expressed His will for Man in Genesis 1:28: "God blessed them, and God said to them, 'Be fruitful and multiply and fill the earth and subdue it and have dominion over the fish of the sea and over the birds of the heavens and over every living thing that moves on the earth.'" God found pleasure in His creation. Man is the only creation God verbally blessed, revealing He enjoyed His human creation most of all! He found such delight in Man that He wanted many more men, enough to fill the earth!

From the beginning of time, God provided for His people. Not only did God bless the human creation, He gave an inheritance to Man. "Then God said, 'I give you every seed-bearing plant on the face of the whole earth and every tree that has fruit with seed in it. They will be yours for food'" (Genesis 1:29). God gave what He enjoyed—His creation—to the creation He enjoyed most—Man!

God honored Man as the greatest creation—the creation most closely resembling Him—by entrusting Man with the great responsibility and special privilege of governing creation. Man would have the opportunity to experience God from a new perspective. By ruling and influencing creation, Man could gain understanding, respect, and appreciation for God's position as the Supreme Ruler, Provider, and Caregiver for creation.

Before God created Man, He looked at the things He had made, and he deemed it all "good" (Genesis 1:25). God gave the highest mark of approval on man by proclaiming him "very good" (Genesis 1:31). God enjoyed man the very first day He created him!

Glorify—v. to honor with praise, admiration, or worship; extol.[8]

Man and Woman were made for God's glory. God is glorified through their very existence; their unique design showcases His image. When Man and Woman carry out God's will, His purposes, for their lives, it is a testimony to God's glory and honors Him.

1 Corinthians 10:31
"So, whether you eat or drink, or whatever you do, do it all to the glory of God."

1 Peter 4:11
"Whoever speaks, as one who speaks oracles of God; whoever serves, as one who serves by the strength that God supplies—in order that in everything God may be glorified through Jesus Christ. To him belong glory and dominion forever and ever. Amen."

Think about it!

1—What characteristics of God are revealed when a husband and wife multiply and fill His earth?

2—What characteristics of God are revealed when a husband and wife govern His creation?

3—What characteristics of God are revealed when husband and wife eat the food He provided?

Pray about it!

Pray using the **ACTS**-model, which stands for **A**doration (praise), **C**onfession, **T**hanksgiving, and **S**upplication (request, ask).

Creator God,
*I **adore** You, for You are a powerful God. You said, "Let it be," and it came into being. You gave life to words and brought words to life!*

*Your words gave me life, worth, and purpose. I **confess** that I don't always find my worth in You. I sometimes find my worth in people's opinions of me, in my possessions, and in the positions of status I hold.*

***Thank You** for creating me as Your image-bearer and verbally affirming me as "very good." I **ask** You to help me to believe Your powerful words—to believe that my worth comes from You and only from You. Help this image-bearer discover the true character of her Creator. Reveal to me the delight of reflecting Your character to the world! Lead and empower me to fulfill Your purposes for my life. God, showcase Your glory through me! In Jesus' Name, Amen.*

10 - Defined by God

Our journey continues in the second chapter of the book of Genesis, which provides a different and more detailed perspective of woman's creation...of our creation!

It was a beautiful day on earth, the sixth day of the earth's existence. I imagine the sun shone brightly. The land was a plush green carpet of grass and shrubs. Blooming flowers painted brilliant explosions of color throughout the land. The signs of life were all around. The happy songs of birds filled the air while their flying dances added excitement in the skies. The playful feet of animals rustling leaves and brushing against the grass created soft background music. Sunlight reflected off the seas like a spotlight showcasing the waves' splendid green and blue hues. Every so often, a fish emerged from the water and dived right back in, a whimsical reminder that mystery and adventure lay in the depths.

Genesis 2:7 says, "Then the Lord God formed the Man of dust from the ground and breathed into his nostrils the breath of life and the man became a living creature." Next, God exercised his hospitality skills when he invited Man to make himself at home in the beautiful garden God planted in Eden. God thought of every detail to ensure Man had a wonderful stay in the Garden. God made sure there was good soil for the Man to cultivate. God made sure there were rivers to water the Garden. He also added trees to enhance the beauty of the Garden and to produce good fruit.

After God provided a gorgeous home for Man, the essentials to make him successful in cultivating the land, and ready-made, tasty snacks he could grab from the trees and plants, He promised to provide a companion for Man! "Then the LORD God said, 'It is not good that the man should be alone; I will make him a helper suitable for him'" (Genesis 2:18).

Adam had relationship with God, and it was the best thing on earth. He must have eagerly anticipated what it would be like to have a compatible mate designed especially for him by the Author of relationship! There is not a dull moment in the story as God did something you would never expect and may find humorous. There was a spectacular parade in the Garden of Eden as God brought the cattle, every beast of the field, and every bird of the sky to Man for him to meet and name! What a scene that must have been!

Can you imagine being in Adam's position, looking into the eyes of a rhinoceros and wondering, "Is this the companion for me?" After a definitive, "No," did he signal the next creation in line to come forth? I can just imagine him peering curiously into the eyes of a giraffe as he stood on his tiptoes, then into the eyes of a sparrow that landed on the back of his hand, next a pig as he squatted to the ground, and a skunk as he held his breath! (Hmmm, maybe smelly skunks didn't roam the Garden.) Next came a tiger, a robin, a cow, an owl, a zebra, a bear…and on and on until dusk. "But for Adam there was not found a helper fit for him" (Genesis 2:20).

When I put myself in Adam's shoes, I think I would have grown discouraged looking at all of creation and not finding a companion. "God, is there a mate for me? Will I be alone forever?" These are the questions I would have asked. Is it possible that Adam might have understood the fear and disappointment that many single women and men experience?

God had the vison for Adam's compatible helper all along, so the process of considering a compatible companion served a purpose. Perhaps it prepared Adam to receive the gift to come. Perhaps it taught him to trust God. Even while Adam slept, God continued His work to bring His Plan to fruition! "So the LORD God caused a deep sleep to fall upon the man, and while he slept took one of his ribs and closed its place with flesh. And the rib that the LORD God had taken from the man he made into a woman and brought her to the man" (Genesis 2:21-22). God was faithful to fulfill His promise, and He did not disappoint!

When Adam saw God's gift, he pronounced, "This at last is bone of my bones, and flesh of my flesh; she shall be called Woman, because she was taken out of Man" (Genesis 2:23). If a guy said that to you today, you would probably think he was weird or needed to come up with a better pick-up line! Yet, on the first day the human race existed, those were passionate words! Adam wasn't saying, "Well, she's *okay*." His words might be translated, "Whoa! She's GORGEOUS! I'll take her!!!" Adam's words were filled with passion, certainty, and excitement. He knew woman was exactly what he needed.

It's interesting that Adam had been asleep while God formed Woman and did not witness her creation from his rib. Yet he *knew* when he saw her that they shared a connection. Without a doubt, she belonged to him. After sizing up the compatibility of a rhinoceros, a cow, and a sparrow, Adam must have thought Woman was incredibly lovely and special!

I wonder if God let Adam sleep because he was exhausted from shopping through the long line of animals. Perhaps God wanted him to be well-rested when he met Woman. After all, you only get one chance to make a first impression! How wonderful that Woman entered the world and immediately received *attention, acceptance,* and *adoration (the Triple A's)!* God certainly knew what He was doing. It seems that the long process of matchmaking prepared Adam to receive God's gift of Woman with deep appreciation and sincere thankfulness.

God knows how to give the perfect gift. Everything God does is for His glory, and Man and Woman created a glorious picture of God. Man's rugged framework and life purpose displayed the bolder attributes of God—His authority, leadership, strength, protection, and provision. God chose to complete His self-portrait by designing Woman to showcase His softer attributes. Her curvy framework and "helper fit" design outlined God's grace-filled, gentle, caring, nurturing, and supportive qualities. Woman was yet another way God blessed Man with relationship, and she would help Man appreciate his relationship with God even more! What a gift!

God's passion for relationship was evident in His creation of Woman. Out of nothing, He made earth, and sky, and sun, and plants, and trees, and birds, and animals, etc. Out of the dust of the earth, He made Man. Yet, out of life, God made Woman. For the first time in all of His creation, God borrowed from life to create life. God didn't just speak her into being; her formation was intense. God engineered a mate for Man and helped prepare Man to receive the gift! He intentionally put Man to sleep and concentrated His energy on her making. He deliberately borrowed from life. He carefully removed a rib from Man and used it to sculpt a helper fit for him. Then, He orchestrated the meeting of the two destined to be together. It was after God made Woman, that for the first time ever, He looked at creation and proclaimed it was not only good, but "very good" (Genesis 1:31).

Once again, we see God's passion for relationship when God gifted Woman with the unique ability to give birth to children. She reflects the beauty of God, the Creator, who brings forth life, and nurtures, cares for, and loves His children. Through Woman, God made it possible for Man and Woman to fulfill His commandment to "be fruitful and multiply and fill the earth" (Genesis 1:28). Through Woman, He brought forth all the men and women of the Bible. A descendant of Adam and Eve was Mary, whom God chose to carry His One and Only Son in her womb and usher Him into the world as a baby. Mary "found favor with God," and He entrusted her to mother and raise Jesus, who would impact the world in the greatest way possible (Luke 1:30).

Through Woman, God made a family—a very BIG family! His family is made up of all the people who believe in Jesus as their Lord and Savior and are committed to Him. His family is often referred to as the Body of Believers, or the Church.

God's Word says the relationship of a man and woman in marriage is symbolic of Christ's relationship with the Church (Ephesians 5:25-33). Jesus loves, nurtures, and cherishes the Church. The man's role in marriage symbolizes Christ while the woman's role symbolizes the Church. In this way, woman represents all the people whom God loves and for whom God holds a special place in His heart. Essentially, Woman represents the Bride of Christ.

Think about the brides you've seen at weddings. The bride is the most beautiful person in the room; she is radiant and joyful. She encompasses purity and dignity. She is admired and honored. Have you ever watched the groom at a wedding? His eyes light up when he sees his bride; he desires to be with her. He is tender and loving towards her. "As a bridegroom rejoices over the bride, so shall your God rejoice over you" (Isaiah 62:5).

Below are some of the ways our Creator defined us; may we always see ourselves through God's eyes!

Woman—(n.) The female human being; Formed by God; ***Uniquely designed:*** Worshipper, Image-bearer/"softer" side of God; Wife or "Helper"; Mother or "Nurturer"; Co-heir of God's inheritance; Co-ruler of creation; Full of purpose/World-changer; ***Special representative:*** Bride of Christ/the Church/the People God loves; Loved, Nurtured, Cherished, Admired, Honored, Beautiful, Radiant, Pure, Dignified, Joyful, Rejoiced over, ***"Very Good."***

Think about it!

1—On a scale of 1-10, how much does your definition of yourself match God's definition of you?

> *1 = I have a really hard time believing I am a person of worth.*
> *5 = I believe I have worth but only in 50% of the ways listed above.*
> *10 = I have full confidence that I have worth in God's eyes in all the ways listed above.*

2—Using the definition of "Woman" in this Reading, which descriptions do you have difficulty accepting about yourself?

Pray about it!

Sweet Father,
I praise You, for You are a powerful, bold, protective God who is equally tender, peaceful, and giving. I am in awe that a God as wonderful as You would create me to reflect Your softer side. Thank You for creating me with passion, purpose, and joy. Thank You for pouring Your heart into me and for making me beautiful.

Sometimes I don't feel that beautiful or kind, and I may never match up to the world's very long list of what makes a woman a woman. But I bear Your image. I am beautiful in Your sight. You have proclaimed me "very good." And You are the Only One who really counts!

Let Your creativity, love, and words define me. Help me to remember that You rejoice over me as a bridegroom rejoices over his bride! Shape my life to reflect the beauty of who You are so that the world will see the true beauty of a woman and the God who made her! In Jesus' Name, Amen.

11 - United as One

T he evening news gives us a glimpse into our world: family feuds, divorce, kidnappings, bullying, discrimination, theft, scandals, murders, war, death…just to name a few daily happenings. Imagine living in a perfect place like the Garden of Eden. The setting for Genesis 2:25 is the Garden of Eden where "the man and his wife were both naked, and felt no shame." The first Man and Woman were in a place much different than the world we know today. They felt no guilt, no pain, no embarrassment, no humiliation—even with their bodies completely bare. They were free from burden, relaxed, and happy! Perhaps they felt similar to how we feel when we're on vacation!

I don't know about you, but I think clothes are fun, and a visit to my favorite clothing stores is always a treat. Even so, I do grow tired of the laundry pile that I can never completely wash away because I keep wearing clothes and adding to the stack! Just think what life would be like if we didn't wear clothes and could walk around shamelessly naked like Adam and Eve. There would be no stress over getting stains out of your pants or ironing those stubborn wrinkles out of your shirt. No decisions about what to wear each day. No worries about clothes not fitting well. No panicking when there are no clean panties. No outgrowing or wearing out your clothes or blowing too much of your paycheck on new clothes (and earrings, purses, shoes, and…). No need to sew up a hole or replace buttons. Think of all the time we would save! As much as I like clothes, life without clothes seems kind of nice!

Walking around "naked" in the Garden and feeling "no shame" also meant that Man and Woman weren't hiding or putting on a facade. They felt the freedom to simply be themselves. The best part is that they were completely known and completely loved. They were not judged on their appearance or fashion sense.

Genesis 3:8 says, "And they heard the sound of the LORD God walking in the garden." In verse 9, "The LORD God called to the man and said to him, 'Where are you?'" Apparently, God did not keep His distance from Adam and Eve. He walked and talked with them. He had a relationship with them. No wonder Adam and Eve were happy: They were able to enjoy genuine relationship with God and with each another!

How strong was the relationship between Adam and Eve? "And the rib that the LORD God had taken from the man he made into a woman and brought her to the man. Then the man said, 'This at last is bone of my bones and flesh of my flesh; she shall be called Woman, because she was taken out of Man.' Therefore a man shall leave his father and his mother and hold fast to his wife, and they shall become *one* flesh" (Genesis 2:22-25). Become "*one* flesh"—that's an intimate connection! Ephesians 5:32 also refers to this one-flesh connection. "This mystery is profound, and I am saying that it refers to Christ and the church."

WAIT! What?

The marriage relationship...
is a *one*-flesh connection...
a bond so tight that it reflects the relationship
of Christ and the Church (everyone who believes in Christ).

Jesus and His followers are TIGHT. Check this out:

Romans 8:38-39
"For I am sure that neither death nor life, nor angels nor rulers, nor things present nor things to come, nor powers, nor height nor depth, nor anything else in all creation, will be able to separate us from the love of God in Christ Jesus our Lord."

Jeremiah 31:3
"I have loved you with an everlasting love."

John 3:16
"For God so loved the world, that he gave his only Son, that whoever believes in him should not perish but have eternal life."

Hebrews 13:5
"I will never leave you nor forsake you."

THAT is some major love! We are creations made in His image, greatly valued and deeply loved by Him.

The husband's role is symbolic of Christ, who is the leader of the Church. The wife's role is symbolic of the Church, those who believe in Jesus and follow Him. Their roles are different, yet the roles are complementary. As image-bearers of God, Man was made to exemplify the stronger side of God, and Woman was made to exemplify the softer side of God. When Man and Woman are united in marriage, it is a beautiful union, a one-flesh connection that reflects the glory and love of God!

Think about it!

Let's begin to look at the roles of husband and wife to help us better understand their one-flesh connection. This unity that gives us greater insight into Jesus' love for us.

1—Read Ephesians 5:22-33. What keyword was used to summarize what the husband is called to do to lead to oneness in the marriage relationship? Count how many times the husband is exhorted to do this.

2—What two words were used to summarize what the wife is called to do to help foster oneness in the marriage relationship?

The husband is told to *love, love, love* his wife. He is exhorted to *love* his wife so that the power that comes with his position will not be abused and so that he will deeply cherish and care for his wife as Christ does His bride, the Church. How much did Christ love His Church? "Christ loved the church and gave himself up for her" (Ephesians 5:25b). THAT, my friends, is the greatest love of all!

Pray about it!

Heavenly Father,
You are true love. Thank You that I am forever loved by You. In my lifetime, many will tell me they love me with words, but You are the One who put Your love into action. Thank You for sending Your Beloved Son to a dying world in need of true love. Jesus loved me to death. Thank You that He loves me every moment of every day to eternity. Because of Jesus, I will never know a day that I am not loved. Thank You! In Jesus' Loving Name, Amen.

12 - Love, Respect, Honor

Let's pick up where we left off yesterday. The marriage relationship is a one-flesh connection, a bond so tight that it reflects the relationship of Christ to the Church (everyone who believes in Christ). The husband's role is symbolic of Christ, who is the leader of the Church. The wife's role is symbolic of the Church, those who believe in Jesus and follow Him. Their roles are different, yet the roles are complementary. As image-bearers of God, Man was made to exemplify the stronger side of God, and Woman was made to exemplify the softer side of God. When Man and Woman are united in marriage, it is a beautiful union, a one-flesh connection that reflects the glory and love of God!

Ephesians 5:22-33

"Wives, submit to your own husbands, as to the Lord. For the husband is the head of the wife even as Christ is the head of the church, his body, and is himself its Savior. Now as the church submits to Christ, so also wives should submit in everything to their husbands.

Husbands, love your wives as Christ loved the church and gave himself up for her, that he might sanctify her, having cleansed her by the washing of water with the word, so that he might present the church to himself in splendor, without spot or wrinkle or any such thing, that she might be holy and without blemish. In the same way husbands should love their wives as their own bodies. He who loves his wife loves himself. For no one ever hated his own flesh, but nourishes and cherishes it, just as Christ does the church, because we are members of his body. 'Therefore a man shall leave his father and mother and hold fast to his wife, and the two shall become one flesh. This mystery is profound, and I am saying that it refers to Christ and the church. However, let each one of you love his wife as himself, and let the wife see that she respects her husband.'"

In his role, the husband takes on the strength of God to lead his wife with knowledge and wisdom, provide for her needs, protect her, comfort her, help her flourish in her relationship with God, and initiate them to take action towards their God-given purposes. To strengthen their union, the husband is told to *love, love, love* his wife. He is exhorted to *love* his wife so that the power that comes with his position will not be abused and so that he will deeply cherish and care for his wife as Christ does His bride, the Church. How much did Christ love His Church? "Christ loved the church and gave himself up for her" (Ephesians 5:25b).

To strengthen their union, the wife's role is to *respect* her husband and to *submit* to his leadership as the Church submits to Christ's leadership. In doing so, she ultimately respects and submits to Christ (who is leading her husband). The Greek word for *respect* means to "revere, fear." In the Greek, *submit* means "to subject oneself, place oneself in submission." To better understand these concepts, let's take a closer look at the example of Christ. Not only does He hold a role of leadership over the church, but He also holds a role in which He respects and submits to the Father.[9]

God the Father had a Plan to send a Savior to rescue His people from sin and restore His relationship with them. Christ knew that all things were made for God's glory, and everything was done for God's glory. God the Son was a willing participant in the Plan. He respected the Father's position of authority and submitted to the Father's lead, knowing it would bring attention to God's glory. He also recognized that following the Father's lead would help the Father accomplish His Plan and would please Him. Christ knew He was loved by His Father, and He wanted people to know the Father's love. He helped God with His Plan! Christ wholeheartedly supported the Plan.

In the same way, a wife unites with her husband to provide a picture of God's glory to a world in need of a Savior. Both are created in His image, the man reflecting the stronger side of God and woman reflecting the softer side of God, and come together to complete the picture. It is all part of God's Plan. The wife recognizes that her husband has been placed in a role of authority by God, and she gives him the respect due that position. Even as he provides for her, protects her, and comforts her, he is being a leader for her. She places trust in her husband and actively supports him in his role. When he leads, she responds.[10] Respecting and submitting to her husband are about more than following a decision or direction. Ultimately, the woman sees past herself to a HIGHER VISION to honor and please God for His glory. She supports His Plan, in which she helps her husband realize his God-given potential as a man while he loves her in the pursuit to achieve her God-given potential as a woman.

Through our human eyes, the wife's role may seem like a lesser role than that of her husband but not through God's eyes. Both roles, though different, are critical to achieving *oneness* and fulfilling the shared purpose of the husband and wife.

Interestingly, God made Woman out of Man's rib. He could have made her out of earth's dust, out of an animal, out of Man's feet, etc. Yet, He made her out of the Man's side, symbolizing that she was created in spiritual equality with Man. Matthew Henry said, "The woman was made of a rib out of the side of Adam; not made out of his head to rule over him, nor out of his feet to be trampled upon by him, but out of his side to be equal with him, under his arm to be protected, and near his heart to be beloved."[11]

My pastor, Randy Pope, taught me that the person in the role of submission is in a position of honor. He described it like this: God the Son submitted to God the Father when He died on the cross. God the Father and God the Son were equal in power and glory. They had different roles in God's Plan. God the Father, who was in the position of authority, honored His Son by seating Him at the right hand of God, the place of highest honor.[12]

Mark 16:19
"So then the Lord Jesus, after he had spoken to them (the disciples), was taken up into heaven and sat down at the right hand of God."

Both the husband and the wife are "very good" in God's eyes. They are equal in power and glory. In 1 Peter 3:7, husband and wife are referred to as "co-heirs of grace," and the husband is exhorted to honor his wife.

People often joke about marriage, referring to their spouse as a "ball and chain," implying they feel like a prisoner and likening their spouse to a large, heavy metal ball with a chain that is usually attached to a prisoner's leg by a manacle. That picture falls short of God's glory. That picture lacks vision, a HIGHER VISION, where a husband and wife are willing to give themselves up to serve each other with a loving desire to see each other grow in Jesus. "Therefore, a man shall leave his father and mother and hold fast to his wife, and the two shall become one flesh" (Ephesians 5:30-31). In verse 32, it says, "This mystery is profound…"

Imagine how many glorious pictures would be painted for a world in need of a Savior *if only* more husbands and more wives would dare to embrace that HIGHER VISION.

Think about it!

You don't have to be married to learn how to respect and submit to authority in a way that honors God. Let's explore what God has taught you already!

1—Think of 1 person you lead. *(For example, you may be a babysitter, camp counselor, have some degree of authority in your job, hold a position in a club at school, as a small group leader at church, have younger siblings who look up to you, etc.)* Has the person you lead ever disrespected your authority or fought your leadership? If so, how? In what ways did his/her disrespect cause disunity and hinder progress towards a goal?

2—Think of 1-2 people in a role of authority/leadership over you who love you well. How have they shown you love and honor? Is it easy or hard to respect and submit to their leadership? And why?

3—Jesus was an authority over His disciples. Discover the insight Jesus shared with His disciples about the heart and character of a God-honoring leader by reading Luke 22:24-30. How can you be a greater servant to those you lead?

Remember this exhortation as you follow the lead of others: "Obey your leaders and submit to them, for they are keeping watch over your souls, as those who will have to give an account. Let them do this with joy and not groaning, for that would be of no advantage to you" (Hebrews 13:17).

Pray about it!

Father God,

I praise You because You are a strong leader! You brought order and stability to the husband-wife relationship. You clearly defined the roles so that man and woman would know what is expected of them, how to live in unity, and how to achieve their shared goals.

Thank You for Christ, who is an example to me of how to respect and submit to authority in a God-honoring way. When it comes to leading others, I confess that I do not always follow my authority as Christ did. I confess I...

Empower me to be a strong, impactful follower who is a joy to those in authority over me.

Father, Thank You for being an authority who doesn't take advantage of His power. Thank You for loving, serving, and honoring those who follow You! In relationships where You have placed me in a position with authority, empower me to be a strong, impactful leader who loves well, serves humbly, and honors people as creations made in Your image.

Father, help me to pay more attention to leaders and the relationships between leaders and the people they lead. Please grant me further insight into the roles of leader and follower, husband and wife, man and woman. May I be a joy to You as a follower, a leader of others, and a woman made in Your image. In Your Son's Name, Amen.

13 - Say Goodbye

In the Garden, God provided leadership to Man and Woman when He gave them one limitation, or boundary. "And the Lord God commanded the man, saying, 'You may surely eat of every tree of the garden; but of the Tree of the Knowledge of Good and Evil, you shall not eat, for in the day you eat of it you will surely die'" (Genesis 2:16-17). Genesis 3 tells the story of how satan, disguised as a serpent, tempted the Woman to eat from the forbidden tree. To eat or not to eat? Hmmm.

She gave in to his manipulation and took a big, juicy bite.
Chomp…chew, chew, chew…gulp.
She also offered the fruit to her husband.
Chomp…chew, chew, chew…gulp.

"And they heard the sound of the LORD God walking in the garden in the cool of the day, and the man and his wife hid themselves from the presence of the LORD God among the trees of the garden. But the LORD God called to the man and said to him, 'Where are you?' And he said, 'I heard the sound of you in the garden, and I was afraid, because I was naked, and I hid myself'" (Genesis 3:6-10).

Remember the blessings of *oneness* Man and Woman enjoyed in their relationship with God and with one other? It all perished with a juicy bite. Bye, Bye, freedom. Hello, shame.

Note>>>The fruit from the Tree of the Knowledge of Good and Evil was thought to be a fruit unique to the tree (and not an apple). Since an apple is usually used to depict this Bible story, we'll refer to the fruit as an apple.

The choice was made. When we make a choice, we are *choosing* something and *not choosing* something else. When Man and Woman chose to eat from the Tree of the Knowledge of Good and Evil, they also chose not to obey God's command. Their choice meant they sinned against God. Man and Woman knew their choice was wrong. After taking the fruity bites, "they knew they were naked. And they sewed fig leaves together and made themselves loincloths" (Genesis 3:7).

Every choice we make has consequences (results, effects). Sometimes the consequences of our choices are good. Sometimes the consequences of our choices are bad…really, really bad. No fruit could have tasted delicious enough to outweigh the consequences Man and Woman were about to face.

First, they had to face the One whom they had sinned against. "{God} said, 'Who told you that you were naked? Have you eaten of the tree of which I commanded you not to eat?' The man said, 'The woman whom you gave to be with me, she gave me fruit of the tree, and I ate.' Then the LORD God said to the woman, 'What is this that you have done?' The woman said, 'The serpent deceived me, and I ate'" (Genesis 3:8-13).

Omniscient God knew Man and Woman had sinned against Him before He came to them. God could have given them the silent treatment. He could have come to them, yelling and accusing them of sinning. Instead, He came to them *graciously*. He came to them and asked them what happened.

God gave them a chance to tell the story from their perspective. In doing so, God gave them the chance to say, "I'm sorry." But, they didn't apologize. Perhaps they were so used to God's love and respectful way of treating them that they didn't always recognize it or appreciate it. Perhaps they were too busy thinking of themselves to see the loving God who was with them. "If we confess our sins, he is faithful and just to forgive us our sins and to cleanse us from all unrighteousness" (1 John 1:9).

Their sinful choice not only placed Man and Woman in a bad position, but it also placed God in a different position. God, who is Holy and always does the right thing, needed to take His place at the judgment seat. Because of their sin, the loving God who handed out blessings to them had to hand out punishment.

God decided on a verdict and punished the guilty, beginning with the serpent, then moving to the Woman, and ending with the Man.

Judging the serpent – Genesis 3:14-15

"Because you have done this, cursed are you above all livestock and above all beasts of the field; on your belly you shall go, and dust you shall eat all the days of your life. I will put enmity between you and the woman, and between your offspring and her offspring; he shall bruise your head, and you shall bruise his heel."

Judging Woman – Genesis 3:16

"I will surely multiply your pain in childbearing; in pain you shall bring forth children. Your desire shall be for your husband, and he shall rule over you."

In a short, two-sentence judgment, Woman became the recipient of a lot of pain and suffering. She took a blow in the two areas that are unique to her as a Woman: bearing children and being a helper fit for Man. Learning more about the pain experienced in childbirth is easy. Just ask mothers you know about their labor processes. You will find that most stories will make you cringe, maybe even leave you scared to death. The birthing process has the potential to be excruciatingly painful. It's called "labor" for a reason!

With the announcement of the second part of the judgment, Woman's relationship with Man became complicated. "Your desire will be for your husband, and he shall rule over you." The Hebrew word for *desire* means "stretching out after, a longing."[13] Since the first day she entered the world, Woman had all the love she needed. She had never doubted that God loved her and that Man loved her. However, due to her sin, she would yearn for and crave man's *attention, acceptance,* and *adoration* (the *Triple A's*). Sin would hinder Man's ability to lead with wisdom and love. The Woman would have to submit to an imperfect husband while wrestling with her own sin-tainted heart.

Judging Man - Genesis 3:17-19

"And to Adam he said, 'Because you have listened to the voice of your wife and have eaten from the tree of which I commanded you, 'You shall not eat of it,' cursed is the ground because of you; In pain you shall eat of it all the days of your life; thorns and thistles it shall bring forth for you; and you shall eat the plants of the field. By the sweat of your face you shall eat bread, till you return to the ground, for out of it you were taken; for you are dust, and to dust you shall return.'"

Because of his sin, Man would move from paradise to common ground, complete with thorns and weeds. The choice food of the Garden would no longer be his feast; he must eat the herbs of the field like the animals He governs. The changing of the ground would negatively affect his work, and his work would distract him from his relationship with Woman.

At the close of Genesis 3, Man called his wife Eve, which means "mother of all the living." This name change is a reminder that God blessed them and said, "Be fruitful and multiply and fill the earth" (Genesis 1:28). Though God was on the judgment seat, He showed them compassion. They sinned against God, yet God intended to be faithful in fulfilling His promises to them. Eve made a choice for self, herself. Adam made a choice for self, himself. God made a choice to love. God had a Plan. Through their offspring, He would provide a Savior. "For the wages of sin is death, but the free gift of God is eternal life in Christ Jesus our Lord" (Romans 6:23a).

Next, the Great Judge graciously provided Adam and Eve with clothing, a parting gift as they exited the Garden. Though it may seem harsh that God drove them out of the Garden, it was another gracious gesture on His part. If Adam and Eve had eaten from the Tree of Life after sinning, they would have lived forever as sinners (Genesis 3:20-24).

Adam and Eve were set to live forever in paradise, but that apple-bite caused them to start the dying process. Bye, bye, God. Bye, bye, paradise. Hello to a much different world and much different relationships.

Think about it!

The man's once pleasurable work became difficult, consuming, and exhausting. Let's use a word picture to help us envision how the change in Man's work and the Woman's intensified desire for her husband impacted their relationship.

To illustrate this, we might draw a man using a shovel to forcefully break the surface of the hard dirt beneath him. Beads of sweat cover his forehead; he has been working since dawn to prep the ground for seed. His work will not be completed until well after dusk. His back is turned to his wife, for he is focused on his work. The wife, wanting the husband's attention, reaches out her hand to touch him. The wife desires to feel close to her husband, to talk and laugh with him, but he is consumed by his work. Her eyes fill with tears.

1—Draw the word picture (or your own adaptation).

2—Remember the ladies' stories you read about in Reading 2? If you take a closer look, in many of the ladies' stories, you will see traces of *desire* for a man. Re-read the stories from Reading 2 and highlight the phrases/sentences that show the Genesis 3:16 desire.

Pray about it!

Dear God,
You are an incredibly loving God. You didn't hold back when it came to loving Man and Woman. You spent quality time with them. You gave them everything with the exception of only one thing—fruit from the Tree of the Knowledge of Good and Evil. Out of love, You warned them of the consequences of eating from that tree. When they committed evil against You, You didn't waver in Your love for them.

You are an amazing God—holy and relational, just and compassionate, loving in all Your ways. God, I don't want to take You for granted. Empower me to love You! I pray in Jesus' Name, Amen.

14 - Wounded

When Adam and Eve made their choice to eat from the Tree of the Knowledge of Good and Evil, did they fully understand the choice they were making and the corresponding consequences? Whether they did or not, they knew God's heart and character. They knew He was a loving God who had taken "very good" care of His "very good" creations. God provided Adam and Eve a home in paradise to enjoy freely with just one boundary. "And the LORD God commanded the man, saying, 'You may surely eat of every tree of the garden, but of the tree of the knowledge of good and evil you shall not eat, for in the day that you eat of it you shall surely die'" (Genesis 2:16).

In their book *Boundaries*, Dr. Henry Cloud and Dr. John Townsend say, "Boundaries define us. They define what is me and what is not me. A boundary shows me where I end and someone else begins, leading me to a sense of ownership."[14]

God's boundary (or limit) was more than reasonable. As their authority, God deserved to be respected through the honoring of His rules. He graciously gave Adam and Eve a wide variety of other delicious foods to eat. They certainly weren't starving! The boundary wasn't created to make them suffer. God made the boundary for His glory, for their protection, and most for their personal growth. When the boundary was honored, it:

guarded them spiritually,
guarded them emotionally,
guarded them physically,
protected them from falling into temptation,
protected the heart of who they were (i.e. who they were designed to be),
preserved their ability to fulfill their purpose,
kept them close to God and in right relationship with Him, and
kept them close to each other, enjoying *oneness*.

The idea of a boundary may have been a lot for Adam and Eve to digest, but God warned Adam: "But of the tree of the knowledge of good and evil you shall not eat, for in the day that you eat of it you shall surely die" (Genesis 3:17). God clearly communicated His boundary and its consequences. How did satan the serpent get them to eat from that fruit tree and ruin their lives? Genesis 3:1-7 and Matthew Henry's Commentary[15] helped me take a closer look at the story. Let's take a closer look at what happened together!

Serpent: "Did God actually say, 'You shall not eat of any tree in the garden?'"

{The serpent questioned Woman about God's commandment, as if God didn't mean what He said and as if God's Word wasn't true.}

Woman: "We may eat of the fruit of the trees in the garden, but God said, 'You shall not eat of the fruit of the tree that is in the midst of the garden, neither shall you touch it, lest you die.'"

{When the conversation began, Woman was already near the tree. Her first mistake was coming near to her shady temptation. Her second mistake was engaging in conversation with a snake. A creepy, chatty snake should have been a red flag to her that something wasn't quite right. We don't know if she stayed because she was paralyzed by shock or curious to see what would happen. It's possible that in her innocence, she didn't have experience in dealing with evil and just didn't do well when her faith was tested. Yet, the fact that the sneaky snake questioned God should have been another red flag. His tone and nonverbal body language may have been warning signs, too.}

Serpent: "You will not surely die. For God knows that when you eat of it your eyes will be opened, and you will be like God, knowing good and evil."

{The serpent flat out lied—another red flag. The serpent denied the consequence that would come if Woman ate from the tree. In doing so, he spoke against the character of God and the trustworthiness of His Word—yet another red flag. The serpent twisted the whole concept of the tree, suggesting it would be to her advantage to eat from the tree—a contradiction to God's Word and manipulation to get her to do what he wanted. The snake's slander created doubt and confusion in the Woman's mind. In Genesis 3:17, the command to not eat from the tree was given to Man before Woman was created. It seems she heard the command secondhand, which may have contributed to her confusion.}

Woman: "So when the woman saw that the tree was good for food, and that it was a delight to the eyes…"

{Woman went beyond speaking words in a conversation to looking at the shady temptation. Her move to action reveals she began to take the serpent's words to heart. She mistakenly placed her trust in a stranger (or rather, an unfamiliar snake) she didn't know anything about. She looked at the fruit-filled tree with pleasure, seemingly forgetting about all the pleasure she already experienced eating from the wide variety of "free-for-the-taking trees" found in the Garden.}

Woman: "…and that the tree was to be desired to make one wise…"

{Through her eyes, Woman saw that intellectual benefits would come from eating the fruit. She wanted to know what God knew—a big red flag. In her mind, she convinced herself that she could know all that the Omniscient, Omnipresent, Eternal Creator of the world knew. If she had only asked, God probably would have enjoyed teaching her about all kinds of things. Essentially, Woman wanted to be like God. What she failed to recognize was that she was already like God; she was made in His image.}

Woman: "…she took of its fruit and ate, and she also gave some to her husband who was with her, and he ate."

{Woman stole. She took something that belonged to God, something He had not given to her. Woman led in eating the apple with her husband following her lead. This meant their roles were reversed. God's structure for oneness was disregarded.}

Scripture indicates that in *The Fall*, Woman was deceived by satan. During the Genesis 3:13 conversation: "The LORD God said to the woman, 'What is this you have done?' The woman said, 'The serpent deceived me, and I ate.'" 1 Timothy 2:14 says, "And Adam was not the one deceived; it was the woman who was deceived and became a sinner." When God handed down a curse to Adam, He began by saying, "Because you have listened to the voice of your wife and have eaten of the tree of which I commanded you, 'You shall not eat of it…'" (Genesis 3:17). This indicates that Adam knew he was sinning when he allowed his wife to lead in eating the apple.

Think about it!

A good boundary will serve to grow and strengthen relationships. When a good boundary is not respected and upheld, relationships end up wounded (harmed, hurt, broken). Our words and actions can cause others to feel loved or hated, respected or disrespected, trusted or betrayed, encouraged or manipulated. Below are actions that happened as part of *The Fall*. Think about how each action hurt the person who was sinned against and the relationship. Do the actions reveal disrespect, manipulation, betrayal, slander, or deceit?

1—Woman trusted an unloving serpent over the God to whom she belonged.

2—Woman made an important decision without consulting her husband.

3—Woman stole from God.

4—Woman enticed her husband to eat the fruit, to sin.

5—Man did not consult God (or heed God's previous instruction) before eating the fruit.

6—Woman ate the fruit.

7—Man ate the fruit.

Pray about it!

All-Knowing God,
Thank You for creating the Bible so that I can know You. Thank You for providing the Bible so that I can know the good boundaries that were designed to protect me from evil. Enable me to claim the prosperous, hope-filled future You have planned for me.

(Psalm 119:33-40) "Teach me, O LORD, the way of your statutes; and I will keep it to the end. Give me understanding, that I may keep your law and observe it with my whole heart. Lead me in the path of your commandments, for I delight in it. Incline my heart to your testimonies, and not to selfish gain! Turn my eyes from looking at worthless things; and give me life in your ways. Confirm to your servant your promise, that you may be feared. Turn away the reproach that I dread, for your rules are good. Behold, I long for your precepts; in your righteousness give me life!" In Jesus' Mighty Name I pray, Amen.

15 - Bitter Aftertaste

"But the LORD God called to the man and said to him, 'Where are you?'" (Genesis 3:9-13). It was the moment of truth…

Man: "I heard the sound of you in the garden, and I was afraid, because I was naked, and I hid myself."

God: "Who told you that you were naked? Have you eaten of the tree of which I commanded you not to eat?"

Man: "The woman whom you gave to be with me, she gave me fruit of the tree, and I ate."

God: "What is this that you have done?"

Woman: "The serpent deceived me, and I ate."

When it was time to fess up, the Man blamed the Woman for the choice he made. The Woman blamed the serpent for the choice she made. The moment of truth—the time to come clean—was not truthful, pure, nor loving.

Both the Man and the Woman admitted the obvious: "I ate." A simple "I ate, and I'm sorry!" would have been nice. Instead, both of them watered down their confession by dragging someone else through the mud with them. Though Woman enticed Man to eat the fruit, the choice—to eat or not to eat, to obey God or not to obey God—was *his* choice. Though the serpent deceived Woman, the choice—to eat or not to eat, to obey God or not to obey God—was *her* choice.

In his confession, Man described the Woman as "the woman whom you gave to be with me" (Genesis 3:12). His words seem to **insin**uate that God gave Man the Woman to harm him as if God tempted him to sin.

Blaming God for their sin wasn't the best idea, and God was not amused. Before He announced the curses to Man, He reminded Man of why he was receiving a curse: "And to

Adam he said, 'Because you have listened to the voice of your wife and have eaten of the tree of which I commanded you, 'You shall not eat of it…'" (Genesis 3:17).

What Man and Woman did was *blame shifting*. This occurs when a person consciously makes a choice and follows through on her (or his) decision by taking action. When she is held accountable (called to explain or give an account) for her actions, she blames someone else for what she has done. In blame shifting, a person fails to take responsibility for her choices and actions. Blame shifting brings no good; it hurts people and relationships.

Woman was deeply wounded by Man's blame shifting. She remembered the moment when Man first laid eyes on her. He thought she was breathtakingly beautiful. He didn't hesitate to pursue her. He verbally expressed his pleasure in her with those passionate words from Genesis 2:23: "This is now bone of my bones and flesh of my flesh." He affectionately named her with a name that boldly proclaimed that she was intimately connected with him, "She shall be called Woman, for she was taken out of Man."

He was proud of her, and he was proud to be united with her. On the day of *The Fall*, she saw a different side of her husband.

Woman and Man had always been *one*, partners who walked through life together. But in that moment of truth, Man didn't stand up for Woman. When faced with a trial, he didn't even stand with her. He blamed her for doing him harm. It's likely his words were spoken with an angry tone as he said, *"That* woman you gave me…"

His words cut her like a knife. His words seemed to validate her as a failure. She failed to bear the loving image of God. She failed to help her husband claim the plans God had for them. Now, the husband for whom she was made to be a "helper fit" no longer found her acceptable. He didn't want to claim her. "A wife of noble character is her husband's crown, but a disgraceful wife is like decay in his bones" (Proverbs 12:4).

The Silence of Adam is a book written by Dr. Larry Crabb, a noted counselor and seminary professor, scholar Don Hudson, and counselor Al Andrews. The book presents an excellent case to support the theory that Adam was with Eve the *whole* time she was being tempted. It says, "Adam was not only silent with the serpent, he was also silent with Eve. He never reminded her of God's word. He never called her to a larger vision. He did not join his wife in battling wits with the serpent. He passively listened to her speak, rather than speaking with her in mutual respect."[16]

If Adam was with Eve throughout *The Fall*, then Eve had some severe wounds inflicted by his words. Imagine you were Eve tempted by a strange snake. How would you feel if your husband, who knew God's command with certainty and who had the strength and power to stop the sin, just stood there? How would you feel knowing he stood there and did nothing AND blamed you for his sin?

In the moment of truth, Adam and Eve found themselves in a big mess. "For the wages of sin is death" (Romans 6:23). When they sinned, Adam and Eve saw the death of many things:

Their physical bodies grew weaker every day.

They saw the immediate death of their innocence, happiness, peace, freedom, love, life in paradise, true relationship.

The relationship of Man to God, Woman to God, and Man to Woman would never be the same.

They lost it all. Their perfect lives were over. Sin's bitter aftertaste would remain with them for the rest of their lives.

At the end of every day, there would be no one to blame but themselves.

Think about it!

"A common boundary problem is disowning our choices and trying to lay the responsibility for them on someone else. Think for a moment how often we use the phrases, 'I had to' or 'She (he) made me' when explaining why we did or did not do something. These phrases betray our basic illusion that we are not active agents in our dealings. We think someone else is in control, thus relieving us of our basic responsibility. We need to realize that we *are* in control of our choices, no matter how we feel." Dr. Henry Cloud and Dr. John Townsend[17]

1—When you realize you have sinned or are about to sin, do you seek to be honest and take responsibility for your behavior? Or do you brainstorm excuses and blame others? And why?

2—God is extremely gracious to us when we take responsibility for our choices. Based on the scripture passages below, what are the blessings/benefits He grants us?

    Proverbs 19:9

    Hebrews 4:13

    James 4:6-12

    1 John 1:5-10

Pray about it!

Pray using the **ACTS**-model, which stands for **A**doration (praise), **C**onfession, **T**hanksgiving, and **S**upplication (request, ask).

Dear God,
*I **adore** You for You are a God of integrity.*

*I **confess** that I struggle to live with integrity. I confess that I…*

***Thank You** that the Bible is my guide for knowing what is truth or a lie and knowing good from evil.*

*I **ask** that You give me the strength to resist temptation, to speak the truth, to act justly, and to take responsibility for my actions. Give me the wisdom and discernment to know when someone is blaming me for their actions. Empower me not to take responsibility for others' actions. God, be glorified in my thoughts, words, and behavior. In Jesus' Strong Name I pray, Amen.*

16 - Rotten Apple

Adam and Eve were the first father and first mother of the human race. Essentially, they were our great, great, great, great, great, great, great, great, great, great, great, great, great, great, great, great, great, (well, you get the point) grandfather and grandmother. Unfortunately, their poor food choices make them seem not-so-great and far from grand. For today, we'll call them Mom and Dad for short.

The way Mom and Dad lived their lives carried their influence far beyond the Garden of Eden. Their stories impacted every person who has lived and died, every person who is currently living, and every person who will one day be born into the world. With a Holy, Wise, Almighty God guiding, loving, and supporting them, Mom and Dad had unlimited potential. They could have lived up to the title of "grand" and accomplished "great" things in their lives. Mom and Dad could have left their children and grandchildren a remarkable legacy. But we all know how their stories ended. What began as a fairytale of sorts turned into a horror story.

Where their stories end is where our stories begin. We follow in the footsteps of a mom and dad who failed miserably. They had it all, and they lost it all. When they lost it all, they didn't just lose it for themselves. They lost it for all of us. When God created Adam and Eve, He built worth and purpose into Man. Not only was He showing His favor to Man, but He was also making a covenant, or promise, to Man. God promised relationship to Man, and that promise required something of Man—to obey God. That meant not eating from the Tree of the Knowledge of Good and Evil. God's covenant with Man included God's blessing on Man to "be fruitful and multiply and fill the earth and subdue it," and so, God's Covenant was for all of Mankind. Adam represented all Mankind. Together with Eve, Adam disobeyed God and His covenantal requirement.

Romans 5:12
"Therefore, just as sin came into the world through one man, and death through sin, and so death spread to all men because all sinned…"

Romans 5:18
"One trespass led to condemnation for all men…"

Romans 5:19
"For as by the one man's disobedience the many were made sinners…"

The legacy Mom and Dad left us is one of sin, separation from God, struggle, pain, and suffering. When we were born, we entered a world where all had been lost long before we took our first breath. "Behold, I was brought forth in iniquity, and in sin did my mother conceive me" (Psalm 51:5). *Gee…thanks…Mom and Dad.*

Does it make you mad that Mom and Dad did that to us? It made me mad! In my eyes and in the eyes of the majority of their descendants, Mom seems to have taken the brunt of the Fall. Thousands of years after her death, she is the butt of many jokes. She is often ridiculed as the one who brought Dad down. On the canvas of Dad's life, his story would most likely be depicted with Mom offering him an apple she had first sampled. On the canvas of Mom's life, her story would be illustrated with a red apple in her hand as she makes small talk with a silly-looking snake. It all goes back to Mom and that apple. How lame for one's most memorable contribution to the world to be symbolized with a piece of fruit that rots!

I just didn't understand. Mom had it all—a blessed marriage, beauty (inside and out), a nice place to live, lots of delicious food, a variety of pets, plants she didn't have to water, and the blessing of children to come. Even if those things were taken away from her, she had the most important thing anyone could ever have: She had a relationship with God and lived in His glorious presence every day. He was *with her* to love her, to lead her, to empower her. But she lost it all, and she ruined life for the whole human race. *If she had never sinned,* I thought, *then my life would not be a horrible mess right now. How could she do that?* Have you felt that way about Mom? What thoughts or feelings have you had about her?

I wanted to hate Mom for what she did. I tried to hate her, but God's Word cut through my hatred. "For the word of God is living and active, sharper than any two-edged sword, piercing to the division of soul and of spirit, of joints and of marrow, and discerning the thoughts and intentions of the heart" (Hebrews 4:12). Included below are the truths and thoughts that poked and prodded my heart.

Matthew 7:4-5
"Or how can you say to your brother, 'Let me take the speck out of your eye,' when there is the log in your own eye? You hypocrite, first take the log out of your own eye, and then you will see clearly to take the speck out of your brother's (or father's, or sister's, or mother's) eye."

Romans 3:23
"For all have sinned and fall short of the glory of God."

John 8:2-11
"The scribes and the Pharisees brought a woman who had been caught in adultery, and placing her in the midst they said to him, 'Teacher, this woman has been caught in the act of adultery. Now in the Law Moses commanded us to stone such women. So what do you say?' This they said to test him, and that they might have some charge to bring against him. Jesus bent down and wrote with his finger in the ground. And as they continued to ask {Jesus}, he stood up and said to them, 'Let him who is among you be the first to throw a stone at her.' Jesus stood up and said to her, 'Woman, where are they? Has no one condemned you?' She said, 'No one, Lord.' And Jesus said, 'Neither do I condemn you; go, and from now on sin

no more.'"

Here are some reasons Eve deserves our respect:

Ephesians 6:2-3
"Honor your father and mother (this is the first commandment with a promise), 'that it may go well with you and that you may live long in the land.'"

Genesis 1:27
"So God created man in his own image, in the image of God he created him; male and female he created them."

Think about it!

1—If another woman besides Eve had been the first woman in the Garden of Eden, would she have sinned? Why or why not?

2—Ask yourself, "If I was the first woman in the Garden, would *I* have been able to resist the temptation to eat the apple?"

3—If you blame Eve for your failures, is that blame shifting? Why or why not?

"Following Eve's Footsteps"—A CREATIVE CHALLENGE!

As I pondered God's Word and applied it in my life, I began to see Mother Eve was more than a thief who stole from God and robbed me of my fairytale story. God's Word helped me see her as a person with thoughts, feelings, and desires. Respecting her, instead of condemning her, brought a whole new perspective to the story of *The Fall of Man*.

I invite you to put yourself in Eve's shoes—I mean bare feet—and walk her path for a few miles. Re-read the story of *The Fall of Man* in Genesis 3, and pretend you are Eve. Seek to understand who she was and what she experienced.

Because this CREATIVE CHALLENGE can be extremely impactful in your life, I encourage you to give it your best effort and not skip over it. The CHALLENGE is to creatively share the story of *The Fall of Man* from Eve's perspective, showing how it impacted her. The CREATIVE part is up to you. For example, those who like to write might write about *The Fall of Man* as if Eve was journaling about it. Others might capture Eve's experience in a sketchbook. From scrapbooking and photography, to dance choreography and acting, to vlogging and songwriting, choose your CREATIVE way to share Eve's experience.

Here are some questions to consider as you re-read the story: What did she see? What did she hear? What did she smell? What did she taste? What did she feel? What thoughts ran through her head? What desires filled her heart?

Do your best to complete this **CREATIVE CHALLENGE** in the next 7 days. When posting your creations on your social media accounts, tag @aimforhimblog and use hashtags #LovebyDesignBook and #AimforHim.

Pray about it!

Heavenly Father,
I praise You, for You are a relational God who loves His people. Thank You for making Yourself known to me. I confess that I judged Eve. Your Word tells me that all have sinned. I am a sinner, and I have no right to condemn Eve or blame her for my sin. Please forgive me.

Eve was made in Your image. She is "the mother of the living." She is my mom, and You have commanded me to honor her. You placed the story of mom eating that apple in the Bible for a reason. Show me what I can learn from her story that I can apply in my life. Father God, glorify Yourself through my story. In the Name of Jesus, Amen.

(Genesis 1:27, Romans 3:23, Ephesians 6:2-3, 1 Corinthians 13:4-8)

17 - Eve's Footsteps

I took the CREATIVE CHALLENGE and imagined myself in Eve's place as she acclimated herself to a whole new world tainted by sin. May God ignite your imagination as you follow Eve's footsteps in your own CREATIVE CHALLENGE.

Eve's Story

I walked in the Garden naked and doing so felt good, comfortable, and right. Then one day, walking around naked didn't feel good anymore; being naked felt shameful, uncomfortable, and wrong. I remember those cherubim who stood guard at the Garden gates. They were always so kind and friendly. But on the day that sin entered the world, the cherubim's stern faces, solemn stares, and the force with which they moved us out of the Garden were perhaps some of the most frightening memories of that dreadful day.

I can hardly bear to remember how angry God became and how much He hated sin. I had never seen Him find displeasure or disappointment in anything. But on that day, the God who deeply loved Adam and me and loved us more than any fish, bird, plant—more than anything in the world He created—ordered us out of His presence. God made us "very good," but when sin entered our hearts, there was nothing good in us.

My eyes were opened that day I fell. I began to see a whole new world, the place that exists outside of the love of God. It's a lonely, painful, sad, hopeless place. I'll be honest with you. For a while, I was really angry at God for making us leave the Garden. After all, it was just a piece of fruit, right? But the more I remembered all those fun times Adam and I shared with God, I couldn't convince myself that God made us leave unfairly. If there's one thing I know for certain about God, I know He is loving. He would do anything for Adam and me.

God is Holy. Oh—the beauty and majesty of His Holiness—I'll never forget what an awesome God He was to behold. Many times I would sit in silence before Him, taking in the magnificence of His exquisite glory radiating from Him. What a gift it was to be in the presence of His Holiness. Now that my heart is filled with sin, it is unclean—too impure to be near God. His Holiness cannot be in the presence of impurity—no way. If I were to see His face in this sinful condition, I would actually die. I understand now that He had no choice except to order us to leave. In fact, He was gracious to do so.

As hard as it is to admit, I realize that I must accept the blame for my sin-filled actions and face the consequences. God said, "You may surely eat of every tree in the garden, but of the tree of the knowledge of good and evil you shall not eat, for in that day that you eat of it you shall surely die." His words were clear. His warning was strong. Yet, I was greedy. I wanted to be like God. I wanted His wisdom and goodness. When I reached for that fruit, I was trying to take a handful of God's glory. What in the world was I thinking? What I didn't realize was that I had a relationship with God Himself. I had everything I could possibly have in life. I reached for that fruit because I desired to be like God. What I failed to see was that I was already like God, for He made me in His image.

If only I had been strong—strong enough in my love for God—to say, "No," and turn and walk away from the Tree of the Knowledge of Good and Evil. If only I had taken some time to think before I acted. If only I had realized that God's Command, His Truth, was all I needed to make wise decisions. But I ate from *that* eye-opener, hope-stealer, life-ender of a tree! Ughhh!!!

Now I must live with the results of my sin. The consequences never seem to end. I used to spend lots of time with Adam; we always had so much fun together. Now I hardly see him. He has to work such long, hard hours just to put food on the tree stump table and clothes on our backs. As much as I love Adam, sometimes my heart feels a loss of love for him; sometimes I feel hatred towards him. I can't fully explain it, but I know those terrible feelings are connected to the sin that has made its home in my heart.

I hate this new world, partly because I've seen how good things can be—God's best. I desperately miss being around God. There is nothing I can do to make myself good enough to gain entrance into God's glory again. I wish all this pain could end with me. It's bad enough that I have to suffer; it's even worse to watch my children suffer, too. They don't know the beauty and tranquility of the Garden. All they know is the ugliness and turmoil of this so-far-away-from-God place in which they live.

I watched my older boy, Cain, bring God fat portions from his flock as His offering. Cain's actions were thoughtless and careless; he doesn't understand the Holiness of God. He doesn't comprehend that God is worthy of the best he has to offer…and so much more. His actions reveal to me that sin is reigning in his heart.

I wish I could say that Cain's only struggle is whether to eat from this tree or that one. But the sin my son battles seems more complicated than my sin battle in the Garden. Cain was jealous of his younger brother, Abel. Over time, sinful thoughts kept building inside of him, and he killed his brother. *He murdered his own brother.* My son is a cold-blooded killer. My dear Abel is dead. I had to bury my own son. I never ever experienced such loss and grief in the Garden. There's nothing I can do for my children; sin is not just my problem or Adam's problem. Sin is now every person's problem.

My eyes saw the birth of sin in mankind, and I have watched sin grow into an untamable monster. I lived in Paradise. I experienced the goodness of life with God. It is horrifying to see how far sin takes us away from God and how quickly it ruins lives. The reality of it all is hard to swallow. I can hardly bear the heaviness and emptiness I feel in my heart. I am glad I won't live to see sin and its effects centuries from now because it will all be much too great for my human heart to bear.

If I could go back and do things over, I would run as fast as I could from that tree. I might even take a piece of fruit and smack that sly snake right between the eyes. I would take it all back if I could, but there's nothing I can do to make things better. Nothing. Only God has the power to change things.

I hope that my children, my grandchildren, their sons and daughters, and all of Adam's and my descendants will one day get to see God face-to-face. I want them to know the glory and wonder of being close to Him. God is such a loving God. He values relationship and wants to have relationship with the people He created. I know He hates sin. As hopeless as this world seems, I believe God's love for His people is so great that He will do *something* to help us. Holy God, please forgive us our sins, and bring Your people near to You again!

Think about it!

Eve had a unique perspective on the relationship between God and His people. God brought her into the world, and she quickly learned that she was made in His image (and so was Adam). God came to Adam and Eve, and He pursued a personal relationship with them. God came to them, and they came to know Him.

In the Bible, we read that God is Holy, and we try to grasp in some way what that means. In the beginning, God's glory dominated Eve's world. When Adam and Eve sinned, they denied God's calling to live as His people, and her eyes were opened. She fully understood how heinous her sin was because she had experienced God's perfection. How gut-wrenching and hopeless it must have been to know only the beginning of the story. Imagine what hope it would have brought Eve to read the Bible stories of God pursuing and restoring relationship with His people through a covenant, or promise, of what He would do.

Look up the following Bible verses, and as you read, pretend you are Eve! How would Eve respond to what she learns through these verses?

Genesis 12:1-3

Genesis 17:1-8

Exodus 6:1-8

Matthew 1:23

John 1:14

John 3:16

1 Corinthians 6:19

Revelation 21:1-5

Pray about it!

Holy God,
I praise You, for You are Perfect in every way! Help me to understand the magnitude of Your Holiness. In light of Your Holiness, help me see the darkness of my sin. Thank You that you came to Your people and were with them. Eve didn't appreciate what she had in You until she was separated from You. Teach me to appreciate and enjoy You more and more, for I do not want to take You for granted. In Jesus' Holy Name I pray, Amen.

18 - Life Lessons

A s you have been working on the **CREATIVE CHALLENGE** of *"Following Eve's Footsteps,"* what has it been like to see sin and the world from Eve's perspective? Have you had any new revelations about Eve or yourself?

Following Eve's footsteps led me to view Eve from an entirely different perspective. As I sought to understand who she was and what she experienced, I began to appreciate her. My contempt for her melted away. Compassion emerged.

As the first Woman, Eve had a lot resting on her shoulders. She had to embrace her design. She was created as the beautiful, softer side of God, and she had to learn how to live out that design. She had to understand what it meant to be *one* with Adam with no other married couples to model it for her, no marriage counselors, no marriage seminars, and no books like this one to guide her! Plus, God wanted her to help Adam with ruling creation and filling the earth—two HUGE responsibilities. Eve definitely had a lot to learn.

Is it possible that Eve felt so overwhelmed by all the things she didn't know that a desire to figure it all contributed to her reaching for the full-of-knowledge tree?

I found Eve relatable. Sure, I've never talked to a snake in the literal sense, but figuratively, I've fallen prey to some sneaky snakes in my life! What about you? Can you relate to any of the following statements about Eve?

She had a relationship with God; He was there to love her, lead her, and empower her.

She forgot that she had everything she needed in God and reached for something more.

She made a bad decision and placed her trust in an unsafe place.

She made her heart vulnerable and ended up hurt.

Her sin caused a mess in her life.

Her sin negatively impacted her relationship with God and another person.

When I first followed Eve's footsteps, I was wading through the aftermath of that destructive dating relationship. My life was a mess, and I realized I had every single scenario in common with Eve.

(Hard swallow.)
(Deep breath…exhale.)

Then *my* eyes were opened, and I saw the cold, hard truth: If I had been Eve, tempted with the fruit, I would have done the SAME thing she did. Anticipating a sweet bite, I would have reached for the apple and sunk my teeth into it. I would have failed, too! *OUCH!!! Ughhh!!!*

In that moment of truth, *Eve's Story* became much more than a Bible Story. *Eve's Story* is *My Story.* The truth is…*Eve's Story* is *Your Story,* too. It hurts, doesn't it?

Eve's Story—*Our Story*—are marked by failure. All of us are BIG, FAT SINNERS. I craved for *My Story* to have a MUCH different ending from her story. Don't we all want that?

Is there anything else we can learn from *Eve's Story?* Is there any more wisdom to glean from her failure? Could the footsteps that led Eve far from God lead us any closer to Jesus? The answer is YES! In a sense, Eve is a mentor who has gone before us in the world. She gained invaluable life experience from which we can learn and grow.

Eve's Story shows us our pure PURPOSE.
Through Eve, we understand how we were made—by God, in His image—and why we were created—to glorify Him and enjoy Him forever.

Eve's Story shows us our powerful POTENTIAL.
Eve helps us see that we can have tremendous influence in our husbands' lives, in the world in which we live, and in the hearts of future generations.

Eve's Story shows us our pathetic PURSUIT.
Her devilish conversation with the serpent reveals that we are too quick to abandon our purpose and disregard all we have to take hold of something that seems better.

Eve's Story shows us our perilous PREDICAMENT.
Her pursuit leaves her a sinner and takes her far away from the Garden and the heart of God. She can do nothing to change her situation. Like Eve, we are sinners who need a Savior to rescue us.

Eve's Story reveals our PURPOSE, our POTENTIAL, our PURSUIT, and our PREDICAMENT.

When she was following after God and His Word, she was on the path to becoming everything God created her to be. God's likeness in her made her beautiful, "very good," full of purpose and potential. When she stopped pursuing God to pathetically pursue evil, she ended up in a perilous predicament. Eve's Story is an important reminder. We need a Savior and must be intentional about following His lead every day.

In her book *Let Me Be a Woman*, Elisabeth Elliot posed this question: "What sort of world might it have been if Eve had refused the Serpent's offer and had said to him instead, 'Let me not be like God. Let me be what I was made to be—let me be a woman?'"[18]

As women, we would recognize the worth of human life and treat creations made in His image with dignity.

We wouldn't put ourselves down.

We would stop competing with other women and cheer them on to become all God had in mind when He created them.

We would seek to be helpers, not manipulators.

We wouldn't have to be right; we would value unity with others over getting our way.

While dating, we wouldn't compromise the heart of who we are for the sake of gaining *The Triple A's—attention, acceptance,* and *adoration.*

Once married, we would cultivate our homes into loving, safe refuges where our husbands find compassion and can be themselves.

We would raise children who realize they have a future and a hope and are loved unconditionally.

God's glory would be revealed to the world through our love instead of through our sin.

We would enjoy a growing, love relationship with God.

Those are just a few ways the world would be a better place if we chose to take hold of our glorious destiny. The world needs you to be you, and it needs me to be me!

Think about it!

1—Ponder your pure PURPOSE. Read 1 Corinthians 10:31, Psalm 73:25-26, and Micah 6:8.

2—Ponder your powerful POTENTIAL. Read Matthew 5:14-16 and 1 Peter 3:1-2.

3—Ponder your pathetic PURSUIT. Read Isaiah 53:6.

4—Ponder your perilous PREDICAMENT. Read Romans 3:23 and Romans 6:23.

5—On a scale of 1-4, rank the life lessons (1=easiest life lesson to embrace and 4=hardest life lesson to embrace.)

Your pure PURPOSE =

Your powerful POTENTIAL =

Your pathetic PURSUIT =

Your perilous PREDICAMENT =

Reminder: Continue working on the *"Following Eve's Footsteps"* **CREATIVE CHALLENGE** introduced in Reading 16. When posting your creations on your social media accounts, tag @aimforhimblog and use hashtags #LovebyDesignBook and #AimforHim.

Pray about it!

Dear God,
Let me be a Woman.
*Let me live with **PURPOSE**.*
*Let me move forward in reaching my **POTENTIAL**.*
*Let my **PURSUIT** be You and not the apples of temptation.*
*Lead me on the right **PATH** to take hold of my glorious destiny.*
In Jesus' Glorious Name I pray, Amen.

19 - Our Perfect Path

Today, we get to walk the path Eve never got to walk. Eve reached out her hand to take a piece of God's glory. Not only did she disobey God's command, but she also disrespected her Creator, a God worthy of ALL of her praise and honor. She abandoned what God created her to be in hopes of becoming something better and ended up becoming something much worse. Her sin separated her from her Heavenly Father. She was under the curse of sin, doomed to die with no hope of returning to her Heavenly Father's loving arms. That was Mother Eve's legacy, and it was our legacy...*until* God gave us Jesus.

John 3:16
"For God so loved the world that He gave His only Son, that whoever believes in him should not perish but have eternal life."

Romans 5:6-8
"For while we were still weak, at the right time Christ died for the ungodly. For one will scarcely die for a righteous person—though perhaps for a good person one would dare even to die—but God showed his love for us in that while we were sinners, Christ died for us."

Romans 5:18-19
"Therefore as one trespass led to condemnation for all men, so one act of righteousness leads to justification and life for all men. For as by the one man's disobedience the many were made sinners, so by the one man's obedience the many will be made righteous."

John 14:6
"Jesus said to him, 'I am the way, and the truth, and the life. No one comes to the Father except through me.'"

Our perfect PATH is Jesus.

He is your perfect PATH—no matter what you've done. No matter how unworthy you feel. No matter how long you've been resisting God or running from Him. Remember that Jesus walked, struggled, and persevered in making His way to the cross for you. Jesus went to the cross with arms open wide...*for you*...and died *for your sins*. Because of what Jesus did, you can run to a loving, merciful God who will lift you up in His arms and hug you close to His heart. "If you confess with your mouth that Jesus is Lord and believe in your heart that God raised him from the dead, you will be saved" (Romans 10:9).

Now is a good time to talk to God, if you desire.

I came to know Jesus as my Lord and Savior a week before my 21st birthday. Before meeting Jesus, I was a girl wandering aimlessly with no hope. The day I entered into a relationship with Him, my life changed forever for the best. My life turned to the perfect PATH, and Jesus filled my life with purpose and hope. At the point in my journey when I sought to embrace and learn from Eve's Story, I had been a Christ-follower for five years. Walking the PATH He paved for me brought me tremendous joy. I knew Jesus was the perfect PATH for me.

Those who knew me when I became a Christian often described me as "passionate" in my relationship with Jesus. Yet, somehow my relationship with the guy from the church singles' group almost destroyed me. That failed relationship was a temptation, a great trial. Once called "passionate," I felt such sorrow and remorse for not loving Jesus well. He *died* for me, and I *abandoned* Him. Jesus gave me everything, and I selfishly thought I needed more. Devastated by the sting of shame, asking His forgiveness didn't seem like enough.

Have you ever felt that saying, "I'm sorry," to a Holy God didn't seem adequate to restore your relationship with Him? Have you ever felt that apologizing to a Glorious God didn't seem to justify your leaving a path leading straight to hell to gain a pathway to heaven?

It can be extremely difficult to see and accept the reality that sin exists in our hearts. Even more difficult is accepting the truth that God loves us and wants to have a personal relationship with us. Accepting these truths are steps taken toward God and steps in the right direction!

When Adam and Eve realized they were sinners, what did they do?
They hid from God. They felt great shame.

What did God do?
He graciously came to them and talked with them.

What did Adam and Eve fail to do in response?
They didn't take responsibility for their sin. They didn't say, "I'm sorry."

What did God do?
He acted justly as their sin deserved, yet He was gracious to them. God didn't give up on Adam and Eve. God doesn't give up on us, either!

God's GRACE...it is a GREAT GIFT. Our sin earns us death. Because God is gracious and loving, He sent Jesus to die for our sins. Jesus bore the punishment for our sins. He came to earth and lived a sinless life, overcoming sin. He died, yet He was victorious over death and rose again. He ascended into heaven, where He is preparing a place for us. Jesus trailblazed a perfect PATH for us.

When we come to God, believing Jesus died for our sins, was buried, and rose again, God sees us through the blood of Jesus. "In him we have redemption through his blood, the forgiveness of our trespasses, according to the riches of his grace, which he lavished upon us, in all wisdom and insight" (Ephesians 1:7-8). Saying "I'm sorry" to God with a heart that truly means it is enough because Jesus graciously did ALL that was needed to restore our broken relationship with God. My pastor, Randy Pope, summarizes it like this:

"We had it ALL.
We lost it ALL.
Jesus did it ALL.
We get it ALL."[19]

On that cross, Jesus said, **"It is FINISHED,'** and he bowed his head and gave up his spirit" (John 19:30). Those who believe in Jesus now have hope. "It is FINISHED." Those who believe in Jesus can find forgiveness for their sins. "It is FINISHED." Those who believe in Jesus can have relationship with God here on earth. "It is FINISHED." Those who believe in Jesus are no longer doomed to die forever but will live in Heaven eternally, no longer separated from God. "It is FINISHED." One day, sin will have absolutely NO hold on us. "It is FINISHED." We will be completely free and completely loved. "It is FINISHED." Because God so loved you and me, our legacy changed for the best. "It is FINISHED."

Praise God! Thank You, Jesus, **"IT IS FINISHED."**

Think about it!

1—Read the following verses, and take notes on how God extends His grace to us:

Ephesians 2:4-10

Hebrews 4:16

Psalm 103:8-12

Pray about it!

If you know with all your heart that you are ready to accept Jesus as your Lord and Savior, pray a prayer something like this, but make it your own!

Dear God,
You are a Holy God. I know I am a sinner. I have sinned against You, and I am truly sorry. Thank You for loving me and sending Jesus. I want Jesus to be the Savior of my life. I believe He died for my sins, was buried, and rose from the grave. I want Jesus to be my Lord, too. Help me to place Jesus first in my heart and life, and empower me to follow His example. I love You, God! I pray in Jesus' Name, Amen.

20 - His Resurrection Power

In His great power, God spoke the world into existence. His power sent Jesus into the world through a woman. Through His power, Jesus bore the sin of the world on the cross. "On that cross, Jesus said, 'It is FINISHED.' and He bowed his head and gave up his spirit" (John 19:30). God's power raised Jesus from the dead and made Him victorious over death. Through His power, our sins are forgiven, and we are made pure. "For as high as the heavens are above the earth, so great is his steadfast love toward those who fear him; as far as the east is from the west, so far does he remove our transgressions from us" (Psalm 103:11-12). That is the power of His resurrection.

The dating relationship had ended, but the guilt and regret over my sin tortured me. Night after night, month after month, tears flooded my eyes, and cascaded down my cheeks. The weight of my sin had taken my heart captive. God had forgiven me, but I struggled to *believe* He had forgiven me, and I struggled to forgive myself. I struggled to experience the power of the resurrection.

One night in my Bible reading, Psalm 55:22 leaped off the Bible pages and tugged on my heart: "Cast your burden on the LORD, and he will sustain you." These particular definitions for *cast* struck me: "*To throw or hurl; fling; to throw off or away.*"[20] The Hebrew word for *cast* means "to hurl."[21] The concept of casting my burden met inspiration and became an activity that helped me deal with my sin.

After several nights of "casting my burdens," I returned to my bedroom another night to read God's Word, journal, cry, and cast some more burdens. If the tears didn't come after reading the Bible, they would always come after journaling. But on this particular night, no tears appeared. Puzzled, I sat still for a while, waiting for the tears to surface...

No tears came. *Hmmm.*

I had no more tears left to cry! My heart—it felt light and free!

I burst out laughing!

Jeremiah 31:13
"For I will turn their mourning into joy and will comfort them and give them gladness for their sorrow."

2 Corinthians 5:17
"Therefore, if anyone is in Christ, he is a new creation. The old has gone; behold, the new has come."

For months, I had been sitting in the ruins that used to be my life with a broken, bleeding heart, unable to move beyond the pain and shame. On that tearless night, God lifted me up, carried me out, and set my feet on solid ground. Though the consequences of my decisions would stay with me for a while, I knew my sin was in the past. It was FINISHED. I was forgiven by God, and He gave me the faith to forgive myself! My relationship with Him was restored!

I was free to move forward. Because Jesus rose from the grave, I could rise from the ruins around me and walk a path full of purpose, potential, and righteous pursuit—a PATH He paved for all who trust in Him. God made me new and gave me a new day, a fresh start. That's the power of His resurrection. "I want to know Christ and the power of his resurrection and the fellowship of sharing in his sufferings, becoming like him in his death, and so somehow to attain to the resurrection from the dead" (Philippians 3:10-11).

Are you struggling to find forgiveness and freedom from sin's shame? Do you find yourself waking up day after day, facing the pain of your sin over and over again? Is your heart aching because someone hurt you? Are you struggling to forgive someone? Below is the activity I created to help me find forgiveness and freedom from sin. If your heart is burdened now or in the future, I pray that this application activity will help you find rest for your soul.

Think about it!

Psalm 55:22
"Cast your burden on the LORD, and he will sustain you."

"Cast Your Burden"—APPLICATION ACTIVITY

On a piece of paper, draw a big cross. Secure the cross to a wall. Back up from the cross so that you're standing or sitting some distance away from it. Take some time to visualize Jesus on the cross, dying for you. Spend some time thinking about the pain, the anguish, He felt on the cross.

Next, close your eyes, and remember the promise God gave us in 1 John 1:9, "If we confess our sins, he is faithful and just to forgive our sins and to cleanse us from all unrighteousness." Remember that God is always faithful to fulfill His promises and extremely gracious to His people. Whatever sin is heavy on your heart, confess it to God and ask forgiveness.

With eyes closed, visualize the sin you confessed and all the pain (spiritual, emotional, and physical) the sin has brought you. Visualize all of the pain, all of the emotion, and all of the shame in your heart coming together. From the top of your head, from the tips of your toes, and from your fingertips, it's all coming together and forming one big ball inside your stomach.

Next, act as if you are vomiting. Visualize the ball of pain moving up your throat to the back of your mouth and then moving up and out of your mouth. Open your eyes, and visualize the ball of pain rapidly coming out of your mouth and moving across the room and onto the cross. You are casting the ugly, horrible sin on the cross, the place where Jesus already bore that sin for you. When the ball of pain hits the cross, visualize it exploding into pieces and fading into nothingness. Let that ball of pain die at the cross. It's no longer your pain to bear. Jesus bore that pain already, so let the pain die. It is FINISHED. Say it aloud, "It is FINISHED."

Suggestions:

If you think it would be more impactful for you, write the sin that comes to mind on a piece of paper. As you think about that sin, write down the thoughts that come to mind on the piece of paper. Crumble the paper into a ball, symbolizing the sin and the emotions surrounding that sin coming together. As you cast your burden on the cross, throw the paper ball to the cross.

The burden I felt was so deep-rooted that I would cast one sin, and another sin would come to mind. I repeated this casting activity over and over, night after night, for several consecutive nights. Though exhausted emotionally, my heart felt lighter with each burden I cast on the cross.

Do you have a burden to cast? Take time now to cast it on the cross.

Pray about it!

Dear Father,
I come to You with a sinful heart in need of Your goodness. I cling to Your promise that You will always be faithful to forgive my sins when I confess them. Please forgive me for…

As far as the east is from the west, take this filth out of my heart. Make me right with You. Make my heart pure again. With Your resurrection power, rescue my heart from dead-end paths, and turn my heart's desire to life-giving paths that lead to Heaven with You. Flood my heart with Your goodness. Thank You for Jesus, who died for every single sick sin of mine and defeated death. In Jesus' Powerful Name, Amen.

"Create Your Canvas"—A CREATIVE CHALLENGE!

Supplies: small to medium-sized artist's canvas or sketchbook | colored pens, markers, or paint set/paintbrush

When it comes to applying God's Truth in our lives, we must seek to understand God's Word and our life experiences. Our life experiences build upon one another and are connected in some way. They provide clues to who we are, what we value, what we desire, what we believe, and what motivates our behavior. In an earlier Reading, I described how God taught me to observe and interpret my dating relationships like a painting on a canvas. Now, it's your turn to create your canvas of dating relationships! Complete this activity before you reach Reading 25 where you'll begin interpreting your canvas. Due to the nature of this activity, I don't encourage you to share your canvas on your social accounts.

Directions:

If you have experience in dating:
Record significant experiences you've had with guys that went beyond friendship. Examples include: your first date, first kiss, dating relationships, etc. Experiences can be recorded by drawing pictures, titling the experience, writing a name, including your age when it happened, etc. By the most impactful experiences, draw a big dot.

If you have not yet experienced dating:
Record significant interactions you've had with guys that went beyond friendship. Experiences can be recorded by drawing pictures, titling the interactions, writing a name, including your age when it happened, etc. By the most impactful interactions, draw a big dot.

If you have not yet had interactions with a guy that went beyond friendship:
You get to bring your canvas to life however you desire! A suggestion is to turn your canvas into place to record inspiring things you discover through this book. This might include Bible verses, quotes, images that come to mind as you read, ways to apply scripture, how you envision your first date, or personal definitions you'll create further into the book.

21 - Heavenly Husband

I knew I wanted to marry a godly man. If you want a godly man, then work on becoming a godly woman. That concept made sense, so I came up with a list of things to work on while I waited for God to bring that special, godly man into my life.

One of the things that many of my married friends struggled with was spending time in God's Word daily. I knew if I was struggling to have a quiet time as a single woman, it would only become more difficult when I married. I set goals of reading through the Bible in a year and having time with God every day, with the hope that those disciplines would become lifelong habits. With God's help, I successfully read through the Bible in a year, missing my quiet time with Him only three or four days total for the whole year!

During that time, I was working at a parachurch organization where I met Linda, who was the epitome of a southern belle. She had perfect posture, stylish clothes, a beautiful face, flawless makeup, a striking mix of silver and dark gray hair, a bright smile, a distinctly southern accent, a bubbly personality, and a way of capturing everyone's hearts.

Linda was in her 50s and single when I worked with her. She lived her life in such a way that demanded respect from men. She didn't manipulate or flirt with men to obtain respect. Linda loved being a woman and enjoyed being honored by gentlemen who opened doors for her, slowed their stride so she could walk in front of them, and listened to what she had to say. Men sensed that she appreciated and enjoyed them being gentlemen, and men seemed to enjoy treating her well.

Anyone who knew Linda knew that she was "tight" with God. She would boldly proclaim, "God is my husband." I had never heard of that concept. It comes from Isaiah 54:5: "For your Maker is your husband, the LORD of hosts is his name; and the Holy One of Israel is your Redeemer, the God of the whole earth he is called." As a single young woman who wanted to marry one day, the concept of God being my husband intrigued and encouraged me. I discovered that the concept encouraged other young women, too.

I was eating lunch with Jackie, a precious 14-year-old girl in my discipleship group. She had her whole life ahead of her, yet she was very concerned about something. No, she wasn't worried about a test at school or peer pressure. With a deeply distressed look on her face, she asked, "What if no one wants to marry me?"

I comforted her, "I think you'll get married one day to a great guy. Do you know that you already have a husband? God says He is your husband."

Her whole face lit up in excitement. "Really, I'm married?"

I smiled and nodded.

"COOL!" she exclaimed.

We talked about the qualities of God that made Him a good husband, and then we moved on to other topics. I think Jackie was relieved that she didn't need to worry about a husband. She already had a husband—a heavenly one!

That conversation with Jackie helped me see my personal folly. With tremendous determination, I had set out to become consistent in my quiet times. My motive? To prepare myself to be a godly wife one day. *But if God is my husband,* I thought, *then I'm already a wife.* I realized that I should spend time in God's Word daily to enjoy my husband of today—God! If I continued to live only for the future, then I would miss out on the present blessings of being with my Heavenly Husband! Just like Eve in the Garden, I had God, but I was looking for satisfaction in something else!

How about you? As you read God's Word, do you approach it as an opportunity to enjoy God? Are you applying your heart to get to know Him—to understand His Word, His character, and His ways?

As you have been reading this book, are you seizing each day's reading as a way to enjoy God? Are you giving careful thought to answering questions at the end of each day's reading? Are you praying the prayers with your heart?

Carolyn, my spiritual mentor, would often say, "We stop to eat at a fast food restaurant when there's a banquet table prepared for us." We often settle for so much less than what God has given us. Because He did it ALL, we get it ALL. We get to enjoy relationship with God *today.* "This is the day the Lord has made; let us rejoice and be glad in it" (Psalm 118:24).

I believed God was sovereign in my life. I believed He would provide an earthly husband for me if that was part of His Plan. I realized it was foolish of me to work so hard at becoming a godly wife for an earthly husband God might not provide. Desiring to read the Bible daily was a great goal; I simply went about it the wrong way! In a sense, I was *working* for my future. I was working on reading the Bible daily for a future with an earthly husband, but the work had already been done. Jesus did it ALL. Through His work on the cross, Jesus prepared a future for me in Heaven!

Better than an earthly husband who may (or may not) come and a marriage that may (or may not) last, Jesus had united me with a Divine Husband who would love me forever! Because of His work on the cross, ALL I had to do was rest in Him and enjoy relationship with my Heavenly Husband.

Think about it!

What did God mean that He is our husband? Let's find out! Before you read Isaiah 54, here is some background information on the passage:

The prophet Isaiah spoke these words as a prophecy (divinely inspired prediction about the future) over the Israelite people. This prophecy is thought to foretell the coming of Christ and how He will build His Church (the Body of Believers, His Bride). When Isaiah spoke this prophecy, the Israelites (Jewish people) were in captivity. It was common for the Israelites to think of God as a husband to His people. During their captivity, the Lord had forsaken them. Since they thought of Him as a husband, they related being forsaken by God to being a widow who had been abandoned. Isaiah prophesies that God will return to His people, rescue them from slavery, establish, defend, and prosper them.

Read Isaiah 54:1-17.

1—Throughout this passage, God instills hope in His people. List the things He says He will do for His people.

2—Imagine you are one of the Israelites held captive in the passage. How would the knowledge of your prosperous future affect your thoughts and actions?

3—How do you want the knowledge of your future in Heaven with God to affect your thoughts and actions?

Reminder: Continue working on the *"Create Your Canvas"* **CREATIVE CHALLENGE** introduced in yesterday's reading. Complete it before you reach Reading 25. Due to the nature of this challenge, I don't encourage you to share your canvas on your social accounts.

Pray about it!

Heavenly Husband,
You are faithful to Your promises and to Your people! Thank You that You came to me. You pursued my heart. You have loved me with an everlasting love. Your love redeemed my life and our relationship. I don't want to take You for granted. I desire to love You with all my heart. Show me how to love like You love. Every day, I desire to acknowledge and enjoy Your loving presence. Let every breath I take, every move I make, every thought I construct, and every word I select reveal Your presence in my heart and life. In Jesus' Name, Amen.

22 - Sharing His Life

The unmarried woman and the married woman have something in common: They have a Heavenly Husband. "For your Maker is your husband, the LORD of hosts is his name; and the Holy One of Israel is your Redeemer, the God of the whole earth he is called" (Isaiah 54:5). Does it seem like a tall order to relate to God as a Heavenly Husband when you're human and you've never been a wife? I was a Christian for five years before discovering God was my Heavenly Husband. I must have been a terrible wife all of those years!

So how do we take the truth that God is our Heavenly Husband and apply it in our lives? It begins by allowing this biblical truth to change our perspective. Though we may have thought we were going through life alone, we are not alone. After God proclaims He is a Husband to His people in Isaiah 54, He says, "For the mountains may depart and the hills be removed, but my steadfast love shall not depart from you, and my covenant of peace shall not be removed." He reminds us of His presence in Hebrews 13:5c, which says, "I will never leave you nor forsake you." Our Heavenly Husband sent His greatest love to us when He sent Jesus, Emmanuel, which means "God with us." Jesus is our Way to God, and He promised, "I am with you always, to the end of the age" (Matthew 28:20b).

My friend, Carol, has been married over 40 years. She described marriage to an earthly husband this way: "When a man asks a woman to be his wife, he is inviting her to share his life." *Share* is defined in the dictionary as "to participate in, enjoy, receive, etc., jointly."[22] Sharing his life is an opportunity for the wife to get to know her husband more and to deepen her relationship with him. What does a wife do to get to know her husband? She spends time with him, talks with him, and listens to what he has to say.

In a sense, our Heavenly Husband has invited us to share His life—the ups and the downs, the sorrows and the joys, and eventually, eternal bliss in Heaven! He promised, "I love those who love me, and those who seek me diligently find me" (Proverbs 8:17). Our Heavenly Husband is an open book—as long as our Bibles are open!

As we read and study the Bible, we can discover all kinds of things about our Heavenly Husband. We can learn what He likes, dislikes, values, what's on His mind, what grieves His heart, and what brings Him joy. The Bible reveals how God views challenges and handles stressful situations. It allows us to see our Heavenly Husband at work achieving His goals and at rest.

Sharing a husband's life means sharing his vision, or purpose, in life. Our Heavenly Husband's Vision is to be united with His people in Heaven, worshipped as the one true God, and enjoyed by His people forever. Revelation 7:9-12 describes His vision: "After this I looked, and behold, a great multitude that no one could number, from every nation, from all tribes and peoples and languages, standing before the throne and before the Lamb, clothed in white robes, with palm branches in their hands, and crying out with a loud voice, 'Salvation belongs to our God who sits on the throne, and to the Lamb!' And all the angels were standing around the throne and around the elders and the four living creatures, and they fell on their faces before the throne and worshiped God, saying, 'Amen! Blessing and glory and wisdom and thanksgiving and honor and power and might be to our God forever and ever! Amen.'"

Sharing a husband's life means sharing his vision and supporting the accomplishment of that vision. Heaven with God is a vision that's easy to get behind! We're blessed because our Heavenly Husband has clearly defined how His Vision will be accomplished, known as His Mission:

John 3:16
"For God so loved the world, that he gave his only Son, that whoever believes in him should not perish but have eternal life."

Matthew 28:18-20
"And Jesus came and said to {his disciples}, 'All authority in heaven and on earth has been given to me. Go therefore and make disciples of all nations, baptizing them in the name of the Father and of the Son and of the Holy Spirit, teaching them to observe all that I have commanded you. And behold, I am with you always, to the end of the age.'"

Let's review: Our Heavenly Husband has loved us by sharing His Vision and Mission with us. One of the greatest ways we love our Heavenly Husband is to wholeheartedly embrace His Vision and become active participants in His Mission. Our lives have value and purpose beyond our comprehension!

Vision:
For God's People to be united with Him in Heaven, worshipping Him as the one true God and enjoying Him forever.

Mission:
To make disciples (or followers) of all nations.

Did you know that God's Vision and Mission are woven throughout the Bible? Did you know that the Bible tells One BIG Story? Though it is made up of 66 books, 39 Old Testament books followed by 27 New Testament books, ALL the books tell One BIG Story. It's the Story of God's Glory and Rescue Plan for His People. It goes like this:

The Story begins in Genesis. Not long into the story, Adam and Eve sin, and their relationship with God is severed. In the Old Testament books, God makes a promise to redeem the people He loves and sets His plan in motion. In Matthew, the first book of the New Testament, God sends His Son to redeem His people. In the New Testament books, God makes a way through Jesus for His people to experience relationship with Him again and builds His church. The Story ends with the book of Revelation where Jesus reunites His followers with God in Heaven for all eternity!

Reading the Bible from the perspective that every book and every story is part of a BIGGER Story, we see the BIG picture of who God is and all He did to rescue the people He loves—to rescue us! As you read the Bible, remember these key points:

Every small story in the Bible points to the BIG Story—John 3:16.
The message of Old Testament stories is *Jesus is coming*.
The message of New Testament stories is *Jesus has come!*

A theme distinctly woven throughout the BIG Story of the Bible is *suffering*. The very Mission we share with our Heavenly Husband was set into motion when Jesus came to seek and save the lost, and later, was pierced for our transgressions and crushed for our iniquities (Luke 19:10, Isaiah 53:5). Through the suffering of Jesus, we are re-united with God. Suffering is a crucial part of the perfect PATH to knowing our Heavenly Husband.

Philippians 3:10-11 (NIV)
"I want to know Christ and the power of his resurrection and the fellowship of sharing in his sufferings, becoming like him in his death, and so, somehow, to attain to the resurrection from the dead."

I don't know about you, but when my heart is aching, I only share my deepest heart with friends I love and trust and who accept me as I am. What an honor that Jesus would share His sufferings with you and me! Jesus endured many trials and hurts during His life on earth that are recorded in the Bible. Isaiah 53:3 describes Jesus this way: "He was despised and rejected by men; a man of sorrows, and acquainted with grief." When you read about His sufferings in the Bible, imagine that Jesus is sitting across from you, telling you about what happened to Him, and sharing His heart with you. Jesus is one with God the Father, so His heart reveals the Father's heart.

When I'm in the midst of a trial, it's easy to believe the lie that I'm all alone and that no one understands what I'm feeling. Have you ever felt that way in your suffering?

Hebrews 4:15 reminds us: "For we do not have a high priest who is unable to sympathize with our weaknesses, but one who in every respect has been tempted as we are, yet without sin." When we share our hearts with Jesus, we don't have to fear being rejected or misunderstood. With Jesus, we can be ourselves. When we share our hearts, we find acceptance, understanding, encouragement, and support.

Not only does Jesus share His sufferings with us, but there is *fellowship in His sufferings*. Every suffering we face, Christ has already suffered for us. Our sufferings are His sufferings. There is fellowship with Jesus, and ultimately, with our Heavenly Husband. "Let us then with confidence draw near to the throne of grace, that we may receive mercy and find grace to help in time of need" (Hebrews 4:16).

Think about it!

1—When it comes to sharing your Heavenly Husband's Vision, how committed are you on a scale of 1-5? (*1 = I don't believe in it. 5 = It has become my vision, too.*)

2—When it comes to supporting God's Vision through the Mission of making disciples, how are you doing? What do you need to become more effective in making disciples? (Training, prayer, accountability, service opportunities, etc.)

3—What trial are you facing right now? How did Jesus face the same sort of trial? How can this trial help you relate more to Jesus and to your Heavenly Husband?

Reminder: Continue working on the *"Create Your Canvas"* **CREATIVE CHALLENGE** introduced in Reading 20. Complete it before you reach Reading 25. Due to the nature of this challenge, I don't encourage you to share your canvas on your social accounts.

Pray about it!

Heavenly Husband,
Thank You that every day, I am surrounded by Your love and peace and will be forevermore! I ask that, through the Holy Spirit, You would give me a growing desire to spend quality time with You, to listen to what You have to say, and to learn more about You! I want to learn about Your character, interests, experiences, perspective on life, likes, and dislikes. Let our times together deepen our relationship.

Thank You for inviting me into Your Story. Your Vision and Mission are also my Vision and Mission. Make it my heartbeat to glorify You, to delight in You, to follow wherever You go, to make disciples. When I'm suffering, turn my heart to Jesus to experience the intimate fellowship of sharing in His sufferings. Draw me so close that our hearts beat as one. I love you! In Jesus' Name I pray, Amen.

23 - Godly Husband

Not only did Isaiah 54:5 give me a Husband, but it also gave me tremendous comfort as I walked through the aftermath of my unhealthy dating relationship with the guy from the singles' group. Soon after the relationship ended, I left that church. It took me a while before I could attend church again. My heart was still hurting, and I didn't want to engage in conversation with anyone new. I just wanted to go to church, sing praise songs to God, hear His Word preached, and leave.

I eventually found the strength to visit new churches because I believed my Heavenly Husband was very near to me. Jesus is the way to God, and as my relationship with Jesus grew, I felt closer to God. Each Sunday, I imagined that Jesus escorted me into the church balcony and sat in the seat next to me! I realize that probably sounds crazy, but hold on—I'm about to tell you the crazy part! One Sunday, as I was sitting in the balcony with Jesus, waiting for the church service to begin, someone came and sat on Jesus!

Ok, the person didn't actually sit on Jesus, but the person sat in His seat! That made me mad! Seriously, I was mad! I told you I wholeheartedly bought into Isaiah 54:5!

I laugh about it now, and I also remember it fondly. You see, my Heavenly Husband made me feel protected, loved, and joyful during a painful season in my life. I leaned on Him, and He helped me press through the pain. It was the start of a deeper relationship that I will forever treasure!

It's guaranteed that a human husband will sometimes fail you, but your Heavenly Husband will never let you down!

Your Heavenly Father is wise and trustworthy and will always lead you down the right path. His love is true, and He will always be faithful to you. "I have loved you with an everlasting love; therefore I have continued my faithfulness to you" (Jeremiah 31:3).

Your Heavenly Husband continues to pursue your heart and is your greatest encourager. He is always gracious to forgive you when you mess up. "If we confess our sins, he is faithful and just to forgive us our sins and to cleanse us from all unrighteousness" (1 John 1:9).

Your Heavenly Husband also gives very nice things to you! "Every good gift and every perfect gift is from above, coming down from the Father of lights with whom there is no variation or shadow due to change" (James 1:17). God is the perfect Husband!

I think most every girl who wants to marry desires a husband with whom she can completely be herself and be completely loved. How would you like a husband who is always *attentive* to you, *accepting* of you, and absolutely *adores* you? That is what you'll find in your Heavenly Husband! He meets your needs for the *Triple A's!* "And my God will supply every need of yours according to his riches in glory in Christ Jesus" (Philippians 4:19).

God created love. Only the Author of Love could love you perfectly!

1 Corinthians 13:4-8 (known as the Love Verse)
"Love is patient and kind; love does not envy or boast; it is not arrogant or rude. It does not insist on its own way; it is not irritable or resentful; it does not rejoice at wrongdoing, but rejoices with the truth. Love bears all things, believes all things, hopes all things, endures all things. Love never ends."

What's in your cup?

When it comes to God being your Heavenly Husband, is your cup half empty or half full?

We may seek after the *attention, acceptance,* and *adoration* of men, but we don't need these things to be content and joyful. We have everything we need in God! "And my God will supply every need of yours according to his riches in glory in Christ Jesus" (Philippians 4:19).

In the story of the burning bush, God told Moses to call Him, "I AM," because God was EVERYTHING Moses would ever need and more! I came up with a visual to help me remember that God is my EVERYTHING. He is my All in All. I hope you will also find it helpful in remembering He is *your* EVERYTHING.

Imagine you have a cup, a mug actually. It's one of those really nice, handmade porcelain mugs that are great for holding hot chocolate (or coffee). Pick your favorite color(s) for your cup.

Your cup symbolizes your life. Imagine that your cup is filled to the rim with the best hot chocolate that exists! Think about how comforting it is to wrap your fingers around a big, warm cup of hot chocolate on a cold winter's day. Your cup is full because God has given you everything you need.

Since God is a gracious, giving God who gives us more than we ask or imagine, your cup overflows with a fluffy topping of whip cream and delectable chocolate shavings! How does that sound?

God fills your cup. Then, He throws in a little "extra," the overflow of His blessings!

The healthy *attention, acceptance, and adoration* you receive from a man (or anyone) will always be extra. So, when God provides you a boyfriend or an earthly husband, remember that your Heavenly Husband fills your cup. Your boyfriend or earthly husband is the overflow of God's gifts in your life.

Think about it!

The Bible provides several descriptions for a godly husband to help us understand what a godly husband does and his character traits. Using the verses that follow, create a role description.

1—ROLE DESCRIPTION: **"GODLY HUSBAND"**

Ephesians 5:22-33
RESPONSIBILITIES AND CHARACTER TRAITS:

Example: He is the head, or authority, in relationship with his wife. (Leader)

1 Peter 3:7
RESPONSIBILITIES AND CHARACTER TRAITS:

Proverbs 3:11, 28
RESPONSIBILITIES AND CHARACTER TRAITS:

2—Once the role description is completed, read through it from the perspective that God is your Heavenly Husband. Write down your thoughts/insights.

"God Fills Your Cup"—A CREATIVE CHALLENGE!

This Creative Challenge is inspired by the *What's In Your Cup?* section of today's Reading. If pottery painting stores are popular where you live, then visit one! Design and paint your own coffee mug or drinking cup. If you are going through the book with a group, make it a group outing! When you post an individual or group photo on your social accounts, tag @aimforhimblog, and use hashtags #LovebyDesignBook and #AimforHim.

Reminder: Continue working on the *"Create Your Canvas"* **CREATIVE CHALLENGE** introduced in Reading 20. Complete it before you reach Reading 25. Due to the nature of this challenge, I don't encourage you to share your canvas on your social accounts.

Pray about it!

Sweet Heavenly Husband,
*I **adore** You, for You are the BEST husband! You are my EVERYTHING. "Whom have I in heaven but you? And there is nothing on earth that I desire besides you. I **confess** that "my flesh and my heart may fail, but {You are} the strength of my heart and my portion forever" (Psalm 73:25-26).*

***Thank You** for filling my cup! I am a blessed woman because You have filled my cup with...*

*I **ask** You to help me to remember that I have everything I need in You. When my heart wanders and I begin to find my satisfaction in things or in people, show me my folly quickly. Strengthen my heart to repent from making idols out of things that pleasure only for a short time. Lead me to repent from making idols out of imperfect people who could never measure up to You. Help me to recognize all of the blessings You pour into my cup, ponder them, treasure them, and give thanks to You.*

May the graciousness and love You have lavished on me overflow from my heart into the lives of others so that they may know You, the One who truly satisfies the longing heart. In Jesus' Name, Amen.

24 - Godly Wife

D o you ever imagine what it will be like to see Jesus face-to-face? Thomas, one of the twelve disciples, heard Jesus preach, watched Him perform miracles, talked with Him, ate with Him, and prayed with Him. After Jesus died and rose again, He appeared to Thomas, but Thomas didn't recognize Him. Though he had spent time with Jesus, Thomas didn't know Jesus well enough to know for certain it was Him. Jesus had to convince Thomas it was really Him in John 20:27-29.

Jesus: "Put your finger here, and see my hands; and put out your hand, and place it in my side. Do not disbelieve, but believe."

Thomas: "My Lord and my God!"

Jesus: "Have you believed because you have seen me? Blessed are those who have not seen and yet have believed'"

I may not have a good grasp of what that day will be like when I meet Jesus in person, but I have high hopes. When united with Jesus, I want to recognize Him the minute I lay eyes on Him. I desire to know Jesus as deeply as I can in this life so that when we come face-to-face in the next life, I will recognize Him as my Lord and Savior. I long to know Jesus as my best friend, my prince of peace, my safe place, my #1 confidant, my strength, the One who lifts my head, the One who wipes my tears, the One who walks with me, my biggest fan, my delight, and my first and greatest love!

I hope to be so close to Jesus that when I am finally with Him, I won't waste time questioning and doubting Him. Instead, I want to love Him as He would want to be loved. When I tell Jesus, "I love you," I desire for my words to mean something special, now and for all eternity.

Jesus told doubting Thomas, "I am the way, and the truth, and the life. No one comes to the Father except through me. If you had known me, you would have known my Father also. From now on you do know him and have seen him" (John 14:6-7).

In Exodus 33:18, Moses made a bold request, asking God to reveal Himself. Moses had the ultimate opportunity on this side of Heaven to actually meet with God on Mount Sinai! A portion of their conversation is recorded for us in Exodus 33:18-23.

Moses: "Please show me your glory."

God: "I will make all my goodness pass before you and will proclaim before you my name 'The LORD.' And I will be gracious to whom I will be gracious, and will show mercy on whom I will show mercy. But you cannot see my face, for man shall not see me and live. Behold, there is a place by me where you shall stand on the rock, and while my glory passes by I will put you in a cleft of the rock, and I will cover you with my hand until I have passed by. Then I will take away my hand, and you shall see my back, but my face shall not be seen."

Because God is holy, so perfect and pure, sinful people cannot exist in His full presence. God is far too glorious for us! He deserves our utmost respect and worship, but our sin makes it impossible to honor Him as He deserves. He could have forgotten about us and left our relationship with Him undone. Instead, He stayed true to His mission: *"For God so loved the world, that he gave his only Son, that whoever believes in him should not perish but have eternal life" (John 3:16)*. His grace opens up a door for us to meet with Him, to truly know Him.

Are you entering into His presence with all of your heart?

Have you ever imagined what it will be like to enter Heaven and see God the Father? Sometimes when I pray, eyes closed, I sit silently for several minutes. I envision Jesus escorting me to God. We're walking together, neither one of us uttering a word. We don't need words. My heart is at peace in His presence.

We approach two gigantic doors, swinging open slowly. We enter into a bright room. Walking through a long stream of waist-high, white, fluffy clouds, we eventually emerge at a majestic throne. God the Father is there, and His glory is shining bright.

God's glory radiates as far as the eye can see. I fall to my knees and bow before my Heavenly Father. My head gently lifted—by the Holy Spirit or maybe an angel—and I SEE HIM. Immediately my heart comes alive with a song—this is the One whom my soul loves. He is my God and my Heavenly Husband. "We love because he first loved us" (1 John 4:19). To know Him is to know love in its truest form!

When you marry, God will still be your Heavenly Husband. God will always be your #1 Husband. Remember, God fills your cup, and an earthly husband will be the extra, overflowing blessing of God. All women, married or not, are to honor God with their lives. "So, whether you eat or drink, or whatever you do, do all to the glory of God" (1 Corinthians 10:31).

Proverbs 31 helps us understand what it means to be a godly woman who glorifies God in everything she does. The Proverbs 31 Woman also happens to be a wife and mother. Read Proverbs 31:10-31, and highlight verses that articulate your heart's desire.

Here are notes on the character of a godly woman and how she honors God as her #1:

- She is of great worth (v.10)
- Trustworthy, a blessing to her husband (v.11-12)
- Hardworking (v.13-15, 24)
- Thinks through decisions before taking action (v.16)
- Has the spiritual, emotional, and physical strength needed for her tasks, spiritually prepared for the troubles a day holds (v.17, 25)

- Recognizes that she has valuable skills and sees value in the product she produces, diligent worker, confidently sells her products (v.18-19, 24)
- Helps those in need (v.20)
- Does not fear the future, cares for her family and has prepared them for the days to come (v.21, 27)
- Resourceful, dresses nicely (v.22)
- Supports her husband as he serves others in a position of leadership (v.23)
- Wise, kind, role-model (v.26)
- Appreciated and celebrated by her husband and children (v.28)
- Honored by her husband (v.29)
- She lives her life for the glory of God, and her God honors her. (v.30-31)

Think about it!

Yesterday, we created a Role Description for a godly husband. Using the verses included below, let's create a role description for a godly wife.

1—ROLE DESCRIPTION: **"GODLY WIFE"**

Genesis 2:18
RESPONSIBILITIES AND CHARACTER TRAITS:

1 Peter 3:1-6
RESPONSIBILITIES AND CHARACTER TRAITS:

Ephesians 5:22-33
RESPONSIBILITIES AND CHARACTER TRAITS:

Pray about it!

As you think about honoring, loving, and supporting your Heavenly Husband, I encourage you to pray scripture over your life. Proverbs 31 is a passage I have prayed over my life. If I could learn to relate to my Heavenly Husband in excellent ways pleasing to Him and honor

Him as my #1, then I believed I would be a godly wife to an earthly husband. When your relationship with God is right, healthy, and growing, then everything else in your life will fall into place. Here are some suggestions of how to pray Proverbs 31:10-31 over your life:

- Start your prayer: Heavenly Husband, make me a Proverbs 31 Woman.

- Continue your prayer: Read verses 10-31 aloud. As you read, personalize the highlighted verses. For example: Verse 12, "She does him good, and not harm, all the days of her life" becomes "God, make me a woman who does my Heavenly Husband good, and not harm, all the days of my life."

25 - Help or Hinder?

God designed a human husband and wife to experience a deep connection with each other. In Ephesians 5:22-33, we learned that the marriage relationship reveals God's glory as the husband and wife become *one,* painting a picture for the world to see how deeply Jesus loves His Church. That is no small assignment. It is a profound purpose to pursue. Marriage is not for wimps or quitters!

Marriage is a covenant relationship where two people make a promise to each another that unites them together. Their commitment to each another reflects the truth that God is always faithful to His promises and His people. In light of God's glory, the marriage commitment is a serious commitment. It requires that we Love God and Love People as Jesus did.

My friends, Jim and Pam, have a super sweet, loving marriage—the kind I always hoped and prayed God would give me one day. Pam told me that sometimes it seems easier to love her husband than it does to love God. After all, she can see Jim, hear his voice, hold his hand, look into his eyes, laugh with him, hug him, eat dinner with him, go to the movies with him, etc.. She said Jim helps her keep the right perspective. He reminds her, "We're just here to help each other make it to the end."

Helping each other make it to the end is about more than Jim and Pam. It's about more than having kids, paying the bills, making it through the ups and downs of life together, and one day retiring. That's why Jim's statement is so powerful. It reminds Pam of the HIGHER VISION that their relationship is part of the BIG Story of God's Glory and Rescue Plan for His People.

As you think about dating, what does it mean to help a boyfriend make it to the end?

As I thought about that question, one woman came to mind. Her name? Bathsheba. If you've heard of her, then you know that she was a pretty one, but her story was not always a pretty one! (Bathsheba's story is in 2 Samuel 11. Matthew Henry's Commentary[23] helped me understand her story.)

There's so much to learn from this story. For today, let's focus on Bathsheba's influence in David's life.

After some time had passed since David's adulterous affair with Bathsheba, God, through the prophet, Nathan, helped David realize the extent of evil in his actions. David sincerely confessed his sin to God and repented. In Psalms 51 and 52, David expressed his gratitude to God for being gracious and forgiving towards him.

Before he became the king of Israel, David walked with God and found favor in His eyes. God described David in Acts 13:22: "And when he had removed him {the king before David}, he raised up David to be their king, of whom he testified and said, 'I have found in David the son of Jesse a man after my own heart, who will do all my will.'" David was a man made in the image of God for His glory. That was David's potential.

On the canvas of David's life, a black mark exists. 1 Kings 15:5 says, "David did what was right in the eyes of the LORD and did not turn aside from anything that he commanded him all the days of his life, except in the matter of Uriah the Hittite." The matter of Uriah the Hittite refers to David's affair with Bathsheba, which seems to have led to tens of thousands of deaths and a curse: "Now therefore the sword shall never depart from your house, because you have despised me and have taken the wife of Uriah the Hittite to be your wife" (2 Samuel 12:10).

The ugliest design on David's canvas is shared with Bathsheba. When a woman comes into a man's life, she will either help him grow closer to God or help him grow distant from God. She will either help him make it to the end in a God-honoring way, or she will hinder him from reaching the end in a God-honoring way. Bathsheba was an outwardly beautiful woman who left a not-so-beautiful mark on a man's life. When she entered David's life, she was more of a curse than a blessing to him.

We know David was not innocent as related to the sin. We also know that before the rendezvous with Bathsheba, David had been open to the advice of others. He had even listened to a woman named Abigail, who bravely confronted him about a sin he was about to commit.

"And David said to Abigail, 'Blessed be the LORD, the God of Israel, who sent you this day to meet me! Blessed be your discretion, and blessed be you, who have kept me this day from bloodguilt and from avenging myself with my own hand! For as surely as the LORD, the God of Israel, lives, who has restrained me from hurting you, unless you had hurried and come to meet me, truly by morning there had not been left to Nabal so much as one male'" (1 Samuel 25:32-34).

Abigail helped prevent David from committing the murder of many. That is something Bathsheba did not prevent.

As I thought about the story of Bathsheba and David, I realized that every man I date and the man I marry will all be men made in the image of God for His glory. My presence in a boyfriend's or husband's life will either help him grow closer to God or influence him to grow distant from God. Will I *help* him make it to the end in a God-honoring way, or will I *hinder* him from making it to the end?

What kind of woman did I want to be in a man's life? I decided:

I don't want to be a Bathsheba.
I want to treat men with respect as made-in-His-image-creations.
I want my presence in a man's life to be a blessing and not a curse.
When I marry, I want my husband to achieve his potential in God; I want to help my husband make it to the end as a man after God's own heart."

Think about it!

Today, you'll begin using the canvas you created!

1—For every guy who left a mark on your canvas, ask, "Did I *help* or *hinder him* in making it to the end?" Optional: Draw a box around those you hindered and a cross next to those you helped.

Note: If guys have not made a mark on your canvas, that's a good thing and won't be a problem at all. Throughout the book, I will continue to share my own dating experiences, and you can learn from my mistakes and successes! As you read my stories, ask, "Did Aimee *help* or *hinder him* in making it to the end?" and "Did he help or hinder Aimee in making it to the end?"

2—Did any of the guys on your canvas help you make it to the end somehow? Describe.

3—Describe the kind of woman you want to be in a man's life.

Pray about it!

Prayer suggestions:
- Express to God that you don't want to be a Bathsheba.
- Ask God to make you a wife who helps your future husband make it to the end and doesn't hinder him.
- If you feel led to confess sin to God, use Psalm 51 as a prayer. It was written by David.

What happened to Bathsheba?

Well, we can't leave a Christian sister in the mud. There seems to be evidence that Bathsheba repented of her part in David's fall. She was actually married to David when God called him a man after his own heart.

David and Bathsheba are a man and a woman who failed God and faced the consequences. We know for certain that David humbly repented of his sin and was forgiven by God. David was later blessed by God and became known as a righteous king, acclaimed warrior, musician, and poet. Though Bathsheba seems to disappear into the pages of the Bible, she was David's wife when God prospered him. Some believe she wrote several Proverbs and may have written Proverbs 31, the description of *The Woman Who Fears the Lord*.

God blessed David and Bathsheba with a son, Solomon, who became king of Israel when David died. God blessed Solomon, making him a great king who was known throughout the world as one of the wisest, wealthiest, and most powerful men. If you have sinned Bathsheba-style in a relationship with a guy, or your heart is weighed down by another sin, you can find forgiveness and restoration in God. "If we confess our sins, he is faithful and just to forgive us our sins and to cleanse us from all unrighteousness" (1 John 1:9).

26 - Read My Lips

As God helped me interpret my canvas, I discovered several themes. Here are 2 noteworthy themes:

Theme #1

When I began dating as a teenager, kissing naturally went along with the territory. I knew a lady didn't kiss on the first date and maybe not for two or three more dates, but that was the extent of my kissing convictions. Most of my friends had kissed a boy long before me.

I experienced my first kiss at 15. At 25, as I sought to honor God in my dating relationships, I began thinking about kissing in a different light after a friend asked me, "How many guys have you kissed?" It took me a while to answer her question. I had a hard time counting all of the guys I had kissed. I had trouble remembering some of their names (so embarrassing). I didn't even remember some of their faces.

My friend's question caused me to do some addition more eye-opening than anything I had calculated in math class in high school and college combined! I realized I had kissed almost every guy I had dated over the past 10 years. God could keep me single for 10 more years. If I kept kissing every guy I dated, then I wouldn't have enough fingers and toes to keep count of all the mouths my tongue visited! Those calculations grossed me out!

In light of God's BIG Story, I'm certain that my kisses did not help any of those guys make it to the end.

Theme #2

I met Curt at college. Curt was a great, godly guy. We had a few dates here and there, but our friendship never grew into much more. We did kiss a few times, but that was such a small part of our times together. In the back of my mind, I had always wondered if Curt and I might end up together.

A year before I met Curt, he had gone through a difficult trial in which he was terribly betrayed by a girlfriend. On one of our dates, Curt opened up to me about a part of his story that he had shared with very few people. His heart was still grieving, and I could sense that he needed more healing. In my personal prayer times, I began to pray for God to heal Curt's heart. Though I wanted more with Curt than friendship, I truly cared about him as a Christian brother and wanted him to be healed, whether I benefitted or not. I prayed for him numerous times. I prayed for him years after we stopped spending time together.

As I was struggling with my sinful part in the dating relationship with the guy from church, Curt came to mind. I decided to call him.

Curt told me he had found the woman he would marry. I jokingly responded, "Well, at least I know now that we weren't meant to be together." We both laughed. I remember thinking: *Well, I've lost pretty much everything in my life. It just makes sense that I would lose that hope, too!* Ultimately, I wanted the best for Curt, and I was happy that he was happy.

Tearfully, I confided in Curt about how I had fallen away from God and felt scared. Curt responded, "Aimee, you have an awesome heart for God. Don't ever lose that passion." He repeated with firmness, "Don't ever lose that passion." He continued, "Remember the day you were saved. Think back to that day, and remember that Jesus died for you. Remember the joy you felt that day when you came to know Him. Don't you dare let your heart get hardened."

Curt said God had changed his heart since I had last seen him. He shared that God helped him realize he was struggling to trust others and had closed off his heart. He said God opened up his heart, and trust was no longer an issue for him. He credited God using our short time together to lead him to that revelation.

After the conversation with Curt, I marveled at what God had done. God used Curt, a person I respected and trusted, to realize that I needed God's help to learn how to trust again, and it would take time. I had the same need I had prayed for God to fill in Curt's life. Hearing about God's faithfulness to move Curt beyond the pain, heal his heart, and bring him joy was a tremendous faith-builder! I wrote this in my journal: *As I think of my conversation with Curt, my eyes well up with tears, and my soul leaps with joy. Father, I am humbled that You would use me as part of Your plan to heal and bless a brother in Christ. Your ways are too precious!*

I had never told Curt about the specific way I prayed for him. God had been faithful to answer my prayers (and others' prayers for Curt). God had been faithful to restore the heart of His Beloved son, which meant He would be faithful to restore my heart. God was gracious to let me hear the rest of the story…in the perfect moment…and use it to build my faith.

God used me in a small but meaningful way to help Curt make it to the end, and vice versa.

Interpreting the themes

Theme #1 and Theme #2 describe two very different ways I interacted with guys. One theme reveals how I gave myself away physically (through kissing) to numerous guys. The second theme highlights how I took the time to get to know Curt's heart and pray for him. What caused me to act differently in the themes? The answer lies in my motives.

In Theme #1, what were my motives in kissing all those guys? To be really honest, I'm not sure why I kissed some of the guys, other than they leaned in to kiss me. Other motives include curiosity, no longer wanting to be the never-been-kissed girl, the guy was seriously hot, my own pleasure, and a desire to keep the guy's interest. Do you see the commonality in all of those motives? It was all about me. All the motives were self-centered.

What were my motives in Theme #2? I wanted to explore a serious dating relationship with Curt, but more than that, I wanted God to comfort and help him.

Philippians 2:1-5 says, "So if there is any encouragement in Christ, any comfort from love, any participation in the Spirit, any affection and sympathy, complete my joy by being of the same mind, having the same love, being in full accord and of one mind. Do nothing from selfish ambition or conceit, but in humility count others more significant than yourselves. Let each of you look not only to his own interests, but also to the interests of others. Have this mind among yourselves, which is yours in Christ Jesus."

I truly wanted God's will above my own will. I wanted to live the BIG Story of God's Glory and Rescue Plan for His People and not Aimee's little story. Observing Theme #1 on my canvas makes me feel grieved and disappointed in myself. Theme #2 makes me feel joyful and thankful to have supported God's work in another's life. I behaved differently in Theme #2 than in Theme #1 because I gained a right perspective on God, myself, and guys.

The Golden Rule: Matthew 7:12
"So whatever you wish that others would do to you, do also to them, for this is the Law and the Prophets."

Matthew 22:26-39
"Teacher, which is the great commandment in the Law? And he said to him, You shall love the Lord your God with all your heart and with all your soul and with all your mind. This is the great and first commandment. And a second is like it: You shall love your neighbor as yourself."

Philippians 4:8-9
"Finally, brothers, whatever is true, whatever is honorable, whatever is just, whatever is pure, whatever is lovely, whatever is commendable, if there is any excellence, if there is anything worthy of praise, think about these things. What you have learned and received and heard and seen in me—practice these things, and the God of peace will be with you."

Think about it!

If you've kissed a guy:

1—Of the guys who left a mark on your canvas, which ones did you kiss? In the areas of your canvas where you shared your kisses, write S.W.A.K. (Sealed With A Kiss) or draw lips.

2—Why did you kiss the guys you kissed?

3—How did sharing your kisses benefit you or hurt you?

If you have not yet kissed a guy:

1—As you think about kissing for the first time, what thoughts and feelings come to mind?

2—Do you desire to kiss a guy soon? Why or why not?

Pray about it!

Prayer Suggestions:

- Are you thankful for something you saw on your canvas? Maybe you're thankful for a clean canvas! Tell God thanks!

- Did you see any themes on your canvas you wish were different? Ask God to help you move forward in righteous ways.

- Did you see any weak areas in yourself? Ask God to strengthen your weak spots.

- Did you identify any needs you would like to trust God to meet? Ask God for what you need, including the faith to trust Him!

27 - This Thing Called Love

I met Ryan briefly during my senior year of high school through one of my best friends. During the summer, Ryan recognized me in a music store, approached me, and struck up a conversation with me. I remember that he was wearing a baseball hat, and he looked so cute! So, of course I said, "Yes!" when he asked me out.

For the first year and a half of college, I lived at home and commuted to a local university. Ryan was three years older than me and was working full-time. Ryan and I dated for many months, breaking up once and getting together again for several more months. We committed to date each other exclusively. I don't remember if we talked about marriage, but like most 18-year-old girls, I questioned if Ryan might be "the one." We said, "I love you" to one another more than once.

Ryan was successful at his job. Unlike other guys I had dated, he could afford nice cars, expensive dinners, and pretty much anything he desired. When it came to me, he was very generous with his money. He bought me clothes and music, always paid for our dates, and regularly showered me with flowers. During our time together, Ryan gave me dozens of gorgeous, long-stemmed red roses. Many of these were delivered by florists to my home, so I know he was paying the big bucks for the flowers.

The flowers Ryan sent were beautiful, and I was deeply touched by his thoughtfulness. But as our relationship progressed, the flowers became less meaningful to me. The specialness of the flowers was not tarnished by the frequency by which I received them. The specialness of the flowers was diminished by what happened in our relationship. Ryan seemed to care more about pushing me to experiment sexually rather than caring about me as a person, much less as a girlfriend. At times, he would make demeaning remarks about me or compare me to other young women, always pointing out how they were better than me.

During our second round of dating, I am 99% certain he lied to me. I believe he began dating me again while he was in a serious relationship with another young woman. If I'm right, that makes me the woman with whom he cheated. I was extremely naïve at 18 and 19. I should have been swayed by the 99% to breakup with him, but instead, I let the 1% give me hope that this could be love. Though I didn't fully understand all the unhealthy clues in my relationship with Ryan, my gut ached with misery, emptiness, confusion, anger, and regret. These feelings were signals that the relationship wasn't right.

I questioned if the flowers he sent were just a means of manipulating me and giving me false hope to continue in the relationship. In their own right, the dozens of roses Ryan sent were beautiful. In light of how Ryan treated me, those flowers were ugly. I realized that I would rather be treated with respect and kindness than receive roses. If Ryan's "I love you" meant that I would be manipulated, belittled, controlled, and "bought" with gifts and roses, then I didn't want to be "loved" by him. Most importantly, I realized that I didn't love Ryan. In fact, I couldn't wait to get away from him—far, far away!

Ryan was the first guy to whom I said, "I love you." To this day, I believe that I did not love him. I spoke those three words carelessly and selfishly. Perhaps the only loving thing I ever did for Ryan was walk away from him.

Years later, when I was in my late 20s, single, and still trying to figure out this thing called love, I decided to talk to the "experts"—my married friends! I asked them, "How do you know when you've met "THE ONE"? Most responded, "You'll just know." I was never satisfied with that answer, so I kept asking. Other friends were more helpful. They said things like:

"You'll know because you can be yourself around him, and he will appreciate you for who you are."

"You will be excited about him and will look forward to spending time with him."

"You can accept his faults."

"Both of you will be willing to walk through difficult times together."

"You know you're in love when there is pain and joy in the separation."

"He will know the song of your heart."

My pastor, Randy Pope, has shared an interesting definition for love in several sermons. He says, "Love is a commitment based on the will of God, typically undergirded by an emotion."[24]

Have you ever asked some of your married friends, "How do you know when you've met 'THE ONE' and are in love?" If so, what did they say? If not, ask some married friends this week!

When it comes to love, God is the real expert! "Anyone who does not love does not know God, because God is love" (1 John 4:8). Love begins with God; love is found in God. He is the very definition of love. As we grow in our relationship with God, the more we will understand what it means to love and receive love. The more we will embrace and experience God's love, the more we will grow in our ability to love Him and others. We will also more easily recognize what love is and what it isn't.

The New Testament books of the Bible were originally written in the Greek language. In the Greek, there are three kinds of love: Eros, Philia, and Agape.

Philia—"brotherly love" (friendship; fellowship with others)
Characteristics: Dependent on two or more people's expectations, perceptions, and circumstances.

Eros—"sexual love" (butterflies in the stomach and warm; fuzzy feelings; sensual passion) Characteristics: Dependent on two people's perceptions and circumstances.

Agape—"selfless love" (God's love of humanity; love of one person for another) Characteristics: Involves giving without expectation of anything in return. Based on commitment. Not limited by a person's perception or circumstances.

1 John 4:19
"We love because he first loved us."

John 15:13
"Greater love has no one than this, that someone lay down his life for his friends."

1 John 3:16
"By this we know love, that he laid down his life for us, and we ought to lay down our lives for the brothers."

1 Corinthians 13:4-8a & 13—*The Love Verse*
"Love is patient and kind; love does not envy or boast; it is not arrogant or rude. It does not insist on its own way; it is not irritable or resentful; it does not rejoice at wrongdoing, but rejoices with the truth. Love bears all things, believes all things, hopes all things, endures all things. Love never ends. So now faith, hope, and love abide, these three; but the greatest of these is love."

Think about it!

If you have said, "I love you," to a guy:

1—Near the relationships in which you told a guy you loved him, draw a red heart, or write XOXO.

2—Do you believe you truly loved the guy(s)? Why or why not?

3—Think about the guys who told you, "I love you." Did they treat you in a loving way?

For everyone:

1—What does it mean to say, "I love you," to a friend? A husband? A guy you are dating?

2—Moving forward, what do you want your, "I love you," to mean?

Pray about it!

Heavenly Husband,
I praise You because You are a loving God. I don't fully understand this thing called love, but I know You do! You are the very definition of love! Because You first loved me, I can experience the height, depth, width, and length of love—Thank You!

Please don't let love pass by me. Help me to know love when I see it. Help me to know love when I hear it. Help me to know love when I feel it, as well as, in the absence of emotions.

Teach me to love as a lifestyle and to love well. The more I know You, the more I will know love. Author of love, reveal Yourself to me! In Jesus' Name, Amen.

(1 John 4:8)

28 - What's Next?

Let me tell you about Jake. Awww…Jake. He was a great guy through and through! We dated for about six months during our junior year of high school—my first real relationship. He was my first love.

Jake knew that I didn't want to have sex before I married, and he *always* honored my standard. I know that after our junior prom, people close to Jake poked fun at him for not having sex with me. I find it remarkable that Jake respected me even when it caused him to go against the grain of what his friends were doing, caused him to fight the same raging hormones all of us had, caused him to endure joking, and left him with a sexless prom night! I told you Jake was a great guy!

It was the summer after I graduated high school. I was meeting Jake for lunch at a local restaurant to ask for his advice. Because of how Jake treated me when we dated, he had gained my respect and trust. We were just friends by then and had no interest in dating again; we knew we were not meant to be together. I wanted to ask his advice about Ryan. Remember Ryan? He's the guy who gave me enough roses to fill a florist's shop and told me he loved me. He is also the one who pushed me sexually. I talked to Jake about my relationship with Ryan and shared that I was thinking about losing my virginity to him.

To my surprise, Jake became angry. He expressed that he felt Ryan was not treating me right. Jake went on to share that I was the first girl he had ever dated who was a virgin. *Seriously?*

Jake felt sex was a special thing, and he said he wanted my first time to be special. If our high school romance had continued, he would have wanted to go all the way. He shared that he couldn't do that to me, and that's why he decided our relationship needed to end. He warned me, "This Ryan guy is just taking advantage of you, and you deserve to be treated better than that." *WHOA!* I sat there speechless.

Jake's words impacted me profoundly. I had always been confused about why Jake wanted to breakup. Everything was going great in our relationship, and then suddenly, he began distancing himself. His words made me realize that he backed away so that I would break up with him instead of him dumping me. I ended the relationship, thinking that he just didn't want to be with me anymore, which made the breakup especially painful for me. As I heard the real reason our relationship ended, I realized how much Jake had respected me.

I had loved Jake as much as I knew how to love at 17. If our relationship had continued, I'm 99% sure I would have had sex with him. He knew that if he had straight-up told me the reason he was distancing himself, then I might have chosen to have sex with him in order to keep him as a boyfriend. He was trying to protect me, and he was doing what seemed honorable to him. I didn't know God at that time, but I believe He was looking out for me.

After my lunch with Jake, I continued to date Ryan a couple of months before ending the relationship. Jake's honest words and sincere concern for me caused me to realize that I was allowing myself to be manipulated emotionally and physically by Ryan. I walked out of the relationship with many emotional wounds.

Years later, as I observed my canvas of dating relationships, I realized what a miracle it was that I had not become sexually active. Sure, I had a desire to remain a virgin until I married but it was a surface-level desire. When I asked myself why I didn't want to have sex before marriage, I didn't know why. My best guess was that I had moral parents who tried to live a good life, and that had rubbed off on me. Yet, there was absolutely no conviction behind my desire.

My dating relationships were built on a foundation of sand. When pressured by a guy to experiment sexually, I was tossed back and forth by the winds of uncertainty. I always compromised my standard. If I had kept dating guys who pushed me to have sex, then I would have eventually drowned in the flood. I was a fool in dating relationships.

Jesus shared this wisdom:
"Everyone then who hears these words of mine and does them will be like a _wise_ man who built his house on the rock. And the rain fell, and the floods came, and the winds blew and beat on that house, but it did not fall, because it had been founded on the rock. And everyone who hears these words of mine and does not do them will be like a foolish man who built his house on the sand. And the rain fell, and the floods came, and the winds blew and beat against that house, and it fell, and great was the fall of it." –Matthew 7:24-27

When it comes to hearing God's Word, this passage reminds us that there are two kinds of hearers. The first person hears the Word and does something with the Word: She applies it in her life. She surrenders herself to God, trusts His Word and His Way, and builds her life on a solid foundation. She believes in the BIG Story, and she actively participates in it. Though temptations rain down, troubles overflow, and hard times beat on her door, she overcomes it all. Her rock is the One who overcame the world and will stand victorious in the end.

The second person hears the Word and does nothing with the Word: She may forget it or add it to her collection of knowledge about God. Her heart trusts in her own will and her own way. She builds her life on a weak foundation that has no chance of surviving the storms of life.

(Jesus speaking) "I have said these things to you, that in me you may have peace. In the world you will have tribulation. But take heart; I have overcome the world." –John 16:33

"The grass withers, the flower fades, but the word of our God will stand forever." –Isaiah 40:8

Think about it!

1—Who (or what) has influenced your view of sex? What is their view of sex?

2—What is *your* view of sex?

3—Look at your canvas. Did you feel pressure in any of the relationships to experiment sexually? Why or why not?

4—When it comes to protecting your virginity, what advice and instruction have you been given?

Pray about it!

Heavenly Husband,

I praise You, for You are a God of great wisdom. Thank You for sharing Your wisdom with us through the Bible. I confess that I can be naïve and foolish. I need Your insight and guidance to help me make wise choices in my life, especially when it comes to dating and relationships with guys. Help me understand Your Word and how to put it into practice. Build a solid foundation of truth in my life. When I feel pressure to do what is in opposition to Your Word and Jesus' example, be my rock. Calm my mind, steady my heart, and keep my feet firmly planted in Your truth. In Jesus's Name, Amen.

29 - God's View of Sex

n my late twenties, I discovered that God gave us a "Birds and Bees Talk" in a very surprising source! It's found in the Bible book, Song of Solomon (also called Song of Songs). Never would I have guessed that the Bible included a descriptive story of how a husband and wife thoroughly enjoyed sex together!

The Song of Solomon is the 22nd of 66 books of the Bible. Neatly tucked away in the middle section of the Bible, this Old Testament book is a treasure waiting to be discovered! Today, we're going to explore the riches it holds!

The Song of Solomon was written by King Solomon, who was one of the sons of David and Bathsheba. Solomon was a very successful king known for his wisdom, wealth, and writings. People from surrounding nations traveled long distances to hear Solomon speak. He composed over 3,000 proverbs and 1,000 songs, some of which are found in Proverbs and Ecclesiastes.

The Song of Solomon is fairly short, with only eight chapters. Its chapters poetically describe the stages of a healthy, God-honoring relationship of a man and woman, from their initial attraction to life as husband and wife. Someday in the future, I encourage you to read all of Song of Solomon. If you have a Bible with study notes and a Bible commentary, you will find those especially helpful in understanding the many poetic phrases found in the text. I sought the help of Matthew Henry's Commentary.[25]

For today, read about *The Honeymoon* of Solomon and his bride in Song of Solomon 4:1-5:1. Make a note of what Solomon calls his wife in Song of Solomon chapter 4 verses 1, 7, 9, 10, and 11. What do these names reveal about how this husband feels about his bride?

In Song of Solomon 4:1-8, the happy groom takes time to compliment his wife. Some of his descriptions may make you wonder if Solomon was a weirdo; his choice of words may even seem like put-downs. However, Solomon's words are nothing but complimentary towards his wife. Esteemed as a gifted poet, his words are music to his wife's ears and translate as love in her heart.

Solomon is an observant guy. He has something sweet to say about his wife's eyes, hair, teeth, lips, mouth, temples, neck, and breasts. Slowly and gently, this happy husband admired, enjoyed, and verbally affirmed his wife's physical features. Then, he seems to get carried away with excitement and pleasure! Verse 7 seems to confirm this when Solomon says, "You are altogether beautiful, my love; there is no flaw in you." The groom was delighting in his bride! Overcome with emotion, he describes the "mountain" and "hill," leaving it up to our imaginations to translate. Yes, ladies, this is in the Bible!

Solomon shows respect for his wife. In Song of Solomon 4:8-9, Solomon invites his wife to move with him, to journey with him. "Come with me," he says. He did not see her as a thing to conquer; he saw her as a partner, an active participant in the sexual experience. He invites her to come with him to experience the peak of sexual pleasure. As they journey to their much-desired destination, Solomon makes a very interesting exclamation in verse 10:

> "How beautiful is your love, my sister, my bride!
> How much better is your love than wine,
> and the fragrance of your oils than any spice!"

Solomon could have commented solely on the sex or his wife's body, but instead, he talks about her love! What this husband and wife were experiencing was more than sex. They were truly making love! The act of sex was being brought alive with love!

A man's sexuality is sometimes described in the Bible as a "spring," Keeping that in mind, re-read Song of Solomon 4:12:

> "A garden locked is my sister, my bride,
> a spring locked, a fountain sealed."

Solomon was making the point that up to this time, his bride had been "locked" or "sealed." In other words, she was a virgin. Solomon respected, appreciated, and helped guard his beloved's purity as a virgin throughout their courtship. Now, as they consummated their marriage, he delighted in being her first sexual partner! He grasps what an honor it is for his wife to unlock her "garden" for him. The union is complete in verses 13-15. The chapter ends with the woman speaking (verse 16).

> "Awake, O north wind, and come, O south wind!
> Blow upon my garden, let its spices flow."

She was a partner in the experience, an active and willing participant. She, too, had respected, appreciated, and guarded her purity. She waited for a time, but that time had finally come to let her guard down, to freely begin to explore her sexuality, and to invite greater intimacy into her relationship with Solomon. It was a precious gift, opened at the right time, with God's blessing upon it.

As chapter 5 begins, Solomon expresses his pleasure and satisfaction in the gift his bride gave him. The pleasure and satisfaction Solomon experienced in his bride's gift to him inspires this poetic response:

> "I came to my garden, my sister, my bride,
> I gathered my myrrh with my spice,
> I ate my honeycomb with my honey,
> I drank my wine with my milk."

She belongs to him, and he belongs to her. Solomon delights in his wife with a passion like that of Adam in the Garden when he first saw Woman. Just as Adam excitedly claimed her as his own, Solomon calls his beloved "mine."

Think about it!

1—Sooooo, what did you think of Song of Solomon?

2—Does it surprise you that a story like this is in the Bible? Why or why not?

3—What does this story tell you about God's view of sex within marriage?

4—Did Song of Solomon influence or change your view of sex? If so, how?

Pray about it!

Dear God,

I praise You, for You are a God full of delight! You gave me the joy of knowing Your Son. Through Jesus, You delivered me from despair and the ultimate doom—hell. You ushered me into unending delight—a relationship with You that will last forever!

You are I AM—You meet my every need, and full satisfaction is found in You. You've promised that when I "delight {myself} in the Lord, {You} will give me the desires of {my} heart" (Psalm 37:4). Show me how to delight in You. Thank You for delighting in me "as the bridegroom rejoices over the bride, so shall {my} God rejoice over {me}" (Isaiah 62:5).

Your love is higher and wider, longer and deeper than I can imagine! Open my mind to understand Your view of the physical union of a husband and wife. Stretch my thoughts to grasp how You entwined the physical with the spiritual! With delight in Jesus' Name, Amen.

30 - Good and Perfect Gift

The Bible book, Song of Solomon, revealed a pleasurable sexual encounter involving a man of faith and a woman of faith on their wedding night. They mutually gave to each other and received from each other. The man, who was created to reflect the strength and safety of God, initiated and led while the woman, who was created to reflect the softer side of God, responded and joined her man in the journey. They were united physically, emotionally, and spiritually in purpose. They were completely free to express their love, unashamed!

Does that remind you of Genesis 2:22-25?

"And the rib that the LORD God had taken from the man he made into a woman and brought her to the man. Then the man said, 'This at last is bone of my bones and flesh of my flesh; she shall be called Woman, because she was taken out of Man.' Therefore a man shall leave his father and his mother and hold fast to his wife, and they shall become one flesh. And the man and his wife were both naked and were **not ashamed**."

It is a profound concept that out of all the people in the world, God brings together two people who "fit" together, who were meant to be together. God orchestrates the events of each person's life and causes both lives to intersect and connect relationally at a certain time and place. Over time, He creates and grows love between them. What God does…it's miraculous!

God could have stopped there, but He went a step further and created marriage. God's creation gives the man and woman an opportunity to express and embrace their love through a deeper commitment, a stronger bond. Again, God could have stopped there, but He chose to go a step further and created sex. This creation gives man and woman the potential to express and explore their love in an even deeper way.

They become *one* through a profound connection of their minds, bodies, and souls. When they experience oneness, they know the greatest intimacy possible in a human relationship. This oneness, this unity, provides a glimpse into the paradise that Adam and Eve experienced in the Garden. It also provides a glimpse into the paradise to come when we are united with God in Heaven and will experience the greatest love and delight that exists! What does it say about God that He would give such a glorious gift to sinners on this side of Heaven?

James 1:17
"Every good gift and every perfect gift is from above, coming down from the Father of lights with whom there is no variation or shadow due to change."

Here's a true story about a couple on their wedding night. They had just enjoyed a beautiful wedding celebration. They were in the car, driving away from the church to begin their honeymoon. Suddenly, the wife started sobbing. Stunned, her husband asked, "What's wrong?" With tears streaming down her face, she responded, "The wedding I've dreamed of my whole life is over, and I will never have another wedding. I've spent my whole life guarding my virginity, and you're going to take that away from me tonight. I will never be a virgin again." Something was wrong with the woman's view of virginity and sex within marriage.

1 Corinthians 7:3-4
"The husband should give to his wife her conjugal rights, and likewise the wife to her husband. For the wife does not have authority over her own body, but the husband does. Likewise the husband does not have authority over his own body, but the wife does."

Not only is sex a gift to God's Beloved ones, but it is also a gift God created for a woman to give to her husband and a man to give to his wife. They yield their bodies to each other. In other words, the wife's body belongs to her husband. The husband's body belongs to his wife.

The woman in the story above valued her virginity as a gift and had been careful not to give it away before it was time. On her wedding day—the day when she could finally give the gift of her body *and* receive the gift of her husband's body—she somehow missed the blessing and joy of God's Plan. Sex is a gift God meant for her and her husband to enjoy.

Many brides spend more time thinking about and planning for the wedding ceremony than the wedding night sex. The grooms, on the other hand, seem to look most forward to the wedding night sex and all of the God-approved sex to come! They anticipate sex and daydream about it (so I've been told)! The groom in the story knew that his bride had "saved" herself for him, and that must have made him feel very special. Imagine how confused, hurt, and unloved he must have felt hearing his bride speak the words, "You're going to take that away from me tonight." The message she sent him (probably unintentionally) was *I don't want to give you this gift because you're not worthy of the gift.*

The bride's beliefs made the gift no longer seem like a gift. God offered her a little bit of paradise on earth, but she settled for less. Sound familiar? Like mother, like daughter. See how easy it can be to follow in Mother Eve's footsteps?

I always hoped God's Plan was for me to fall in love, marry, and of course, make love with my husband. I wanted to experience those miraculous creations, those precious gifts from God. As I thought about what sex would be like with a God-given husband, I knew I would love the man God gave me, and he would love me. In marriage, I wouldn't have to guard myself physically like I had to in dating. I could share all of who I am with my husband, and vice versa.

Genesis 2:25
"And the man and his wife were both naked and were not ashamed."

In marriage, I had the potential to enjoy sex to the max and *without shame*. That sounded like sweet *freedom* to me. In each other's arms, my husband and I could journey together to a rare and wonderfully safe, loving, honest, peaceful, delightful place. We could simply be ourselves, love our hearts out, and be loved beyond belief—a sampling of Heaven on earth!

Have you ever thought of the perfect gift to give a loved one on his birthday or another special day in that person's life? Remember the fun you had picking out the gift? Perhaps you made the gift; remember how you poured your heart into making it? Remember how you couldn't wait to give it to your loved one because you knew he was going to love it? Remember the fun and excitement of watching your loved one unwrap the gift and seeing his eyes light up and a big smile take over his face?

When that perfect gift is opened on the person's special day, it makes the day (and the gift) even more special. In the same way, sex is a gift chosen by God for His Beloved ones. God knows that sex is the perfect gift for our wedding day and a gift to enjoy throughout our marriage!

Think about it!

1—How does the truth of 1 Corinthians 7:3-4 impact your view of virginity and saving yourself for your husband?

2—Think about experiencing the gift of sex with a God-given husband. What do you look forward to?

3—Look up the following verses, and discover how God designed sex as the BEST gift for your wedding day and marriage!

Genesis 1:28 - Sex enables a husband and wife to create _____.

Genesis 2:24 - Sex enables a husband and wife to experience _____.

Proverbs 5:15, 18&19 - Sex brings a husband and wife _____ and satisfaction.

2 Samuel 12:24 - Sex brings _____ to a husband and wife who are hurting, grieving, or stressed.

1 Corinthians 7:3-5 - Sex is a gift that helps a husband and wife resist _____ satan throws their way.

Most people give wedding gifts, such as pots and pans, blenders, crock pots, can openers, coffee makers, china, picture frames, furniture, vacuum cleaners, gift cards, and money. Not God! He went all out and gave the gift of sex—the gift that keeps giving! God's gift gives us oneness with our spouse, knowledge of our spouse, pleasure, comfort, defense against temptation, and children! Sex is the best wedding gift we could receive! God knows how to give good gifts, doesn't He?!

Pray about it!

Heavenly Father,
I praise You, for You are the biggest Giver! Every good and perfect gift is from You! I pray that You would give me a godly husband one day and that You would help us experience the greatest blessings of oneness, including all the physical and spiritual blessings.

Thank You that You don't make me wait forever to unwrap the gift. You only want me to wait for a time, and You do this with my best interests in mind. Help me to be patient and to resist the temptation to unwrap this special gift before the right time so that it will remain as special as You made it. As I wait for "opening day," I ask that You would help me not to get so wrapped up in pleasing a boyfriend, in finding a husband, or in the planning of my wedding day.

Don't let me lose sight of the tremendous delight You intended me to have in the gift of virginity and in the unwrapping of the sex gift. I also ask for all of this for my future husband. In the Name of Your most perfect gift—Jesus, Amen.

31 - In This Together

I was working on staff at a church. It was Tuesday, and like every Tuesday, the church staff gathered together to pray for the church, specific prayer requests submitted by members of the congregation, and to pray for each other. There were about 100 staff members at the meeting. We sat in a huge circle of chairs that almost filled the large meeting room.

This prayer meeting began differently than normal. One of the pastors stood up and said two of our fellow staff members had something to share with us. His serious tone of voice and solemn face indicated we were about to hear something that would not cause us to rejoice. The pastor paved the way for Brad to share. Brad was in his mid-20s, worked in the church in a behind-the-scenes role, and was the guy that everyone was drawn to because he was funny, told the best stories, and was always the life of the party.

Brad stood up to address the circle of his coworkers—all 100 of us. His face and posture reflected a heart in great distress. It was clear he wouldn't make us laugh today. His voice trembled, and the pain in his eyes flowed out as tears as he confessed to us that he and his girlfriend had made bad choices, and she was pregnant.

Brad took responsibility for the sin, saying, "I have disrespected Jennie. I have disrespected women. I have disrespected God, and I have disrespected God's Church. I am very sorry for what I have done, and I ask for your forgiveness." He turned to Jennie and said, "I have robbed you, and I have robbed your future husband. I'm deeply sorry and ask for your forgiveness."

You could have heard a pin drop in the room. I think we all felt paralyzed by the news.

Jennie was sitting down in the chair next to Brad. She looked very sad, and though she held herself together, she must have been holding back a myriad of emotions. Her situation was devastating, humiliating, irreversible, scary, and would change her life forever. This was not a happy moment.

Though I couldn't fully comprehend their situation, I did understand what it was like to experience deep struggle and suffering. In the timeline of my life, I heard their confession just a few years after my relationship with the guy in the singles' group ended and left my life in shambles. That relationship helped me understand how evil my heart's desires are when I'm not relying on God. I saw how easy it is to trust in my own way over God's way. That relationship helped me see how weak I am and how desperately I need Jesus. I knew the all-consuming sorrow felt when a believer sins against God. I just kept thinking, *That could have been me. I'm just like Brad and Jennie; I'm a sinner. It's only by God's grace that I'm not standing in their place.*

I felt a sobering relief that I wasn't standing in Jennie's shoes. I also felt an overwhelming sadness for Jennie and Brad. I can't imagine how hard it must have been for them to confess their sins to their coworkers, including the Senior Pastor, their bosses, and friends. I respected their courage. I felt for them because the consequences of their sin would call for even greater courage in the days ahead.

The pastor who opened the meeting said that Brad and Jennie would need our support in the days to come and encouraged us to love them. Next, he led Brad and Jennie to chairs placed a few feet apart in the middle of the circle. He invited the male staff members who felt led to surround Brad and pray for him. He invited the female staff members to do the same for Jennie. I was drawn by that invitation to help my sister in Christ feel loved.

I was profoundly impacted by that prayer meeting. As I reflected on it, 1 Corinthians 12:12-27 came to mind. The passage describes how those who believe in Jesus are members of one body, the Body of Christ. Each member belongs to all of the other members of the Body. Each member needs all of the other members. "If one member suffers, all suffer together; if one member is honored, all rejoice together" (1 Corinthians 12:26).

I realized that this wasn't just Brad's sin and Jennie's sin. This was *my* sin. It was the sin of every staff member sitting in that room. "For all have sinned and fall short of the glory of God" (Romans 3:23).

The whole Body of Christ suffers when sin gets a foothold in the life of a Christ-follower. In the months that followed, our staff did not forget about Brad's and Jennie's situation. Shortly after the confession in staff prayer, a retreat was held for all the administrative assistants. Both Jennie and I attended that retreat. At one point during the retreat, she became pretty emotional. All of us stopped what we were doing to gather around her as she shared her heart and pain.

Brad and Jennie submitted themselves to the church elders, who walked with them through the church discipline process. The goal of this process is to come alongside church members who have fallen into sin, provide mentors, consistent accountability, and counseling to help them face their sin, embrace forgiveness, and heal spiritually.

Sometime after the initial staff prayer meeting, it was announced to the staff that the elders had determined that Brad's and Jennie's actions merited their dismissal from staff. Church leadership showed grace to Jennie, allowing her to keep her job because as a pregnant woman, they thought she would have a hard time getting hired and qualifying for insurance. Brad had to leave his job, but church leadership extended grace and allowed him time to find a job so that he never had a day that he was unemployed. These updates on Brad and Jennie were difficult to hear because it ushered us deeper into their pain. We suffered as our days of working with Brad were numbered.

As we watched Jennie's baby bump grow bigger and bigger, the usual excitement you would have for a pregnant friend was mixed with sadness. I had many friends, on staff and not on staff, who wrestled with how to treat Brad and Jennie. Some friends couldn't understand how Brad and Jennie could sin sexually and felt anger and disappointment in them. Others found themselves taking sides, depending on whether they knew Brad better or Jennie better. Then there were friends who had experienced God's grace and forgiveness for their own sexual sin who recounted their stories with Brad and Jennie in hopes of encouraging them. "If one member suffers, all suffer together; if one member is honored, all rejoice together" (1 Corinthians 12:26).

Over a decade later, I had the rare opportunity to ask Brad what it was like to confess his sin that day. He shared, "It was hard to face everyone in that circle and confess my sin. It made me more fully understand the gravity of my sin. I felt incredible sadness. I let God down. I dragged a woman down. I let my parents down. I tarnished the Church. I felt tremendous loss. I believed that God had called me to be in ministry as a pastor, but my sin seemed to destroy that dream. I thought of all the people who had believed in me, encouraged me, and taken time to equip and help me to pursue that dream. I felt like I had let all of them down."

Brad continued, "Something very important and healing happened that day. The church's Senior Pastor walked up to me, hugged me, and then faced me, placed his hands on my shoulders, and said, 'I want you to know Jesus forgives you, and I forgive you.' That was so critical for me because those words were spoken by my pastor, my spiritual authority. It felt as if he was both speaking for Christ and for Christ's Body that I was forgiven. He helped me embrace the truth that God truly forgave me for my sin. That day, I realized what I need is this: people surrounding me and reminding me that I'm forgiven."

Think about it!

1—Who is surrounding you? Who reminds you that God loves and forgives you?

If you want to grow in your relationship with Jesus, it is a good idea to seek out a spiritual mentor. A mentor is an older woman, who has been a Christian for many more years than you, has walked the road of life a little longer, and has gained wisdom along the way. A mentor is someone you respect and admire. She has the depth of character embodied in the Proverbs 31 Woman.

A mentor is someone you trust and with whom you feel comfortable sharing your heart. Mentors ask good questions to help us process our life experiences. "The purpose in a man's heart is like deep water, but a {woman} of understanding will draw it out" (Proverbs 20:5). We naturally see ourselves through biased eyes and from selfish perspectives. Mentors can offer a better perspective on our life experiences because they are less connected to the situations we face. They also care about us, want the best for us, want to help us grow as people and as Christ-followers, and will pray for us.

2—Using Titus 2:1-5, create a role description for a godly mentor.

ROLE DESCRIPTION: **"GODLY MENTOR"**
Titus 2:1-5
RESPONSIBILITIES:

3—Spend some time thinking of older women you know who would make good mentors. If you can't think of someone, consider asking a pastor or key leader at your church if he/she knows of anyone. Pray and ask God to help you with the decision of who to approach about mentoring.

Pray about it!

Dear God,

I praise You, for You are a God of companionship and unity. Thank You that all believers are part of the family of God. Thank You that there is always someone there to share life's celebrations and the struggles. Father, teach me how to appreciate this family You've given me, to love and serve other members, and to encourage them in Your truth.

God, I ask that You provide a mentor for me who is older, wiser, kind, self-disciplined, has a close relationship with Jesus, and can help me grow closer to Him! I would especially like a mentor who...

In the unifying name of Jesus, Amen.

32 - Step into Their Shoes

A day or two after the prayer meeting where Brad and Jennie confessed, another staff member and I were drawn to pray together. That other staff member was Chad, who was also my most recent ex-boyfriend. When we were dating, we had set radically high physical boundaries. By God's grace, we did not cross those boundaries. The prayer meeting impacted Chad in much the same way it had impacted me. We knew that we were sinners, and it was only by God's grace that we weren't standing in Brad's and Jennie's shoes.

Chad and I talked about what would happen if we were standing in Brad's and Jennie's place. Chad was a children's pastor. If I was pregnant, we believed the ministry God entrusted to Chad would be undermined and destroyed. He would lose his job, and he may never have the opportunity to serve again as a children's pastor. The parents of the children participating in the ministries Chad led would feel he had broken their trust in him. It was a sobering thought to realize that a sexual sin on my part could have brought a godly man down. I would have been a Bathsheba. I could have caused a dark mark to go on this man's canvas forever.

At that time, I was a volunteer discipleship leader to elementary-age girls. I had such a close relationship with the girls I discipled that I affectionately called them my "Little Sisters," and they called me "Big Sis." If I was pregnant, Chad and I believed my ministry would have been compromised. All of the truth I had shared with the girls about purity and living my life for God's glory would have seemed like a lie to them.

1 Corinthians 12:26.
"If one member suffers, all suffer together; if one member is honored, all rejoice together."

Overwhelmed by God's grace, Chad and I prayed together. We thanked God for protecting us from sexual sin, protecting our hearts, protecting the hearts of the children we were ministering to, and protecting everyone who would have been negatively affected by our sin. We asked God to help us both to remain pure in the years to come. We also prayed for Brad and Jennie.

Praying with an ex-boyfriend about sexual purity and thanking God for His grace is not something that happens every day! The exercise of thinking about what would happen if I sinned sexually and became pregnant led me to realize there was much more at stake than I ever thought. Sexual sin attacks the very purposes for which we were made. God made us to glorify Him, enjoy relationship with Him, and love and serve others, but sexual sin hurts a lot of people and damages a lot of relationships.

The truth is, when we sin sexually, we lose sight of God. We lose sight of who we are in Christ and that we were created for a HIGHER VISION. God gave His Only Son to rescue us from sin. Jesus submitted Himself to God and to His Mission. He graciously laid down His whole life for us. He gave ALL of Himself so that we could be united with God and delight in relationship with Him for all of eternity.

Jesus gave of Himself emotionally, spiritually, and physically for us. Jesus was spit on, beaten on the back with whips, nailed by His hands and feet to the cross, and crowned on the head with prickly-thorned branches. He hung on the cross in absolute agony and died for our sins. The physical body of Jesus was part of God's Plan to redeem His People.

1 Peter 2:24
"He himself bore our sins in his body on the tree, that we might die to sin and live to righteousness. By his wounds you have been healed"

Because Jesus' body was a gift to us, a married woman freely giving of her body to her husband is a snapshot of the greater love God has for us. A married woman lovingly giving of her body to her husband and lovingly receiving his body is a reflection of the glorious union to come in Heaven when we meet God face-to-face.

A single woman who learns to cherish her virginity as part of the BIG Story and guards it paints a profound picture of Jesus. Like Jesus, she loves God the Father and loves others with such a deep love that she submits her body to God's Plan. In doing so, her body becomes an instrument of His righteousness (Romans 6:8-14). She saves herself for an earthly husband provided by God, but most importantly, she waits for her Heavenly Husband. The watching world will always question a virgin. The virgin compelled by the love of Jesus is a profound witness to a dying world that there is a God who saves.

1 Thessalonians 4:3
"For this is the will of God, your sanctification: that you abstain from sexual immorality."

If God's will for us is sanctification, then it must be important. To sanctify means to set apart as holy.

Romans 8:1
"There is therefore now no condemnation for those who are in Christ Jesus."

Ephesians 4:20-24
"But that is not the way you learned Christ! - assuming that you have heard about him and were taught in him, as the truth is in Jesus, to put off your old self, which belongs to your former manner of life and is corrupt through deceitful desires, and to be renewed in the spirit of your minds, and to put on the new self, created after the likeness of God in true righteousness and holiness."

It is God's will that He sanctifies us. He helps us separate ourselves from evil things and evil ways, purifies us, and enables us to live as new creations. This cleansing and renewing of our hearts starts with learning from God's Word and Jesus' example of what God considers good and what He considers evil. Through the power of the Holy Spirit, God enables us to turn from evil things and ways to step towards Him through obedience to His Word. He re-makes us to be pleasing in His sight as He intended when He created man and woman in His image.

With every baby step of obedience we take towards Him, the Holy Spirit helps us grow in sanctification. According to 1 Thessalonians 4:3, avoiding sexual immorality helps us grow in sanctification.

Think about it!

1—Read 1 Thessalonians 4:3-8 and write down God's definition of sexual immorality.

(v.4) Not controlling your body in…

(v.5) Controlling your body in…

(v.5) Controlling your body like those who…

(v.6) To transgress and do…

(v.7) To violate God's standard of how to treat your…

(v.7-8) To ignore…

(v.7-8) To ignore God's gift of the…

When we do something sexually immoral, we sin against God, we sin against our brother, and we sin against ourselves. 1 Corinthians 6:18 says, "Flee from sexual immorality. Every other sin a person commits is outside the body, but the sexually immoral person sins against his own body." We actually sin against our bodies—add that to the definition above.

1 Corinthians 6:18-20
"Flee from sexual immorality. Every other sin a person commits is outside the body, but the sexually immoral person sins against his own body. Or do you not know that your body is a temple of the Holy Spirit within you, whom you have from God? You are not your own, for you were bought with a price. So glorify God in your body."

If you are single and have given your virginity away, then the truth is: You have crossed the boundary line God put in place to protect you and to preserve His gift to you. You have not worshipped Him as He deserves and have sinned against Him. You need Jesus to save you from your sin. You need His forgiveness. You also need His power to move forward. God doesn't expect you to be perfect. That's why Jesus came. He knows you need His help.

"If {you} confess {your} sins, he is faithful and just to forgive {your} sins and to cleanse {you} from all unrighteousness" (1 John 1:9). That is God's promise to you. Pray and receive it. Then let your Heavenly Father lift you up from the destruction around you, set your feet on solid ground, and help you move forward as a new creation.

2—Do you have any close friends or family members who became pregnant outside of marriage? If so, was it hard watching them go through it, and why? Were they well supported? How did you treat them?

Pray about it!

Dear God,

I praise You, for You are Holy and just. You define right and wrong. I can't measure up to Your Perfection. Thank You for loving me despite my imperfections. You came to me when I couldn't come to You. Jesus is Emmanuel, "God with us." He paid the ultimate price for my sin, sacrificing everything for me, including His physical body.

God, I owe You everything! I can't wait to live with You one day, and I am so grateful that Your Spirit lives inside of me now! Use my life for Your glory. Let my body glorify You from the inside out. In Jesus' Name, Amen.

33 - Rebecca's Story

E very choice we make comes with consequences and costs. If you choose to honor God with your body, there will be consequences, and it will cost you something. If you choose to experience sex outside of God's boundary, there will also be consequences and costs.

Four of my friends who became pregnant outside of marriage have graciously granted me permission to share their stories with you. Their stories will help us understand a little better what it is like to cross God's boundary and find out you are pregnant. My friends' stories will escort us into some vulnerable places of the heart.

My friends are extremely courageous and humble to share the details behind the dark places on their canvases. I didn't twist their arms to share. I didn't pay them anything. They willingly chose to share their stories with you. Why? They share because God's love compels them. They see you as their neighbor, and they view the sharing of their stories as an opportunity to love and encourage you in your pursuit of God and of purity.

Rebecca's story

"I found out I was pregnant two weeks before my 20th birthday. I was terrified, mostly fearing how my boyfriend's parents would respond. I never considered anything other than keeping my baby. At the time, I lived in a different state than my parents. When my mom learned I was pregnant, she wanted me to come back home right away and was less than thrilled when I declined. I felt it would be unfair to my child and my child's father to move to a different state. My boyfriend, Trey, and I had already talked about marriage for at least six months before I became pregnant but with no definitive timeline. I was about seven or eight months along when we finally set a date. I was adamant we not rush to marry 'just because I was pregnant.' We got married when our daughter was two months old.

There was a stigma to deal with because I was pregnant and not married. I've always looked younger, so I looked like a pregnant teenager, which made it worse. Despite the judgment I faced, God helped me have joy in my pregnancy. Thankfully, I did not get sick much when I was pregnant and had an easy delivery and a healthy baby.

I couldn't provide for my daughter's basic needs, so I had to put my pride on the shelf and apply for Medicaid and W.I.C. (Women, Infant, and Child Federal Assistance Program). Using the W.I.C. vouchers at the grocery store was very uncomfortable. I realized it wasn't anybody else's place to judge me, and if they did, they were the ones who had to live with that, not me."

What would you say to a young woman who is having or considering having sex before marriage? Rebecca responded:

"What I would say to others and have (including my own teenage daughter), is that Trey and I were lucky. We have great families who supported us. Getting pregnant outside of marriage, having a child, and starting a marriage with a child was not easy or a fairytale in any sense. Trey and I have been committed to making things work. Don't put yourself in a tempting situation because the best intentions have a way of going by the wayside. It's very hard to think clearly in a tempting situation. Birth control simply fails sometimes. My daughter was conceived while using two types of birth control.

I tell teens/young adults to guard their hearts because there are consequences that can't be undone. Any decisions you make in your youth will have an impact on the decisions you make for the rest of your life."

Guard your heart

Proverbs 4:23
"Above all else, guard your heart, for everything you do flows from it." (NIV)
"Keep your heart with all vigilance, for from it flow the springs of life." (ESV)

Guard your heart. Keep it. Watch over it. Why? The heart is an extremely valuable possession. Your heart is yours and is the core of your being. Take a journey to the depths of your heart, and there you will discover who you really are, your authentic self. Proverbs 27:19 says, "As in water face reflects face, so the heart of man reflects the man." Your heart reveals your dreams, passions, desires, what you value most, and your character. It influences your thoughts, words, and actions.

The heart is where you connect relationally with God and with other people. The heart is the source of everything in your life. From it flows the springs of life. No price tag can be placed on the heart, for it is priceless! That is why King Solomon says to look after the heart, to give it special attention.

Because the heart is a "spring of life," everything in your life is potentially affected by what your heart takes in. For example, think of a movie that made you cry. What was it about the movie that moved you to tears?

Whether you felt a connection to a character or a situation in the movie, what you saw touched your heart. What you felt in your heart overflowed into tears.

A spring found in nature is where water flows to the surface of the earth from deep underground. The water collects in pools or runs off into creeks and streams. If the spring was plugged up, then water would no longer flow from it, and life downstream would be threatened. Life depends on the condition of the spring. For example, if the spring becomes contaminated, it becomes unhealthy and has the potential to harm—even kill—the life that comes in contact with it. As long as the spring remains pure, it is healthy and life-giving.

Your heart is like that spring. When you open up your heart to something, you allow it to influence your heart. Then, your heart influences your thoughts, words, and actions. All of this affects your relationship with God, friends, and family, the pursuit of your dreams, your ministry, and everything else in your life. You must ask yourself, "Will opening up my heart to this affect me and my life positively or negatively?"

Think about it!

1—On a scale of 1-10 (with 1 being the lowest and 10 the highest), how much do you guard your heart? Describe.

2—Which 3-5 people or things influence your heart the most? Are any of these people or things negatively affecting you and your life? If so, how can you guard your heart better?

3—Has your heart been broken through a relationship with a guy? Draw a broken heart or tears by the relationships on your canvas that ended with your heart broken.

If yes, what caused your heart to break? If you had a chance to re-do that relationship, what would you do to guard your heart?

Pray about it!

Heavenly Husband,
You are love's Creator. Thank You for loving me when my sin made me unlovable. Thank You for knowing exactly what my heart needed—Jesus. "This is love, not that {I} have loved {You}, but that {You} loved {me} and sent {Your} Son to be the propitiation for {my} sins" (1 John 4:10). Because of Jesus, my heart is capable of loving. My heart was dead, but Jesus brought it alive. Let my heart beat for You!

God, teach me how to love as You love. Show me how to love You with all of my heart, soul, and mind. Be my first love. Teach me how to keep my heart devoted to You. Teach me how to love my neighbor as myself without losing heart. Protect my wellspring of life. Reveal to me if I am opening up my heart too much or too quickly to others. Show me how to guard my heart in a healthy way while opening it up to be used by You to minister to others.

I love you! In Jesus' Name, Amen.

(Matthew 22:37-39, Proverbs 4:23, 1 John 4:7-12)

34 - Katie's Story

Katie's story: *"When I found out I was pregnant, I was 20 years old and had just finished my third year of college. I don't know why I would have been shocked to find out I was pregnant, but I was shocked. You never think it will be you! My heart sank, and I was devastated. I had just left college for the summer, had a lot of time and space between my boyfriend and me, and was able to really think. We had actually broken up about a week before I found out I was pregnant. I remember my first thought was to cry out to God, begging him to hold my heart and my hand and to help me be strong and wise and able to do the right thing.*

I am actually a little surprised that having an abortion was never even an option in my mind. I knew about the devastation that young women who have abortions experience later in life. While for some, an abortion seems to be an immediate solution, I knew that it would be something I would battle the rest of my life. Also, I knew I would be able to raise the baby with the help of family if needed.

Eric, the baby's father, and I got married shortly after I became pregnant. Once I called him, we decided this was the best thing for us to do. I don't think I would advise that to others. I really had to put aside the fact that I was pregnant out of marriage and take a serious look at Eric and his character. I knew that he loved God and wanted to follow God. I knew that this was a man who would truly love me and the baby and would be committed to caring for us and being a family.

I did not go back to college, and we lived in the same community where Eric grew up. It was a long way from my hometown and my family and friends. For the most part, everyone was very supportive, helpful, and positive. Yet, I wish more than anything that an older couple or those close to us would have talked to us and mentored us. We had NO marriage counseling or anything. Eric and I had to grow up really fast. As I look back, I wish I would have asked more questions and reached out for help and mentoring. I wish I had worked through issues as they arose, but it was a time where you just didn't acknowledge there was a problem, and you certainly didn't talk about it."

What would you say to a young woman who is having or considering having sex before marriage? Katie responded:

"I was raised in a Christian home, went to a Christian school and college, and I heard it ALL! I have realized that we come up really short when we only tell young ladies, 'Don't have sex because it's wrong. Wear modest clothes so that you won't make guys lust.' I would start way before that. I would encourage a

young woman to learn about her own heart, and learn to read her heart."

Katie also wanted to encourage you with Psalm 63:1-8:

"O God, you are my God; earnestly I seek you;
    my soul thirsts for you;
my flesh faints for you,
    as in a dry and weary land where there is no water.
So I have looked upon you in the sanctuary,
    beholding your power and glory.
Because your steadfast love is better than life,
    my lips will praise you.
So I will bless you as long as I live;
    in your name I will lift up my hands.
My soul will be satisfied as with fat and rich food,
    and my mouth will praise you with joyful lips,
when I remember you upon my bed,
    and meditate on you in the watches of the night;
for you have been my help,
    and in the shadow of your wings I will sing for joy.
My soul clings to you;
    your right hand upholds me."

The core of who you are

Your heart is the core of who you are, the core of your inner being. Let's use the illustration of an apple for a moment. When you peel away the skin of an apple, you'll find the pulp of the apple. Cut away the pulp, and you will eventually come to the core of the apple. The core is the innermost and most essential part of the apple. It gives structure to the apple. Everything that makes up the apple is built from its core; the apple wouldn't be an apple without its core.

Our heart is like the apple's core. It is the innermost part of who we are as people. It takes some work to get to our core, but it's a worthwhile endeavor. Just as everything that makes up the apple is built from its core, your character and life are built from your core—your heart. Everything in your life flows out of what is in your heart. It influences your thoughts, words, and actions. When you seek to learn about your heart, you are essentially digging deeper into your life's purpose to discover how God uniquely crafted, gifted, equipped, and called you to be a part of His BIG Story. Learning about your heart is getting to know yourself from the inside out.

Think about it!

Learning to read your heart is one of the most important things you could ever do because your heart is your spring of life! If wrong thoughts, wrong beliefs, or wrong behaviors take root in your heart, then your heart will become contaminated and has the potential to harm your relationship with God and with others. An unhealthy heart will hinder you from becoming the woman God made you to be and paralyze you from fulfilling His plans for your life. Learning to read your heart will help keep it healthy and overflowing with life!

"Learning To Read Your Heart"—APPLICATION ACTIVITY

A professional counselor taught me that there are 5 basic emotions: gladness, sadness, anger, love, and fear.

- A good way to start reading your heart is to ask, *Do I feel glad, sad, mad, love, or fear?*

- Ask, *Why do I feel that way?*

- Then, ask, *What do I know to be true? What does God's Word say about my situation?*

  {Note: To find out what God's Word says, use the concordance in the back of the Bible or the search feature on a Bible app or online Bible. Search for the emotion you feel or a keyword that describes your situation.}

- Next ask, *How does what I'm feeling and experiencing line up with God's Word? How does God want me to apply His truth in my life?*

- ### *Pray about it!*
  "Destroy arguments and every lofty opinion raised against the knowledge of God, and take every thought captive to obey Christ" (2 Corinthians 10:5).

Dear God,
You are solid in character. You are good at the core of Your being. All Your ways are good. You have promised to bring about plans for my welfare, for my good, to give me a future and a hope. I claim Your promise. (Jeremiah 29:11)

When chaos takes over my heart, I will rest in the knowledge of Your good character. Help me read my heart's every beat. When my heart is deceived by lies, enlighten my mind to recognize truth. Teach me how to line up my heart with my mind, to balance emotion with logic. Give me faith to trust You with all of my heart.

*With every **sad** beat, You are my Comforter. Turn my mourning into dancing, my sorrow into gladness (Jeremiah 31:13). With every **angry** beat, You are my Defender. Fight for me. Fight for my heart, soften it with grace, and fill it with love, forgiveness, and peace (Exodus 14:14). When my heart beats with **fear,** You are my Safe Place. Let Your Perfect Love turn my fear into faith (1 John 4:18). When I feel **love,** it is because You first loved me and taught me what love is (1 John 4:19). When I am **glad,** it is because of You and Your good work in my life (Acts 2:28).*

God, You are the Hero of my heart! May my heart always beat in sync with Your Spirit! In Jesus' Name, Amen.

35 - Lynne's Story

Lynne's story: *"I was 16 going on 17 when I became pregnant. I did it with my boyfriend. He was my first. I remember shaking with fear and praying. I begged God to not let it be true, and I think it was the first time I truly experienced His presence. My body trembled the rest of the day.*

Telling my parents was so scary. Up until then, I had been the 'good' child. My brother helped me tell them. My parents came in with groceries. When I told them, my mom dropped her bag and went into her closet. I could hear her crying. I felt awful. I really don't remember my dad's reaction, but I knew that I had really disappointed them.

Like my parents, my boyfriend's mom was devastated. She wanted to keep it a secret from his dad, so she didn't tell him. She got together with my parents, and they made the decision about what to do about the baby. At first, I didn't want to get an abortion and wanted to keep the baby. Adoption was not an option in my head. But then I started thinking about what people would think of me and how hard it would be to become a mom at 17. My boyfriend wanted to marry me, but then that is how his parents got together. Although they were still married, I just couldn't see myself married to him forever. He was still immature, and I wasn't done 'living' yet.

My dad took me to get an abortion, and the rest of my family didn't even know about it. I felt shame. Going to the clinic was weird. Everyone knew why I was there, but everyone acted like it was a normal procedure—lots of smiles and everything. They did an ultrasound, and I tried not to pay much attention to it.

At first, I blocked the abortion from my mind. I just went on and actually appreciated more the freedom I had just being a teenager. I didn't have sex again for a while. Then, I started to feel like I was going crazy. I was hungry for love and attention but didn't want any ties. So, I briefly dated a guy who was engaged. We were about to have sex when my mother came home from work early and found us. I think my mom literally beat some sense into me. That is when I realized I was losing it. So, I got back in church for a while. In college, I started questioning my faith."

After some time on the path:

"I started dating an agnostic. He treated me like a princess. For the first time, I thought that maybe I was worth something. He knew about the abortion and didn't judge me."

Fifteen years later:

"On and off, waves of deep sadness came over me. I cried and asked God to forgive me. I knew in my head that He had forgiven me, but the guilt still lingered in my heart. God continued to heal me and help me embrace His promise that I was forgiven. I went to counseling and prayed over it so much that it grew less and less painful to remember. Experiencing such grace from God helped me grow closer to Him.

What would you say to a young woman who is pregnant, not married, and considering what to do? Lynne responded:

"To young women who find themselves pregnant and unmarried, I strongly urge you not to consider abortion as an option. To kill an unborn child can feel unforgivable, and it does more to your emotions than you can even imagine. As someone who desires to adopt, I think women who give up their children for adoption are courageous. I couldn't do it. I have SO MUCH respect for those who do. Because I've been in their shoes, I can't judge them for getting pregnant. But I can commend them for being unselfish and suffering social consequences to give a child life and then being unselfish enough to give the child to someone who is more equipped to care for the child."

Lynne wanted to encourage you with a verse that has meant a lot to her.

"Delight yourself in the LORD, and he will give you the desires of your heart." – Psalm 37:4

"I have learned that by delighting in the Lord, God gives me more healthy desires and patience for the things for which I have to wait. He gives us better than what we would settle for otherwise. He gives us what is BEST for us. I guess experience is what drives home that truth. Also, HE is what truly satisfies—not a man, money, good health, or anything else we tend to chase after will satisfy like Him."

Lynne gave this advice:

"To a young woman in her teens or 20s who is considering having premarital sex, I would say that it is very easy to think that getting pregnant couldn't or wouldn't happen to you, but it can. All of my friends were having sex long before I was, and they didn't get pregnant, so I thought I would be okay. My boyfriend and I used a form of protection, but I still got pregnant. I'd say don't take the chance.

The emotional consequences of premarital sex are ugly. It is still hard sometimes for me to enjoy sex with my husband because I equate it with something dirty and sinful. I still have a mental connection of doing it 'daringly' and remembering the 'excitement' of doing it, which has tainted my sex life with my husband. Sex with your husband can still be beautiful and exciting, but those earlier experiences don't go away. It takes a LOT of prayer and surrender to get past the guilt of not waiting for my husband."

Think about it!

1—Are you surprised at how much Lynne's heart was affected by what she chose to do with her body? Explain.

One day when you marry, you will become one with your husband. The sexual choices both of you made in the past will affect your union. Your sexual history will impact your husband's body, mind, heart, and life. Having sex before marriage can rob your husband of the full blessings of sex, including intimacy, pleasure, satisfaction, comfort, and strength to resist temptation. It can affect the quality, strength, and happiness of your marriage. When an unmarried woman considers having sex with her boyfriend, she probably doesn't consider those consequences long enough.

Having sex before marriage also puts you and your future husband at risk of being exposed to painful, sometimes life-threatening, sexually transmitted diseases (STDs). STD's are a HUGE consequence that can come from having sex, especially sex outside of marriage with multiple partners.

2—Below is a list of common STD's contracted by young women. To learn more about them, visit the Centers for Disease Control and Prevention website (www.cdc.gov), and use the search option.

Chlamydia | Gonorrhea | HPV (Human Papilloma Virus) | Trichomoniasis | Syphilis

Pray about it!

Father God,

*I **adore** You. "Whom have I in heaven but you? And there is nothing on earth that I desire besides you. My flesh and my heart may fail, but {you are} the strength of my heart and my portion forever" (Psalm 73:25-26).*

*I **confess** that I find myself seeking attention, acceptance, and adoration in other people. Please forgive me.*

***Thank You** that You hold my future in Your hands. Your Word and Your Spirit lead me into my future and to all the blessings you lavish on Your children when we walk in Your ways.*

*God, I **ask** You to convict me when I seek to find my worth in a person. Turn my heart back to You. May I "delight {myself} in the Lord, and {You} will give me the desires of {my} heart" (Psalm 37:4). Protect me from having premarital sex and the consequences that are attached to this sin. Grant me faith and patience to wait on Your Good Plan for me. Plant confidence in my heart that my identity is found only in You. Increase my desire to fulfill my role in Your BIG Story and to help others make it to the end. In the Delightful Name of Jesus, Amen.*

36 - Sarah's Story

Sarah was 20 years old, a junior in college, and in her words, was *"loving college life."* She says, *"Finding out I was pregnant was truly one of the scariest and loneliest times of my life. I was so incredibly ashamed that I did not want ANYONE to know. For the longest time, I did not tell anyone other than my boyfriend. When I left college in May, at the end of that school year, I had told none of my friends. That made it seem a bit like it wasn't happening."*

Following is a letter Sarah wrote to her sorority sister to share with her what was happening in her life.

Dear Meghan,

I want to write this to you because I really do consider you one of my closest friends. I'm sure you remember telling me last year that there was a high price for disobedience. Well, I must not have really believed that because it didn't stop me from being disobedient—not only to my parents, but to an even higher authority, the Lord. You know it says in the Bible, "For the Lord disciplines the one he loves..." (Hebrews 12:6). Now, I can say that I am so thankful to the Lord that He didn't let me get by with my sin. I'm sure you have heard the rumors going around about me. The fact is, that yes, I am pregnant. I have seen over the past few months that my sin is no different than anyone else's sin, but my consequences are worse. I am just one of those who has been caught! I am thankful because the Lord has used this in my life and in the lives of family members to make us more like Jesus. However, this is a hard way to learn a lesson!

I want to take this opportunity to tell you and others that if we could see where sin gets us, we wouldn't do a lot of the things we do. I never dreamed that the first lie I told my parents would lead me into a situation like this. If I had, believe me, I would have found a way to obey. The Lord didn't tell us to honor and obey our parents just to hear Himself speak. He has a purpose—to protect us and to provide guidance for us. One thing I've discovered is that "honor" means a lot more than doing what our parents say. It means "to regard our parents highly, to esteem them." I was wrong for the way I acted and talked about my parents. Through this situation, God has restored a relationship with my parents that I was destroying on my own accord.

I cannot condemn anyone for talking about me and spreading rumors about me. Before this happened, I would have done the very same thing. But now, I know what it feels like to be the object of a lot of people's conversations. It's no fun—absolutely awful! I've always been told that gossip can ruin a person's life, and the Bible talks about the tongue as a deadly poison (James 3:8). It's true! I am thankful that I know how it feels, because it has made me think twice before I speak! I want to encourage you to do the same! If someone brings me up, tell them the truth, and then drop it, please. If you know the pain that gossip can cause, you will understand. If not, take my word for it, and don't do it, please! It can't help any situation.

I want you to realize what I have learned in the past few months—thanks only to the Lord!!! I have seen that when we take our eyes off of Jesus and what He has for us (whether we like it or not), we are in trouble. I took my eyes off of Him, and look where it got me. If my going through this can help one person see that doing things your own way rather than the Lord's way isn't worth it, then this is okay! Really though, it's okay anyway because I have seen that without Jesus, I am nothing. I am not able to guide my own life.

I also want you and others to see their parents as their God-given authority. If we didn't need them, He wouldn't have given them to us! You may be just like me in thinking that they really don't know what is best for you, but believe it or not, we don't know everything that we think we do. I would have been spared a whole lot of pain if I had stayed under my parents' authority. You know how I and a lot of others always said that my parents needed to let me make decisions for myself? Well, I made my own decisions against the counsel they gave me, and it sure didn't get me very far! I have talked about this at length with Mom and Dad, and I want everyone to know that I am convinced that Mom and Dad are not trying to hold on to me and protect me forever as their "little girl." They want to help me learn how to make wise decisions on my own. They share the same goals for me as I have for myself. They want me to only be concerned with what the Lord has for me, and that I would want to be more like Jesus. That's all we should be concerned about anyway.

Meghan, it's okay with me for this to become public knowledge. There is no use in trying to hide it! That would just mean more lies, and I have had quite enough of those!! All I ask is that you share this letter with Jessica. Since she is the sorority President, please ask her to consider reading it at the next sorority meeting.

I want to tell you as I close that I am truly sorry for being such a bad witness to everyone this past year. Please forgive me. I want everyone to know that I realize it was my sin that got me to this place. There is no one else to blame but me! I know that God has forgiven me. I can wait on Him and go on with my life, because Jesus died for this sin, just as He did all others. For that, I will always be thankful! One good thing to remember is that we don't hold our heads up because of anything we have or haven't done. We hold our heads up because we belong to Jesus—because of His life in us!

Thank you for accepting this letter for everyone! If you want, please be in touch!

Much love,
Sarah

Think about it!

It took tremendous courage for Sarah to write that letter. She could have written a short letter to inform her friends that she was pregnant, but she went several steps further. She took responsibility for her sin, shared vulnerably from her heart, asked forgiveness for how she may have negatively influenced them, and encouraged them to trust God's authority and plan for their lives.

1—Imagine that you are one of Sarah's sorority sisters. How would you respond to her letter?

2—Did her letter challenge you to think or live differently? Describe.

3—In the letter, Sarah offers several encouragements (listed below). Which of Sarah's encouragements spoke to your heart the most, and why?

Trust God's wisdom. (Proverbs 3:5-8 and John 14:21)
Trust God's plans for your life. (Jeremiah 29:11)
Honor your parents. (Ephesians 6:1-3)
Watch your tongue. (James 3:8-9)
Keep your eyes on Jesus. (Hebrews 12:1-2)

Pray about it!

Creator God,
You are a God of purpose. Everything You do is done for a reason. You are the architect of the world, who fabricated the blueprints for the land, seas, and sky and the destiny of every human being. Your vision reaches for eternity while my eyes struggle to see beyond my current circumstances.

Father, keep my eyes on Jesus, my perfect PATH to You. Let Your wisdom and commandments guide my every step and lead me closer to You. Help me to honor the people around me, especially my parents.

Teach me to utter words that bless others, who are Your image-bearers. Help me resist temptations along the way and enjoy sweet revelations of You. In Jesus' Name, Amen.

37 - Sarah's Story, Part 2

Yesterday, we read Sarah's letter to her sorority sisters. Let's continue with Sarah's story.

"For as long as I could remember, I had been taught and truly believed that abortion was wrong. I remember thinking (only briefly) that it would be the easiest thing to have an abortion and just get rid of the problem. However, I could never think about that for longer than a few minutes at a time. I knew it was wrong, and it would not be the way to solve my problem. Abortion was out! For me, that left two options: 1) Get married and keep the baby, or 2) Place the baby up for adoption.

I had very strong opinions about keeping the baby and not being married. I saw that as a very unfair solution—unfair to the child to have to grow up without a father and unfair to my parents because they would have to carry the burden of providing. I knew that I would be unable to provide for a child in the way that I truly wanted to provide for my children. So that really only left one option that I thought I could live with: Get married and keep the child. This wasn't the dream I had dreamed and planned, but I figured my boyfriend and I could make it work.

With all the determination in me, I went home from college one weekend to tell my parents that I was pregnant AND I was getting married. It was quite a shock!!! A little background to the story is that the father of this child had demonstrated some character issues during the previous year while we were dating, and my parents and I had agreed that he was not the type of man that I should date or marry. I was fully in support of this decision, but unfortunately, I continued to date him while at college. I never admitted this to my parents and frequently lied to them when they asked me how I was doing without him. Then, I turn up pregnant with a boy that they think I am no longer seeing. Like I said, it was quite a shock!!!

I truly believe that what happened over the next several weeks was a miracle, resulting from the power of prayer. My parents were great (after the initial shock wore off). They told me that they would do anything in their power to help me through this, but they begged me not to get married. They had me meet with godly people they believed could help me. A wonderful professional counselor gave me the greatest advice! He told me that everyone had an opinion about what was right and what I should do, but really, the only one that mattered in making the decision was me. I was the one who had to live with this decision for the rest of my life. My counselor advised me to set aside three days and not speak with anyone about the matter—not the father of the baby, not my parents, not my pastor, not even him, my counselor. I think the first miracle was that I agreed to his suggestion. I was pretty hardhearted and determined at that point and was not looking for any opportunity to change my mind.

I told all parties that I was taking three days to make my own decision. I prayed that God would show me what I needed to do. After seeking God, I knew beyond a shadow of a doubt that the baby needed to be placed for adoption. I think the Lord was clearly directing me, and He made it very evident to me that adoption was the right thing for me.

I think the entire situation became much more real and much scarier to me at this point. It had been kind of fun to think about playing house and having a little baby. The gravity of my situation hit me when I realized what I was facing. As scary as it was, I truly knew that adoption was the right decision.

I stayed at home for a bit of the summer and then left to go to the Gladney Center for Adoption in Ft. Worth, Texas. I lived at the Gladney Center for about four months with many others in the same situation. I had a job, lived in a dorm with a roommate and suitemates, cooked my own meals, and was provided counseling about my decision. It truly was a wonderful place to be, and they cared for me very well. I would love to tell you that it was easy to go through all of that, but it wasn't easy at all. I did have a peace, even on the days that I thought my heart was going to break!"

Psalm 3:3
"But you, O LORD, are a shield about me, my glory, and the lifter of my head."

Think about it!

Throughout her letter to her sorority sisters, Sarah gave thanks to God. She even went as far as to say, *"Now, I can say that I am so thankful to the Lord that He didn't let me get by with my sin."* One of the main Bible verses she references is Hebrews 12:6, which says, "For the Lord disciplines the one he loves."

1—Do you find it remarkable that a young woman in Sarah's circumstances could be so thankful for God's discipline? Describe.

2—Read Hebrews 12:1-17 and write down the ways that God's discipline is a blessing to us.

Pray about it!

Faithful Father,
Thank You for Jesus, the Founder of my faith. With the vision of Heaven and its everlasting joy in His sights, He passionately fought for me. Help me to never lose sight of His sacrifice that rescued me from Hell and made the joy of Heaven mine. He shed His blood so sin would not be the final end for me. He shed His blood so that I could be called a daughter of God, my highest calling. Teach me to live with the vision of

Heaven and Your Holiness always before me. Show me how to live in peace with others, to extend to others the grace You have graciously shown me, and to not defile myself or others sexually.

When I sin, don't allow me to think too highly of myself. Turn my heart back to Jesus, the Perfector of my faith. Father, grant me the courage to welcome Your discipline. Provide the strength to endure the pain of discipline to its completion. Thank You that Your discipline is evidence that You love me as Your daughter. Thank You that it will reveal to me the depth of Your love for me, and the mystery of Your grace.

Thank You that You will set my eyes on Heaven again. You will set my feet on the path of righteousness again. You will produce in me a faith that has been tested and found true, produces good fruit, and fills my days on earth with peace and the hope. In Jesus' Saving Name, Amen.

(Hebrews 12:1-17)

38 - God's Children

Today, you will have the opportunity to learn what it is like to be the person whose life is most radically impacted by a young woman's choice to engage in premarital sex—the child who is conceived as a result of that choice. My friends, Kaitlin and Olivia, were conceived out of marriage by different moms and given up for adoption. They open up their hearts and share the wise insights God has graciously given them.

KAITLIN'S STORY

"I've known I was adopted since I was born. My parents didn't want me to feel like I was different, so they always told me I was adopted but not any different than my brother and sister. At first, I was confused and asked, 'Why would my mom not keep me?' When I turned 19, which was how old my mom was when she had me, it hit me that she did it for me. She gave me up to give me a better life. She knew she wouldn't be able to care for me as well as I would need since I have Cystic Fibrosis and all."

What would you say to a young woman who is pregnant, not married, and isn't sure what to do?

"I love the idea of adoption. I am so beyond thankful I am adopted. I can't imagine what it would be like to be pregnant as a young woman and unmarried, but if I could speak to girls who are pregnant, then I would tell them that adoption is a great idea. You don't have to keep in touch with the child. My adoption was closed, meaning I haven't had contact with my birth mom, and she doesn't want me to have contact with her. I am ok with that because I understand that it was hard for her to give me up at 19, and people judged her. I have a great life that I wouldn't be able to have if I wasn't here.

I would also tell them to think about the baby's life. He or she could grow up to be a great doctor who finds the cure for my disease, Cystic Fibrosis, or even becomes the President of the United States, or the CEO of a company that pioneers environmental advancements in the world. I would tell them to get in touch with a counselor or mentor; having a support system is so important!"

What has your journey of adoption taught you about God?

"Adoption has taught me that God is a sovereign God who loves every child that He creates in this world. He wants all of His children to grow up and bring glory to Him."

Kaitlin wanted to encourage you with this:

"Every girl is special, and yes, there are so many pressures in this world to look a certain way, dress a certain way, do this and that with a boy, try out this drug or drink, but none of that is worth it. God wants all of His girls to be strong, powerful women who bring glory to Him. I don't have a perfect body, I can't wear bikinis, I am sick a lot because of Cystic Fibrosis, and I haven't had a relationship with a boy in a while." (Kaitlin was in college when she wrote this.) *"One thing I tell every girl I mentor: 'If you don't see yourself marrying that boy, then why are you wasting your time dating him?'*

Turn to God for everything. It took me 18 years, when I went off to college, to really turn to God and focus on Him and His Plan for me in life. If you spend time every day with God, He will show you so much love, and you will see so many answers in His Word. He is a great God who does everything in our lives for a complete, and most of the time, not understandable reason."

Kaitlin's life verse:
"The LORD will fight for you; you need only to be still." –Exodus 14:14 (NIV)

OLIVIA'S STORY

"My parents were honest with me. For as long as I can remember I have always known I was adopted. During elementary and middle school, I resented the fact I was adopted, and I hated my birth mom for giving me away. My parents raised me holding my birth mom in the highest respect, but I didn't really understand how lucky I was until my freshman year in high school. For so long, I felt that my birth mom didn't want me, and nobody cared. For a long time, that's what adoption meant to me...being unwanted!

I always knew I wanted to get in contact with my birth mom and that I wanted to hear her voice and her side of the story! When I was 20 and a freshman in college, I decided it was time to write her! Three days after writing, I received a phone call from her! I will remember that moment for the rest of my life! A couple of weeks later, I went to visit her in Tennessee, and I had no idea what to expect! I drove past her house probably five times before I turned down the driveway. She was sitting on her porch, waiting for me! She ran to me before I could get out of the car and embraced me!

We spent the weekend staying up until 5 a.m. every night, catching up on the past 20 years. She told me she thought she would never hear from her daughter because she thought I would hold everything against her! She said she gave me up for adoption because she wanted me to have everything I wanted, and she knew she couldn't give me that herself.

I met the rest of my family, including a half-brother. I had finally found the family I looked like, and I felt so welcomed, like I had always been there! I love my birth mom, and I thank God every day for her selfless choice to give me a better chance at life! I talk to her every day and visit her as much as I can!"

What would you say to a young woman who is pregnant, not married, and isn't sure what to do?

"Adoption is the loving option! It's a selfless choice. I am thankful every day for the life my birth mom let me have! Adoption is the hardest choice a woman can make, but it's a choice made out of love by strong women all over the world!"

133

What has your journey of adoption taught you about God?

"Through all of this I have grown a lot in my walk with God! He does have a plan, and everything happens for a reason! Any time I feel doubt in my life and I find it hard to have faith, I think: How many people who are adopted are successful in finding their birth mom and building a relationship with her?! I am alive today because of the brave and incredible choice a woman made 20 years ago as she gave birth in a hospital alone."

JUDITH'S STORY

My friend, Judith, was gracious to provide us another unique perspective on adoption. Judith and her husband, David, have six sons. All of the boys were adopted. Judith says, *"Adoption is a beautiful design. To me, adoption is the most difficult decision the birth mother could make. It does defy a woman's nature. We have so much respect for our boys' birth mothers. They looked beyond themselves at their children and loved them so much to allow them to be adopted. What they did was so courageous. Our six boys are such a joy and gift to us."*

{After years of struggling with infertility, Judith became pregnant. Shortly after learning she was pregnant, she lost the baby.}

"After I lost Bradford, I began to understand the pain of a birth mom to deliver a baby, yet come home with empty arms. All the things that happen to a woman's body when she is pregnant began happening to me, but I had no baby to hold or nurse. I then began praying specifically for birth moms and encouraging others to do so when hoping to adopt.

The decision to allow a child to be adopted is such a gift for a family longing to be parents. It is the greatest blessing they can receive outside of their salvation. Adoption is a picture of God's adoption of us. We are ALL created in His image. When our boys call out for Daddy, I am reminded of us as children, crying out to our ABBA Father. Adoption is such a sweet taste of the love of God for us!"

Think about it!

Kaitlin and Olivia were innocent babies who had no say in the early choices that were made for their lives. A mother's decisions and actions have a radical impact on her children. Kaitlin and Olivia felt confusion and hurt over their mothers' decisions and actions. God, in His grace, stepped in and provided for them. He placed them in loving families and drew them into relationship with Him. He helped them take captive the lie that they were not wanted and see the truth—they are deeply loved. God helped them believe the truth that He created them with great worth and divine purpose. They are part of a BIGGER Story.

Let's say you become a mom one day.

1—What do you want to model for your children about relating to God?

2—What kind of marriage do you want to model for your children?

3—If you have a daughter, what do you want to model for her about being a woman? If you have a son, what do you want to model for him about relating to women?

4—If you discovered you were pregnant today, how would your current circumstances affect all the things above that you desire for your child(ren) to experience?

5—Kaitlin mentioned the importance of having a mentor. How are you doing with finding a mentor?

Pray about it!

Judith wanted to encourage you with Romans 8:12-17. Let's use it as our prayer.

Heavenly Father,
Your Word says, "{I am a} debtor, not to the flesh, to live according to the flesh. For if {I} live according to the flesh {I} will die, but by the Spirit {help me} put to death the deeds of the body, {so that I} will live. For all who are led by the Spirit of God are sons {and daughters} of God. For {I} did not receive the spirit of slavery to fall back into fear, but {I} have received the Spirit of adoption as {a daughter}, by whom {I cry}, "Abba! Father!" The Spirit himself bears witness with {my} spirit that {I am a} child of God, and if a child, then an heir of God and fellow heir with Christ, provided {I} suffer with him in order that {I} may also be glorified with him." In Jesus' Redemptive Name, Amen.

39 - Pure Potential

Some of my most memorable and humorous moments in ministry have come from times spent with teenagers. I was leading a discipleship group made up of four 14-year-old girls. They were each a bundle of pure energy, sheer silliness, and contagious fun! When you put them together, it was like a bag of popcorn cooking in the microwave, busting forth with giggles, storytelling, and playful banter! Each discipleship meeting was an adventure of its own!

The girls and I were in the middle of Bible study on the topic of "Love." None of our previous studies had seemed to grab the girls' attention like this one. Sara, who usually seemed disinterested in group discussions, looked up at me with serious determination and asked, "Have you ever kissed a boy?"

Before I had a chance to respond, Jaclyn blurted out, "She's 27!" I couldn't help but chuckle!

I confirmed Jaclyn's assumption that I *had* kissed a boy, opening the door for the girls to ask more questions:

"How do you know when you're ready to kiss?"

"What's it like to kiss a boy?"

"How do you make your first kiss special?"

Like every teenager, the girls were curious about kissing. The girls' canvases were nice and clean while my canvas had a lot of marks on it. Their perspective was different than mine. They had the potential to enjoy a first kiss that was special. My first kiss was not special at all; I had blown my opportunity. I loved answering the girls' questions because I wanted them to experience life to the fullest (just as your mentors and small group leaders desire for you!).

In the last few days, my friends invited us into their stories. I am immensely grateful to them for opening their hearts to us with profound honesty and vulnerability. I'm honored to know such beautiful, strong, godly women!

If you haven't kissed a boy or dated much, I realize it may have felt awkward or overwhelming to learn my friends' stories and think about sex, pregnancy, abortion, and adoption. It's perfectly fine and normal to feel that way.

I hope you also feel thankful. Why? You have the potential to do things differently. My friends have bestowed on you a priceless tool—perspective! Receive it. Ponder it in light of God's Word. Then apply the wisdom gained in your life, and invite God to paint your canvas with vibrant colors and gorgeous designs!

PERSPECTIVE—RECEIVE IT!

Through my friend's stories, we witnessed how crossing God's boundary of remaining sexually pure before marriage can bring life-altering consequences, devastating pain, and complicated decisions. We learned how the heart—our spring of life—becomes "sick" when we overstep God's boundaries.

We discovered how our choices not only affect us but can produce pain in the hearts of our brothers in Christ, parents, family members, friends, our future children, and others dear to us.

My friends' stories are not new or unique. My friends' stories are the story of Adam and Eve. The characters and scenery have changed, but the basic storyline is the same:

There is a glorious God who deeply loves His people. He has plans for them—"plans for welfare and not for evil, to give {them} a future and a hope" (Jeremiah 29:11). With the health and prosperity of His people in mind, God made and declared a boundary. The Woman and the Man faced a choice: Honor the boundary or disregard the boundary? A choice made and acted upon in just a few moments altered their lives forever. Innocence was lost. Their hearts were wounded. Their relationships were damaged. It's the same story.

PERSPECTIVE – PONDER IT!

In this battle to honor God with purity of body, mind, and heart, there is a real enemy. "Be sober-minded; be watchful. Your adversary the devil prowls around like a roaring lion, seeking someone to devour" (1 Peter 5:8).

Just as satan sought to destroy the lives of Adam and Eve in the Garden, satan opposes everything that God wants to do in our lives. It is NOT satan's mission to help us make it to the end; his goal is to turn our hearts from God and lure us to idolize other things and people.

When satan launched his attack on Eve, He targeted her mind. He knew if he conquered her mind, then he would have a good shot at her heart. This is also the strategy he uses to devour us. His conversation starter with Eve was God's Word. When satan tempted Jesus in the desert, He also used God's Word.

Eve fell prey to satan's attack because she was spiritually weak in some areas. Here are her 4 key weaknesses:

Weak understanding of God's Word

God declared the boundary to not eat from the Tree. His command ended with a period. There was no question about it. Though satan knew God's Word is solid and permanent, he brought the seriousness and certainty of God's command into question. "He said to the woman, 'Did God actually say, 'You shall not eat of any tree in the garden?'" (Genesis 3:2). His wisdom was corrupted, but it succeeded in planting a subtle seed of doubt in Eve's mind about God. If she had been certain of what God said and the message He conveyed, she would not have been so easy to fool.

Weak belief in God's good character

Later in the conversation, satan becomes more aggressive and confidently tells the woman, "You will not surely die" (Genesis 3:4). Satan flat out lied about God's Word! In a more subtle way, he insinuated that God would withhold something good from Eve. Ladies, satan is a slimy snake! "For the LORD God is a sun and shield; the LORD bestows favor and honor. No good thing does he withhold from those who walk uprightly" (Psalm 84:11). If Eve had just taken a minute to think about how good God had been to her—giving her a life in paradise, treating her respectfully, and always communicating truthfully—she probably would have been more loyal to Him.

Pride

Satan throws another lie at Eve when he says, "For God knows that when you eat of it your eyes will be opened, and you will be like God, knowing good and evil" (Genesis 3:5). Satan drew out the selfishness, the pride, in Eve's heart. If he could get Eve to stop thinking about God and focus on herself (the "ME Mentality"), then he knew she would be vulnerable. "Pride goes before destruction and a haughty spirit before a fall" (Proverbs 16:18).

Impulsive decision-making

Eve quickly acted on satan's words. Eve made the decision to eat the apple in the heat of the moment. It's one thing to listen to what a person (or a snake) has to say; it's a whole other thing to receive everything a person says as complete truth. Why did Eve accept the serpent's words as truth? Why did Eve give the serpent *any* credit? What did she know about his character? The passage doesn't seem to indicate that Eve had any sort of relationship with the serpent or any reason to trust him.

When Eve ate the apple, she chose her selfish desires above God's glory and worshipped satan over God. Satan's mission was accomplished. Satan must have been pretty proud of his slick self. We don't want him to be proud of us. Ladies, we need to use our heads! God gave us brilliant minds, but they are no good if we carry them around in our heads all day and never use them! "Do not be conformed to this world, but be transformed by the renewal of your mind, that by testing you may discern what is the will of God, what is good and acceptable and perfect" (Romans 12:12). Satan may be the prince of this world, but "He who is in you is greater than he who is in the world" (1 John 4:4b).

Think about it!

1—As you consider Eve's key weaknesses that made her vulnerable to satan's attack, where are you weak?

Weak understanding of God's Word
Weak belief in God's good character
Pride
Impulsive decision-making

2—Included below are ways to strengthen your mind to battle satan's corrupted messages. Which ones do you want to start applying in your life?

(a) *Ask God to keep your heart humble and soft towards Him and to grant you wisdom and understanding. See 1 Peter 5:6-7 and Proverbs 2:1-12.*

(b) *You need to know the truth with confidence so that you won't be swayed by lies. It's important to make growing in your relationship with God a priority, specifically by consistently spending time in His Word.*

(c) *Decide that you will not automatically accept every message you hear as truth. Don't accept pat Christian answers either! Ask: How does this message line up with what God's Word says? Does this message accurately reflect God's character?"*

(d) *Before making an important decision, take time to think it through. Open your Bible, search for the answers you need, seek counsel from mentors, and be open to the wisdom you discover. See Psalm 119:105.*

(e) *Watch out for pride—the "Me Mentality." Examine your desires, thoughts, words, and actions to see if there is evidence of selfishness and resistance to God's will.*

(f) *Ask yourself: Am I thinking about pleasing, profiting, or honoring self? Am I thinking about loving God and loving others? Am I keeping the BIG Story in mind and eternity? Or am I thinking about worldly things that only matter on this side of Heaven?"*

2—What kind of support do you need to apply these to your life (i.e. help defining personal goals or boundaries, a mentor, prayer, accountability, etc.)?

Pray about it!

Heavenly Father,

You are a brilliant God! Thank You for giving me a mind designed to reflect Your brilliance! Train me to apply my mind to studying Your Word, memorizing key commandments and promises, recognizing Your character, and believing Your promises. Teach me how to utilize my mind to analyze what I read, discern truths from lies, and consider the facts before making important decisions. Guard my mind against my own proud ambitions. Let my thoughts and behaviors be shaped by the desire to seek Your righteousness and Your Kingdom. May I have the mind of Christ! In Jesus' Name, Amen.

40 - Think Purity

"Do you want to save sex until marriage?" I posed that question to my 8th grade girls' discipleship group as we discussed a lesson on how sex was designed for the marriage relationship. Without hesitation all six girls responded, "Yes." Having all grown up going to church and having Christian moms who had talked to them about sex, they had been well exposed to the truth that God intended sex for the marriage relationship. They had accepted God's boundary, believed it was for their own good, and adopted the boundary for their lives.

I loaded up my conversation cannon with the next question and launched it. "How are you going to protect your boundary of not having sex before marriage?"

Silence took over as the girls wrestled with the question. I remained quiet, giving them space to think. Megan eventually piped up and answered, "If you make sure the guy you date is a Christian, then you'll honor God." The girls nodded in agreement. Jules added, "Don't wear skirts that are too short or low-cut tops." I loaded my conversation cannon again.

I fired this cannonball of a hypothetical question into the group: "Okay, imagine you are coming home from a date. The guy turns the car onto the street where you live. You're just a minute from your house, and he parks the car on the side of the road. He leans in to kiss you, and his hand goes up your skirt. What do you do?" GASPS filled the room—shocked, they responded:

"Can that really happen?"

"You're scaring us."

"Did that happen to you?"

"Yes, it did happen to me," I responded. "Now, what are you going to do?"

Silence—they had nothing. It was okay that they didn't have the answers. My goal was simply to get them thinking! You see, one of the biggest mistakes we ladies make in dating is that we don't proactively think about thchoices we have. We tend to let things happen and quickly find ourselves in bad situations. Then it's too late to protect ourselves, and the only choice left is to react in the moment and do the best we can.

Take Eve for example. She was already standing near the tree when the serpent struck up a conversation with her. Even though she knew the tree was bad news, she moved close to it. Eve invited trouble into her life when she placed herself in a tempting place. She could have avoided the whole temptation to eat the deadly apple simply by staying away from the tree! All she had to do was use her head and think: *God said the Tree of the Knowledge of Good and Evil is bad, therefore I don't need to go near it!* When it comes to our sexual purity, we need to stay away from tempting situations.

Like the girls in my discipleship group, many young women believe that they will have a God-honoring relationship if they date a Christian guy. It's easy to think that we can let our guards down when we date a Christian guy, but we don't want to put 100% trust in a guy who is a sinner like us. Remember when Eve ate the apple someone was standing next to her—Adam!

With a few of the Christian guys I dated, we ended up in situations where we wandered too far beyond kissing. That's right, ladies. Just because a guy is a Christian doesn't automatically mean that he knows how to protect his sexual purity, much less your sexual purity. He may not have had parents who talked to him about protecting girls' purity or discipleship leaders who ask difficult questions that make your head explode! Even worse, that Christian guy you date may not even care about his purity, which means he won't care about yours, either.

I'm sorry to be the bearer of bad news, but simply making the choice to be sexually pure won't be enough to keep you sexually pure. My friends Rebecca, Lynne, Katie, and Sarah were Christ-followers who desired to honor God. All of them had chosen to honor God's boundary, and they all ended up pregnant outside of marriage. How did my friends end up in the very situation they wanted to avoid? Apostle Paul explained, "For I delight in the law of God, in my inner being, but I see in my members another law waging war against the law of my mind and making me captive to the law of sin that dwells in my members" (Romans 7:22-24).

The battle

The battle for sexual purity can be fierce as your spiritual desires and your fleshly desires fight on opposing sides! Hopefully, you will be ushered into the battle slowly, but don't be surprised if you are suddenly thrust into it. It might go something like this:

You are with your boyfriend watching a movie, snuggling together on the couch.

Or you are in a dark movie theater on one of the deserted back rows.

Or you are at a friend's party where there is little or no parental supervision.

You begin kissing. Gentle kisses grow into passionate kisses. One minute everything is normal. The next minute, your boyfriend's hand is MOVING inside your shirt OR his hand is UNBUTTONING your jeans OR HIS HAND IS BRUSHING YOUR LEG AND TRAVELING UP YOUR SKIRT! It's your body, but he most likely won't ask permission. He'll proceed to do whatever he wants. By the time you realize what is happening, there is only a small buffer of bra or panties separating his hand from your intimate areas. WHAT ARE YOU GOING TO DO IN THAT MOMENT??? BETTER THINK FAST! WHAT YOU DECIDE TO DO IN THAT MOMENT IMPACTS YOUR FUTURE!!!

It will be easy to pull away when you don't really like the guy. But what will you do when a guy makes a move on you, and you are so shocked that you freeze up? What will you do when you really like the guy and the *attention* he is giving you? What will you do when his touch feels good to your flesh, and you don't want him to stop? What will happen when your hormones are like fireworks going off inside your body, your heart is racing, and you don't want the excitement to end? What will you do when you feel the guy's heart pounding and he's breathing faster and faster because he is experiencing pleasure from your body? What will you do when you think you love the guy? What will you do?

Those scenarios are no fun to contemplate, but if you are serious about honoring God's boundary to save sex for marriage, then you need to think through these situations. You need to be an active participant in protecting your sexual purity.

Apostle Paul continued to describe the mind-flesh battle: "Wretched man that I am! Who will deliver me from this body of death? Thanks be to God through Jesus Christ our Lord! So then, I myself serve the law of God with my mind, but with my flesh I serve the law of sin" (Romans 7:24-25). Paul's words give us great hope. Though we can't trust our flesh to lead us, God designed our minds to protect us from temptation and help us honor Him.

Romans 12:1-2
"I appeal to you therefore, brothers, by the mercies of God, to present your bodies as a living sacrifice, holy and acceptable to God, which is your spiritual worship. Do not be conformed to this world, but be transformed by the renewal of your mind, that by testing you may discern what is the will of God, what is good and acceptable and perfect."

Paul is instructing us to use our minds for self-examination. Do our thoughts, desires, and actions line up with the world's way or God's way? Could any of our current thoughts, desires, or actions lead to destructive consequences down the road? By humbly submitting ourselves to God, He will shed light on self-destructive tendencies and set our minds on life-preserving ways!

Think about it!

For each numbered scenario below:
Think reactively: *What will be my next step if I find myself in this situation?*
Think proactively: *What step(s) can I take to try to avoid getting in these situations?*

If you have ventured beyond kissing to greater physical exploration:

1—Identify relationships on your canvas where you went too far.

Think reactively: *What will I do if I'm in this situation again?*

Think proactively: *What steps can I take to try to avoid getting in this situation again?*

If you have not yet had your first kiss:

1—The following happened to me, but let's pretend it's happening to you. It's Friday, and you and your friends are hanging out at *Kicks,* a teen dance club. (Feel free to laugh at the club's cheesy name.) Everyone circles up on the dance floor. Guys sometimes pull friends out of the circle to dance. For the first time, you get pulled out of the circle by a guy you've never met and begin fast dancing with him. When a slow song starts playing, he pulls you close to slow dance. Then, he moves in for the kiss. If you kiss him, then your first kiss will not be special.

Think reactively: *What will be my next step if I'm in this situation?*

Think proactively: *What steps can I take to try to avoid getting in this situation?*

For everyone:

1—Consider what you would do in the following scenario that happened to me: You are performing with your dance team at a local school. Shane, a guy around the same age, is helping with the show. You ask Shane where the restroom is, and he walks you to a restroom located on a dark hall. When you exit the bathroom, Shane is waiting for you. He says he wants to show you something and leads you into a small closet-size room. As you enter, he turns off the lights, closes the door, and puts his hands on your face.

Think reactively: *What will be my next step(s) if I'm in this situation?*

Think proactively: *What step(s) can I take to try to avoid getting in these situations?*

In case you were wondering: When Shane put his hands on my face, I ran out of the room! I was so scared! I didn't want to see what Shane wanted to show me!

Pray about it!

Heavenly Father,
You are a loving Creator and protector of Your people. With all of my heart, soul, and mind, I dedicate my body to You as an act of worship. I confess that the desire to please my flesh is sometimes greater than my desire to please You. Please forgive me for wandering away from Your safe presence, disregarding Your commandments, and rebelling against You. I plead for Your Spirit to empower me to resist and run from the deceptive cries of my flesh so that I may walk the blessed path that leads me closer to You. Train my mind to identify situations that are likely to compromise my sexual purity and the courage to stay away. Keep me in Your loving arms! In the Protective Name of Jesus, Amen

41 - Renewed Mind

My friend, Claire, is a beautiful, intelligent, friendly, fun, and extremely godly woman. As you can imagine, a lot of guys asked her out when she was single. She once dated my friend, Nate. Though Nate was a nice, attractive Christian guy with a good job, I was shocked Claire would even consider dating him. I actually shared with Claire that I thought she was WAY out of his league! She said I wasn't the only one who thought that. She shared that she questioned their compatibility but wanted to give the relationship a chance.

Claire didn't kiss guys she dated and clearly communicated that boundary to the guys up front. Nate knew with all certainty that he wasn't going to get a good night kiss at the end of a date with Claire. I admired Claire for giving Nate a chance. I also realized that in her mind, it was a risk worth taking. Because her high standards were guarded by clear boundaries, she had nothing to lose.

I asked Claire why she chose not to kiss the guys she dated. She said, *"I kissed a couple of guys, and I just didn't feel right about doing it. I realized the guy I was dating may not be the guy God wants me to marry. If I kiss a guy I'm not meant to marry, then I am kissing someone else's husband. God meant a kiss to be special. I don't want to rob the guy of the specialness of a kiss. I also don't want to rob his future wife. In the same way, I don't want to rob my future husband. I don't want to rob myself, and I don't want other girls to rob me. I'm saving my kisses for my husband."*

That was radical thinking on Claire's part. It's also a fantastic example of how God renews a mind.

Romans 12:1-2
"I appeal to you therefore, brothers {and sisters}, by the mercies of God, to present your bodies as a living sacrifice, holy and acceptable to God, which is your spiritual worship. Do not be conformed to this world, but be transformed by the renewal of your mind, that by testing you may discern what is the will of God, what is good and acceptable and perfect."

I imagine Claire encountered some criticism from her peers for having such a bold boundary. I appreciated that behind her big boundary lay strong conviction. Others must have admired that, too. Claire was highly respected among women and men in the singles' group. Even though a good night kiss was out of the question, she never lacked for a date.

Claire's conviction and boundary served her well. Because she didn't explore the physical, the time she spent on a date was focused on exploring the guy's personality, beliefs, interests, and goals. Her boundary enabled her to get to know the guy and provided the guy a good opportunity to get to know her. Within a few months of dating, Claire and Nate were able to determine that they were not meant to marry. They ended their dating relationship respectfully and amicably. That's right—there was no drama, and they remained friends. In fact, they were better friends after spending time together.

I believe that Claire and Nate brought each other closer to God. What do you think?

Claire's words about kissing reminded me of God's Word: "For the wife does not have authority over her own body, but the husband does. Likewise the husband does not have authority over his own body, but the wife does" (1 Corinthians 7:4). According to God's Word, the husband's body belongs to the wife, and the wife's body belongs to the husband. If that is the case, then when we go too far physically with a boyfriend, we are behaving like we are married and have ownership of the guy's body.

In reality, our boyfriend's body does not belong to us; his body ultimately belongs to the Lord and one day, to a wife the Lord provides. In the same sense, our bodies belong to the Lord first and foremost and one day, might belong to a husband the Lord provides. When we cross God's boundary for sex and go too far in exploring the physical with a boyfriend, then we are giving a guy power over our bodies that he does not rightfully deserve, and vice versa. We need to remember that we are not married, and in the Lord's eyes, we do not belong to anyone but Him.

Do you know what it's called when we take something that doesn't belong to us? Stealing. What does God think of stealing? He hates it and sees it as a hindrance to our purity and well-being enough to identify it as a sin in Commandment 8: "You shall not steal" (Exodus 20:15). Commandment 10 is of interest to us, as well: "You shall not covet (desire wrongfully or without due regard for the rights of others) your neighbor's house; you shall not covet your neighbor's wife {or husband}, or his male servant, or his female servant, or his ox, or his donkey, or anything that is your neighbor's" (Exodus 20:17).

Your neighbor is every man, woman, girl, and boy in your life. Your neighbor is also the guy you're attracted to and the guy you date. Your neighbor is your boyfriend's future wife. Your neighbor is your future husband. What does it mean to love your boyfriend, his future wife, and your future husband as yourself? That is not an easy question to answer. Maybe some perspective will help.

I received an invitation to my high school reunion. It was surreal to realize that 20 years had passed since graduation. I was so different from the girl I'd been in high school. I thought about all the old classmates who would be there. I would see my old boyfriend, Jake. I would also see his wife, Alicia, who was also in our graduating class. During our senior year, I had a class with Alicia, and we became friends. Even so, it was a little weird to think about seeing Jake and Alicia at the reunion. I had kissed my friend's husband. *See what I mean? Weird.*

I thought about the popular girls in my graduating class who had reputations for sleeping around. Though 20 years had passed, I STILL remembered them as…well, you know—girls who slept around! I imagined what it would be like for one of the promiscuous girls to go to the reunion and introduce her husband to all the guys she had sex with and meet the guys' wives. Granted, a girl wouldn't say, *"Honey, I want you to meet Dan. We screwed each other in the backseat of his car."* Still, having sex with a guy isn't something you forget. It would have to be in the back of a woman's mind as she came face-to-face with her past sexual partners at the reunion. *ICK—so awful.* When you're 16 and thinking about having sex with your boyfriend, you just don't think about how your actions might affect you and others decades later.

I had to ask God to renew my mind, to change it, in regards to those women. It had been 20 YEARS since high school. Surely they had changed. It's possible the rumors about them weren't true. It wasn't fair for me to judge them; they deserved the benefit of the doubt. At least, that's how I would want them to treat me. After all, we were created with the same pure PURPOSE and powerful POTENTIAL! God wants us to see one other as He sees us!

Think about it!

The Bible doesn't specify any boundaries on kissing other than you shouldn't covet or kiss another woman's husband—*DUH!* It's not my intention to persuade you not to kiss the guys you date. Ladies, that's your choice to make. You know I'm all about providing perspective and encouraging you to carefully consider your choices. So, let's get started.

1—When it comes to dating, does kissing seem like a lot to give up? Why or why not?

2—What does a kiss mean to you?

3—As you think about dating, do you desire to kiss? If so, what is your plan for giving away your kisses? (For example: Will you kiss on the first date or wait a while? Will you kiss every guy you date?)

4—Examine your kissing plan to see if there are any traces of pride—the "ME Mentality."

Am I thinking about pleasing, profiting, or honoring self?
Am I thinking about loving God and loving others?
Am I keeping the BIG Story in mind and eternity? Or am I thinking about worldly things that only matter on this side of Heaven?"

Pray about it!

Dear God,

I praise You, for You are a merciful God. Thank You for having mercy on me and saving my soul. I don't want to live for myself. I want to live for You. I present my body to You in worship. Show me how to worship You spiritually and physically.

Do not let me be conformed to the world around me. Transform my heart and life by starting with my mind. Reveal to me Your will for me when it comes to my purity in the area of kissing. Aid me in identifying my thoughts and beliefs about kissing and testing those against Your Word. Show me what is good, acceptable, and perfect in Your eyes. Change my selfish thoughts and beliefs into Jesus-centered thoughts and beliefs. Empower me to live out my new convictions in honor of You! In Jesus' Gracious Name, Amen.

42 - Started with A Kiss

WARNING: The author of this book is about to get really honest. This is the part of the book where the young women in her book study were shocked by what they read…and even blushed a little. Consider yourself warned.

In my journey to date in a healthier, more God-honoring way, I decided to make the truth of Romans 12:1-2 more than verses in the Bible. I prayerfully submitted my body, my physical being, to God as a living sacrifice. I prayerfully requested that He reveal self-focused, self-destructive thoughts and lies I had accepted, whether consciously or unconsciously. I asked Him to renew my mind. Transform my thinking. Transform my life. That was some serious praying. With those prayers, I hit the start button on life transformation!

In a letter to believers in the city of Thessalonica, Paul instructs them on how to live in a pleasing way to God and overcome opposition.

1 Thessalonians 4:1-8
"Finally, then, brothers, we ask and urge you in the Lord Jesus, that as you received from us how you ought to walk and to please God, just as you are doing, that you do so more and more. For you know what instructions we gave you through the Lord Jesus. For this is the will of God, your sanctification: that you abstain from sexual immorality; that each one of you know how to control his own body in holiness and honor, not in the passion of lust like the Gentiles who do not know God; that no one transgress and wrong his brother in this matter, because the Lord is an avenger in all these things, as we told you beforehand and solemnly warned you. For God has not called us for impurity, but in holiness. Therefore whoever disregards this, disregards not man but God, who gives his Holy Spirit to you."

1 Corinthians 6:18-20
"Flee from sexual immorality. Every other sin a person commits is outside the body, but the sexually immoral person sins against his own body. Or do you not know that your body is a temple of the Holy Spirit within you, whom you have from God? You are not your own, for you were bought with a price. So glorify God in your body."

Did you catch that?

When we give away our bodies outside of a marriage relationship, we sin against our own bodies. *YIKES!* Our bodies are a dwelling place for the Holy Spirit and set apart for worshiping God.

Here's the question: When it comes to dating, are you treating your body as a place of worship for God? Or are you treating your body like a place of worship for men?

When I answered those questions, I didn't like my answers. Here's where it gets REAL: I had not had sexual intercourse, but I had made my private areas not-so-private to guys' hands and participated in oral sex. Though technically, I had not "eaten an apple" from the Tree of the Knowledge of Good and Evil, I had "touched some apples" on the tree. *(Yeah, that was awkward.)*

How far is too far to go sexually? A lot of women think: *It's okay to do everything that leads up to sex as long as I don't actually have sex.* I thought the same thing at first, but then I realized that even if "taking an apple" doesn't fully break God's Law, it certainly goes against the Spirit of the Law, the righteous intention behind God's commands.

God wants us to save sex for marriage because it will build and nurture the one-flesh connection with our spouse. Sharing our private parts with a guy is an intimate act that creates a bond with him. Do you really want to bind yourself to a "temporary" guy who will only be in your life a few days, weeks, months, or maybe a couple of years? Or do you want to be completely free to bond with your future husband—your soulmate who will make a lifelong commitment to you? Remember, God's love for us is everlasting, and marriage is a covenant relationship designed to reflect His faithfulness to His people.

Conviction called out to me and led me to this conclusion: Engaging in heavy petting and oral sex with guys I dated didn't benefit them spiritually. In fact, it tempted them to move farther away from God. I didn't want to be a Bathsheba—a woman who brought godly men down. Getting too physical with guys didn't benefit me spiritually, either. Exploring the physical with a guy felt good in the moment, but I always felt guilty afterward. It didn't feel edifying. It felt wrong and weighed me down emotionally and spiritually.

Eve made a monumental mistake in the Garden when she placed herself in a tempting situation, coming too close to the wrong tree. In the same way, I knew I was coming too close to having sex when I allowed guys I dated to explore private parts of me. When I thought about what led me into those situations, I discovered a common denominator: Every single scenario started with a passionate kiss.

I pondered the idea of not kissing another man until I knew it was the man God wanted me to marry. It felt bizarre considering such a radical idea. After all, kissing had been a part of all of my dating relationships. I didn't view kissing itself as a bad thing (after all, God created it!), and I thought it was enjoyable (with most guys). Yet, what outweighed any weirdness or desire to hold on to the option of kissing was the strong conviction that I had kissed with the wrong motives. Let me explain.

Kissing had become a meaningless act.

I had kissed every guy I dated, plus some I had not dated. I asked myself the question, *What does a kiss mean?* To me, a kiss now meant a lot. A kiss meant, "I love you." After coming to that conclusion, I didn't want to carelessly throw away my kisses anymore. You see, *love* had taken on a deeper meaning after discovering that "God is love," and "We love because He first loved us" (1 John 4:8, 19). I wanted the kisses I gave my future husband to be special, to be given in the context of true love. If I valued my kisses enough to save them, then I believed God would make my kisses new, pure, special, and loving again.

Kissing had become a distraction.

As soon as I started kissing a guy, it became difficult to go on a date without kissing. There were some dates when I spent more time kissing than talking with the guy. The time that I spent kissing a guy could have been better spent observing his character, learning about his interests, dreams, and goals. Each guy I dated was a creation made in God's image, yet I had placed more value on his physical body than his heart. Additionally, I didn't necessarily date for the fun of it; I dated with the goal of getting married one day. Kissing slowed down the process of getting to know the guys and delayed my determination of whether to continue dating a guy or not. Kissing caused me to invest too much time in guys I was not meant to marry.

Kissing had become a stumbling block.

Passionate kissing usually led to greater physical exploration with guys, which complicated my dating relationships. Remember Ryan, the guy who sent me roses, said he loved me, and pushed me sexually? I wanted to be loved and desired his *adoration* so much that I moved past kissing and into deeper physical exploration with him. Our relationship was not edifying, and he did not treat me well.

I held on to the relationship much longer than I should have because I had given him a piece of myself physically. Ryan could meet my need for love temporarily, and so, I would go back for another "fix." He became an idol to me. My heart didn't feel good about him or happy in the relationship. I even used the physical part of our relationship to try to make the emotional part feel better. It took me a very long time to make sense of things because the physical and emotional had become so intertwined. Ending the relationship was extremely hard because doing so meant that I was leaving a piece of myself behind.

With all of that in mind, I made a big decision. I kissed kissing goodbye for an indefinite amount of time. I determined that I would save my kisses for the man God wanted me to love and marry. To clarify, I decided to not kiss until I knew I loved the man and knew he was the man God wanted me to marry. By no longer giving away my kisses, I knew I would have a stronger border to hold me back from exploring the physical and feeling regret.

Think about it!

For those who have experienced dating or have had significant interactions with guys:

1—Whether intentionally or unintentionally, have any guys tried to manipulate you physically? If yes, did you give any of the guys undeserved power over you?

2—If you have moved beyond kissing to deeper sexual exploration, what has been your motivation?

3—I shared that kissing had become three things to me: a meaningless act, a distraction, and a stumbling block. Has kissing become (or is becoming) any of these things to you? Moving forward, is there anything you'd like to change as related to kissing?

For everyone:

1—Begin thinking about this question: How far is too far to go physically?

Pray about it!

Gracious God,
You are Holy. You are Good. You are my God, and I choose to worship You above all things, above all people, above myself. My heart belongs to You, and I know it is safe in Your hands.

I am Your Beloved creation made to honor You. I offer my body to You; use it for holy purposes. I welcome Your Spirit to move freely within me and through me for Your glory. I offer my mind to You; find any wrong thoughts that have made their home in my heart, and kick them to the curb! Fill my mind with Your truth, and give me revelations of how to apply it in my life.

You wrote my life story, and You know my place in the BIG Story. Please show me Your will for my life when it comes to kissing. Help me to choose what is good and most honoring to You. In the Name of Jesus Who gave His All for me, Amen.

(Romans 12:1-2)

43 - Becoming A Blessing

"I appeal to you therefore, brothers, by the mercies of God, to present your bodies as a living sacrifice, holy and acceptable to God, which is your spiritual worship. Do not be conformed to this world, but be transformed by the renewal of your mind, that by testing you may discern what is the will of God, what is good and acceptable and perfect." –Romans 12:1-2

I was 27 when I dated Troy. I clearly communicated to him upfront that I had committed not to kiss until God brought me together with the man He wanted me to marry. Troy respected my decision and never pressured me to compromise my standard. He willingly adopted my standard, and so it became *our* standard in our dating relationship.

It became our goal to focus on getting to know each another. We dated for two months and never kissed. We had so much fun on our dates. Because we didn't get physically involved, we got to know each other more quickly than we would have otherwise. It very quickly became apparent that we were not meant to marry. Though we dated only two months, God greatly impacted our lives.

Troy sent this e-mail to me:

Aimee,

It was good to run into you yesterday. It was good to see your smile.

You and I would both agree that God works all things to His glory and demands that we view everything that we experience from that perspective. Here are the things I have seen in my life as a result of our having been together:

One is my own restoration (God restoring me). The standards that we set for our relationship, being non-physical and without any early commitments, gave control over to God to allow Him to develop any intimacy or closeness we were experiencing. I was able to see in action for the first time that if we had gone the world's way, there wouldn't have been near the freedom we experienced doing it God's way. I haven't really dated since, but I will never let go of those standards again.

Something else that took more time to understand was why breaking up with you was so hard for me. It took being rejected for that job position for me to really get a handle on it. I started to realize that I was seeing God's love for me based on how He was blessing me. That was a major revelation. I was saying to myself subconsciously, "Look at what God is doing in my life. I must finally be doing it right, or more directly, God must really love me." I realize that to be the man I feel God wants me to be, this problem needs dealing with, plus some others. So I sought discipleship and mentoring with an older man in the church I respect for his strong walk with God to deal with this and other holes I have found in my foundation.

Nothing is by accident. Knowing you has truly moved me forward in my relationship with God. I want to ask you. What do you think was God's purpose in bringing us together for that time on your end?

You have a special closeness, a gift of faith that I have seen in very few people. I can't count how many times you said you felt a presence of calm and comfort when we were together. At the time, I saw those things you said as a confirmation to continue, that God was in control. Now I see it as God simply opening a door for you because He knew that trust was a big issue for you at the time, and He wanted you to be able to trust again. This is simply discernment from my point of view. You may view differently. I was just wondering if my coming into your life had any effect on your life for eternity?

Friends,
Troy

In the last reading, I asked you to begin thinking through an answer to this question: "How far is too far to go physically?" Did the question feel overwhelming?

Keep thinking and praying about the question. Answering that question was one of the biggest steps in the transformation of my dating relationships and deepening of my relationship with God. The boundary to "save my kisses for my husband" took me from a woman whose life was devastated by a dating relationship to a woman who received a thank you note from an ex-boyfriend who was blessed by her.

In his sweet note to me, Troy wrote this: *"Nothing is by accident. Knowing you has truly moved me forward in my relationship with God. I want to ask you. What do you think was God's purpose in bringing us together for that time on your end?"*

My answer to his question:

My time with Troy helped me grow closer to God. I appreciated that he respected me, my convictions, and my boundaries. I was blessed because he sought to know me for who I was and not for what I could give him physically. I had the freedom to be a woman and to live more fully because Troy cared about my purity. Through the few months I spent with him, I experienced the power and protection of God. I was also reminded of how much God values relationship.

In his letter, Troy said, *"I was able to see in action for the first time that if we had gone the world's way, there wouldn't have been near the freedom we experienced doing it God's way."* I, too, experienced and enjoyed freedom in the relationship. I believe that freedom, along with the presence of calm and comfort, were the good consequences of living in light of God's character and truth.

Troy was correct when he said that trust was a big issue for me. I never told Troy about what happened to me with the guy from my former church. Troy sensed this struggle in me because God revealed it to him. That's the beauty of what happens when two people care about each other as creations wonderfully and fearfully made in God's image. He entrusts them with the vision to see each other's need and compels them to pray.

I didn't want to be a Bathsheba, and I had prayed for God to make me a woman whose presence helped the men I dated grow closer to God. I saw Troy's letter as a sweet reminder from God that He was answering that prayer. Through my relationship with Troy, I learned to trust God in a deeper way, and God healed my heart a little more. I never regretted that I didn't kiss Troy. In fact, I received something far better. I reaped the good benefits of a mind renewed and God taking first place in my dating relationships!

Think about it!

Leading up to today's reading, I've shared how God renewed my mind. Today, you read evidence of God transforming me from a fallen woman stuck in devastation to a woman raised in the power of the resurrection and walking in the light of Christ. God transformed me from a Bathsheba into a blessing…from a hindrance into a woman whose presence in a man's life helped him grow in God.

1—How did today's reading inspire or encourage you in your pursuit of purity?

2—Did you know that the word *dating* comes from a Latin word that means "to edify"? In dating, we're to build up the other person, to edify or encourage him. In what ways do you want to spiritually encourage guys you date?

3—Spend some time on this question: When it comes to the physical aspect of dating, how far is too far to go physically? Write down your thoughts, and examine your thoughts using these questions:

Am I thinking about pleasing, profiting, or honoring self?

Am I thinking about loving God and loving others?

Am I keeping the BIG Story in mind and eternity? Or am I thinking about worldly things that only matter on this side of Heaven?"

Pray about it!

Dear God,
You are Creator. Before you laid the foundations of the earth, You knew I would one day walk on the grass, swim in the ocean, and climb mountains. Before I took my first breath on earth, You knew I would need a

Savior to rescue me from sin. As Jesus hung on the cross in excruciating pain, God thought of me. As I dream of getting married one day, I have a Heavenly Husband who loves me with an eternal love.

When I look in the mirror, I see…

When You look at me, You see a "very good" creation and a delighted-in daughter. You see a person redeemed by the blood of Jesus. You see a beautiful reflection of You.

I see a canvas that…

You see a canvas full of pure purpose and powerful potential.

I see an unfinished story that…

You see the GREATEST Story ever told, and You wrote me into the storyline. You developed my character, and in the end, my story will have a happily ever after!

Glorious God, my perspective is too small. Open my eyes to see what You see. Transform my mind to think BIG. May my heart be surrendered to You, beating in sync with Your Spirit. Teach me to dream the dreams You have dreamed for me! Take my hand, and lead me to fulfill my supporting role in Your Story! In Jesus' Name, Amen.

44 - Just Friends

It was the morning after our THIRD breakup. I sat silently for a while, stunned that this was happening AGAIN. (Insert eye roll…head shake…and overall look of frustration. Oh, and add a sigh of exasperation!) We'll call my ex-boyfriend Rob. Here's the story of our emotional roller-coaster relationship.

Round 1

Rob was a Christian guy with a sincere heart for God. He wanted to proceed cautiously with our relationship. After all I had been through in dating, that was fine with me. He defined us as "just friends" and said we would see where God led us. By this time, I had the no-kissing-until-I-am-in-love boundary. Rob and I hung out one-on-one and sometimes in groups and focused on getting to know each other. We shared many common interests and had fun together.

Several times a week, we encouraged each other with heartfelt messages and scripture written in store-bought cards, handwritten notes, and e-mails. His heart leaked into the messages. Inside one card, he wrote, "My heart belongs to you." I don't have any of the messages I wrote to Rob, but I'm pretty confident that my messages followed his lead.

Rob was very discreet about our relationship and had some boundaries of his own. In public, there was no hand-holding or any other physical contact. Though he was trying to protect himself, Rob's boundaries ended up stirring up attention as many people were aware that we were spending a lot of time together. One day, a mutual friend questioned me about the relationship and the "just friends" label. At the end of the conversation, she boldly declared, "I would never date a guy who was too ashamed to call me his girlfriend." *OUCH!* I felt judged by her.

My mentor, Carolyn, would always say, "There is usually always some glimmer of truth in every criticism." I gave some thought to my friend's comment, and this is the truth I extracted: Rob and I were going out on dates, but we were not acknowledging our time together as dates. The "just friends" label lacked integrity—it was a lie. Not long after that, Rob told me he didn't want to be more than friends, and we stopped spending time together. He wrote, "Maybe I'll be able to let go of Rob one day and not be afraid to give up my agenda, so I can give my all to a woman."

Round 1 completed. Rob's cards, notes, and e-mails kept coming, just less frequently. (Yes, you read that right. He kept contacting me after *he* broke up with me.) I eventually went on dates with two other guys.

Round 2

Several months after breaking up with me, Rob pursued me to date again. Our relationship went pretty much like Round 1. He eventually broke up with me around the three-month mark. His cards, notes, and e-mails kept coming, keeping the door to our relationship propped open.

I wrote in my journal:

We have shared our hearts with each other on a level much deeper than "just friends." Sharing with Rob has made me feel good, understood, and encouraged. When he shares deep things with me or spends one-on-one time with me, it draws me closer to him. No matter what I know in my head, my heart interprets it to mean that he is interested in me and wants more than friendship. A man sharing deeply and spending one-on-one time with a woman is healthy when the man's intent is to pursue the woman. But when the intent is not there, then the man is meeting his God-given need for companionship, and the woman runs the risk of giving her heart away dishonorably.

I decided that I would not date Rob again unless he defined that we were in a dating relationship with the purpose of determining if we should marry.

Round 3

Rob pursued me to date again, but his pursuit took a refreshingly different approach. He clearly stated his intentions to pursue marriage and defined next steps. Feeling a connection with him, I chose to follow his lead again.

The first step Rob had in mind was to share his past history with me. He actually handed me a three-ring binder filled with around two hundred typed pages containing his life story! Rob was extremely detailed in telling his story; nothing was left in question. Reading through the binder gave me knowledge of Rob's major life struggles and past dating history (with way too many details). It was an awful lot to drop on a girl! In all fairness, he didn't twist my arm to read it! I think Rob thought his story would scare me away. In retrospect, it should have.

Round 3 of our relationship began, and this time he called a duck a duck by labeling us "boyfriend and girlfriend." The cards, notes, and e-mails ramped up with constant messages of "I adore you!" He even gave me a ruby ring inspired by Proverbs 31:10 (NIV): "A wife of noble character who can find? She is worth far more than rubies."

Things were going great in our relationship. My heart was becoming more and more connected with him. We were approaching that hard to pass three-month mark, and he broke up with me again! He intentionally tried to keep me in the dark about why he was breaking up. I eventually drew it out of him, and it was a complicated, confusing mess of a reason. But darn it, I still had a glimmer of hope in my heart that he might be the man I would marry.

Jeremiah 17:9
The heart is deceitful above all things, and desperately sick; who can understand it?"

If experience told me anything, there was a chance Rob would pursue me again. I knew I needed to make up my mind about him, once and for all. I needed to take my heart back! I took six months off from dating, and that dating break was one of the best things I ever did! I asked Rob to not communicate with me as he had in the past (i.e. no notes, cards, and emails of a romantic nature).

From my journal:

Because we shared our hearts on a very deep level, my heart feels connected to him. If he is not the man that God made me for, then I have to disconnect from him so that I can be free to love the man who can love me. When we take the chance to love another, we also take the chance of getting hurt. I understand that and will fall into the arms of the One who knows my pain in a far greater way than I ever will.

During my dating break, I processed the relationship with my mentors and a professional Christian counselor, journaled, studied the Bible, prayed, cried, and enjoyed creative activities and time with friends. My dating relationship with Rob was one of the hardest relationships to get past. He had been very open and honest to share his story with me, but unfortunately, I knew things about him only a woman he was engaged or married to should know. I felt burdened because of the information I knew about him. I was floating in the middle of an ocean of hurt and loss with the inescapable waves of burden threatening to take me under.

To this day, I regret flipping open the binder cover and my heart to Rob's story.

My relationship with Rob was disheartening. I had established good physical boundaries to protect my purity. I had succeeded in keeping my body out of a relationship. I had succeeded in focusing on getting to know the guy, but that led to a new problem: I opened up my heart too much. *UGHHH!!!* I needed to take more responsibility for my heart, which meant I needed emotional boundaries. *How many boundaries does a girl need? GEEZ!!!*

Have you been in a relationship labeled "just friends" that was actually dating? Have you seen friends experience this bad knockoff of a relationship? Unfortunately, it's a common scenario in dating, but it's easy to avoid with some good boundaries. Your precious heart is WORTH protecting!

During my break from dating, I developed a question to ask myself in dating: *Is this a man I can follow and submit to if I married him?*

When I thought about Rob, his actions didn't consistently match his words. If you can't take a guy at his word and he's constantly changing his mind, then how can you follow his direction and be a helper to him?

I knew I couldn't succeed in those circumstances. I was not the right fit for Rob. To protect my heart, I wrote a letter to myself and listed all of the reasons why I should not date him. I gave a copy of the letter to my mentor and told her to give it back to me if (1) a day came when Rob pursued me again, and (2) I considered dating him. Door closed...and locked.

(If you're wondering, my mentor never had to give the letter back to me.)

From my journal:

I have to say goodbye to Rob because God doesn't want me to walk with a man who can't love me. God loves me much more than that.

Ladies, God loves you too much for you to settle for a man whose heart is unavailable. "Greater love has no one than this, that someone lay down his life for his friends" (John 15:13).

Think about it!

1—Why is taking a break from dating a good idea after a relationship ends? What are some benefits of doing so?

2—Let's say a guy gave you a note that said, "My heart belongs to you." How would that message affect your heart? What can you do in this situation to protect your heart?

3—Are there any relationships with guys (friendship or dating) where you shared too much emotionally? Describe. Was the guy trustworthy?

4—What are the differences in being "just friends" vs. being in a dating relationship? What types of things are appropriate to share in each relationship?

Pray about it!

Heavenly Husband,
You are true love. You are my first love. Don't let me wander from You. When it comes to sharing my heart, grant me discernment to recognize what is appropriate and what is crossing the line. Show me what emotional boundaries I should adopt to help foster healthy sharing. Help me to be discreet in what I share. Protect me from sharing my heart with men who do not deserve it. Keep my heart close to You. In Jesus' Name, Amen.

45 - Emotionally Healthy

This is evidence of God in our hearts: "If I speak in the tongues of men and of angels, but have not love, I am a noisy gong or a clanging cymbal. And if I have prophetic powers, and understand all mysteries and all knowledge, and if I have all faith, so as to remove mountains, but have not love, I am nothing. If I give away all I have, and if I deliver up my body to be burned, but have not love, I gain nothing. Love is patient and kind; love does not envy or boast; it is not arrogant or rude. It does not insist on its own way; it is not irritable or resentful; it does not rejoice at wrongdoing, but rejoices with the truth. Love bears all things, believes all things, hopes all things, endures all things. Love never ends" (1 Corinthians 13:1, 4-8).

Galatians 5:22-23
"But the fruit of the Spirit is love, joy, peace, patience, kindness, goodness, faithfulness, gentleness, self-control; there is no law."

EMOTIONALLY UNHEALTHY VS. EMOTIONALLY HEALTHY

One of the greatest revelations that came out of my six-month dating break and professional counseling was learning what it meant to be an emotionally healthy person—a person whose cup is filled by God. Following are two lists describing emotionally unhealthy and emotionally healthy people. Adjectives included at the end of each character description reveal how the person exemplifies the fruit of the Spirit. Because of our sin nature, no one on this side of Heaven will perfectly meet all of the descriptions of being emotionally healthy, but as God heals the broken places in our hearts, renews our minds, and develops character in us, He moves us into the "Full Cup" side of the chart!

Emotionally unhealthy people / "Empty Cup"

1—Their words and actions do not line up. They often make promises or commitments they don't keep. It's difficult to trust them. They create an environment of instability and confusion. UNFAITHFUL

2—They have dramatic mood swings and allow their feelings to rule them. They have difficulty expressing their feelings and balancing emotion with logic. NOT PEACEFUL

3—They make important decisions impulsively rather than taking time to gather relevant data and think through the choices. They live without boundaries, have a hard time saying, "No," and tend to overcommit to activities. Their lives are chaotic. IMPATIENT / NOT PEACEFUL

4—Their personalities may seem confident, but they are very sensitive. They are overly concerned about what others think of them, work hard to create a certain public persona, and become deeply bothered when someone thinks poorly of them. NOT PEACEFUL / NOT JOYFUL

5—They view themselves as superior to others and put others down. ARROGANT / UNKIND

6—They view others as competition. They often become defensive and harsh towards others (even when others are not criticizing or attacking them). They feel jealous when others succeed. ENVIOUS / IRRITABLE / RUDE

7—They have difficulty giving and receiving love. They seem to feel more comfortable when treated poorly. UNLOVING

8—When conflict arises, they don't take responsibility for their words and actions and blame others. They are unwilling to say, "I'm sorry," They are not forgiving of others and hold grudges. They don't respect others' boundaries. INSISTS ON THEIR OWN WAY / UNFORGIVING / RESENTFUL / NOT PEACEFUL

Emotionally healthy people / "Full Cup"

1—Their actions and words line up. When they make promises or commitments, they do their best to follow through on them. They are easy to trust. FAITHFUL

2—They think before they act. They demonstrate the ability to balance their emotions with truth (i.e. balance head and heart). They are comfortable expressing their thoughts and feelings. PEACEFUL

3—Before making a decision, they take the time to collect relevant data and carefully consider it. They live with boundaries and structure. They often make wise decisions and demonstrate balance in their lives. PATIENT / PEACEFUL

4—They appropriately care about social standards and people, but they are not people-pleasers. They seek to honor God, and if they have done that to the best of their ability, they rest secure. JOY / PEACE

5—They value others as creations made in God's image. They seek to love and serve their neighbors as themselves. LOVING / KIND

6—They are comfortable with who they are in Christ and not threatened by others. They respect the differences of others and celebrate the successes of others. JOYFUL / LOVING

7—They know how to give love and receive love. They recognize acts of kindness and express gratitude. LOVING / KIND

8—When conflict arises, they are willing to work through it. They take responsibility for their words and actions. They are willing to say, "I'm sorry." They seek to understand others, respect others' boundaries, and are gracious and forgiving towards others. GENTLE / FORGIVING / PEACEFUL.

If we are emotionally healthy, then we are more likely to attract guys who are emotionally healthy. It works the other way, too. If we are emotionally unhealthy, we will attract guys who are emotionally unhealthy. As you get to know a guy, here are suggestions for how to guard your heart and mind:

Rely on your community.

"Where there is no guidance, a people falls, but in an abundance of counselors there is safety" (Proverbs 11:14). If you don't know much about a guy, don't go on a date alone with him. Spend time with him in the context of community and seek to build a very basic friendship first. If friends or family members express concern about him, consider what they share.

Observe his character.

Does his behavior reflect the fruit of the Spirit? What are his relationships with others like? Does he put others down? Does he act like he's in competition with others? Does he think he is always right? Is he easily angered? Deep down, is he overly sensitive or emotional? How does he work through conflict with others?

Journal after spending time with him.

Soon after spending time with him, take a few minutes to write a short summary of what happened. Include: (1) what you learned about him/his character, (2) what you learned about yourself, and (3) your feelings—what you feel about him and how you feel after spending time with him. Taking time to process will help you identify unhealthy patterns and relationships.

Think about it!

1—Which numbered descriptions of "Empty Cup" and "Full Cup" people are struggles for you personally?

2—Considering the lists, do you lean more towards emotionally healthy or unhealthy?

Show these lists to a mentor, and spend time discussing the lists. She can help you grow in areas of weakness, so don't be shy to ask for her help, prayers, and accountability.

For those who have experience in dating:

1—Have most of the guys on your canvas been emotionally healthy or unhealthy?

2—If you are currently in a dating relationship with a guy you think may be emotionally unhealthy, talk to your mentor, small group leader, parent, or someone spiritually mature who can help you look at your relationship with discerning eyes.

Pray about it!

Heavenly Husband,
I praise You, for You are I AM. You are my EVERYTHING! Fill my cup with Your goodness. Let my cup overflow with the fruit of Your Spirit—love, joy, peace, patience, kindness, goodness, faithfulness, gentleness, and self-control. God, if there is something emotionally unhealthy mixed into my cup, let it float to the surface for me to see. Give me the courage to face it, take responsibility for it, and surrender it to You. Based on today's reading and what I discovered in my cup, I surrender these areas to You...

Purify me—scoop unhealthy character traits out of my cup, and fill my cup with healthy character. Make me more like Jesus, and use me to love people well and sweeten the world with Your goodness. In Jesus's Name, Amen.

46 - Heart-Attack Relationship

Buckle your seatbelts. Today's journey will be a little bumpy but sit tight. What I share today can help you resist distractions and keep you moving forward on the perfect PATH—Jesus!

A type of relationship exists that attacks our hearts. It involves a bully—the loud, overbearing, quarrelsome, know-it-all who enjoys intimidating and bossing around smaller or weaker people. For most of us, the mention of the word bully brings someone to mind. Who comes to your mind?

Sean comes to my mind. He had spiky, brown hair, was always getting into trouble in our 4th grade class, and was always making fun of someone. I was one of his targets. Sean brought 10-year-old me to tears many times. I'm talking the ugly cry. Pain set up a residence in my heart, and I dreaded going to school each day…*until* my dad called Sean's parents and ended the verbal torture. *Thanks, Dad!*

Bullies eventually grow older and taller, but some of them don't grow up emotionally. They go on to date, and the odds are high that a bully will ask you out at some point. I wish someone had warned me to be on the lookout for bullies because it would have saved me a lot of heartaches. That's why I'm warning you.

My dating relationship that turned my life upside-down and started me on this journey to honor God in every area of my life was a relationship with a bully. My counselor gave this heart-attack of a relationship a name: the Verbally Abusive Relationship.

I thought the Verbally Abusive Relationship was a rare relationship a young woman might encounter only once or twice in her life, but I've discovered that bullies can show up throughout our lives. Verbal abuse can mark all types of relationships: peer to peer, sibling to sibling, parent and child, boyfriend and girlfriend, husband and wife, and boss and employee, to name a few. Thankfully, there are some warning signs that can help us identify a bully boyfriend and a Verbally Abusive Relationship.

The bully boyfriend's behavior is inconsistent.

At first, he might seem confident, stable, and easygoing. Over time, you see a much different side of him. Behind closed doors, he becomes easily unraveled, emotional, and irrational. In public, he may act like the perfect gentleman while in private, he acts like a toddler who didn't get his way.

The bully boyfriend is easily angered.

Small and insignificant things rattle him. His emotion grows quickly out of control and into fits of rage with him yelling. Understandably, you might feel scared in his presence.

The bully boyfriend is critical of you.

At the beginning of your relationship, he might be encouraging and complimentary. As the relationship progresses, he grows critical of you. His natural default is to point out what he thinks you did wrong and tell you what you should do differently.

The bully boyfriend blames you for his behavior.

Your relationship is riddled with problems, and in his mind, ALL of the problems are your fault. He doesn't take responsibility for his own behavior and has difficulty admitting when he's wrong. He might say things about you that are not true. If you try to have a heart-to-heart talk with him about the conflict in your relationship, he dismisses your feelings.

The bully boyfriend tries to manipulate you.

He might manipulate you by indirectly suggesting how you should act in order to make him happy. He may directly tell you what to do or demand you behave in a specific way.

You feel like a different person.

As the relationship progresses, you feel like a different person than when you began the relationship. You feel unhappy, depressed, and confused. You may even feel bad physically. Friends and family express concern for you and your dating relationship.

Verbally abusive relationships are based on lies.

These lies take the form of subtle, negative comments or direct put-downs the bully makes towards you. These lies are in direct opposition to how God created you—as a fearfully and wonderfully made-in-His-image woman full of pure PURPOSE and powerful POTENTIAL. Essentially, your identity, Who God is to you and who you are in Christ, comes under attack.

If you welcome the lies and accept them, then your heart becomes vulnerable to abuse.

If you are currently in a dating relationship with a guy you think might be verbally abusive, do not hesitate to talk to someone. A peer may not know how to help you, so talk to a parent, mentor, small group leader, or pastor. God has planned something FAR BETTER for you than an abusive relationship. I'm proof of that! His arms are open wide for you!

Proverbs 22:24-25: "Make no friendship with a man given to anger, nor go with a wrathful man, lest you learn his way and entangle yourself in a snare."

The descriptions above can help you identify guys who struggle with verbally abusive behavior. The important thing to remember is that it takes time to identify these emotionally unhealthy guys. They usually know how to put on a good act in public. If you become the focus of their attention, then they will be on their best behavior in order to impress you. Be an active observer of guys' character, and guard your heart.

A key trait to watch out for in a guy is ANGER and how he handles it. Verbally abusive guys have deep-seated anger that drives their behavior. They have not learned how to deal with their anger in healthy ways.

As you interact with a guy who is pursuing you (as a friend or to date), pay attention to your feelings—what you feel about the guy and how you feel after talking with him. The Holy Spirit can use feelings to warn you that something is wrong. Use the "Read Your Heart" questions from Reading 34 to help you process your feelings:

"Read Your Heart" Questions

- *Do I feel glad, sad, mad, love, or fear?*

- *Why do I feel that way?*

- *What do I know to be true? What does God's Word say about my situation?*

- *How does what I'm feeling and experiencing line up with God's Word? How does God want me to apply His truth in my life?*

- Pray and "destroy arguments and every lofty opinion raised against the knowledge of God, and take every thought captive to obey Christ" (2 Corinthians 10:5).

Also, remember these suggestions (from yesterday's reading) for guarding your heart and mind as you get to know a guy:

Rely on your community.

"Where there is no guidance, a people falls, but in an abundance of counselors there is safety" (Proverbs 11:14). If you don't know much about a guy, don't go on a date alone with him. Spend time with him in the context of community and seek to build a very basic friendship with him first. If friends or family members express concern about him, consider what they share.

Observe his character.

Does his behavior reflect the fruit of the Spirit? What are his relationships with others like? Does he put others down? Does he act like he's in competition with others? Does he think he is always right? Is he easily angered? Deep down, is he overly sensitive or emotional? How does he work through conflict with others?

Journal after spending time with him.

Soon after spending time with him, take a few minutes to write a short summary of what happened. Include: (1) what you learned about him/his character, (2) what you learned about yourself, and (3) your feelings—what you feel about him and how you feel after spending time with him.

Think about it!

A woman who is most vulnerable to verbal abuse struggles in several of the following ways:

Has low self-esteem
Has a weak understanding of Who God is
Has a weak understanding of who she is in Christ
Doubts God's love for her
Is searching for the Triple A's (*attention, acceptance, adoration*),
Too easily accepts people's opinions and critiques of her as truth
Often discounts her own feelings
her family line contains at least 1 verbally (or physically) abusive relationship

1—Place a check mark next to the descriptions that are weak spots for you. Based on the descriptions above, how vulnerable are you to verbal abuse?

2—Have you dated any guys who were verbally abusive?

3—Read the following verses. How is God's character different from that of a bully?

Hebrews 13:8 -
Psalm 103:8 -
Matthew 11:29-30 -
1 Corinthians 13:4-8 -
Galatians 5:22-23 -

Pray about it!

Heavenly Husband,
You are the God of hearts. Thank You for loving my heart perfectly. Protect my heart from guys who are emotionally unhealthy and emotionally abusive. Empower me to believe the identity I have in Jesus, and grant me confidence in my identity that cannot be shaken.

*In Christ, I am Your child, a woman of God, **Uniquely designed** as a worshipper, Image-bearer/ the "softer" side of You, Helper; Nurturer; Co-heir of Your inheritance; Co-ruler of creation; Full of purpose/World-changer. I am Your **Special representative**—spiritually symbolic of the Bride of Christ/ the Church/ the People You love. I am Loved, Nurtured, Cherished, Admired, Honored, Beautiful, Radiant, Pure, Dignified, Joyful, Rejoiced over by You, God! You verbally defined me as **"Very Good."** May I always see myself through Your eyes! In Jesus' Name, Amen.*

47 - The List

After experiencing the heart-attack relationship with the guy from the singles' group, I decided my wish list for a husband needed to be revised! Things that made the list were *loves God, good sense of humor, tall, dark, handsome, light-colored eyes, smart, older than me,* and on and on. The list was soooo long.

How long is your list?

An overwhelming majority of wishes on my list were related to the man's appearance. I admit that I had a lot of superficial requests. The list was more like an order form for a product with check marks by every special feature. Granted, a man's physical appearance can be a big part of what initially attracts you to him, but it's the heart of the man that is most important. When it came to the important choice of a king to lead God's People, God placed emphasis on the man's heart. But the LORD said to Samuel, "Do not look on his appearance or on the height of his stature, because I have rejected him. For the LORD sees not as man sees: man looks on the outward appearance, but the LORD looks on the heart" (1 Samuel 16:7).

My vain self had to come to grips with the fact that God's best for me might be an earthly husband who had an incredible, loving heart…and who was unattractive to my eyes. *Uhh. Are you feeling my pain?* If God provided a godly husband for me, I wanted to receive His gift with a thankful heart. I prayed this prayer many times:

Dear God,

Thank You for being my Heavenly Husband, and showing me what is important. I pray that You would provide me an earthly husband who loves You deeply. God, help me to accept the man You want me to marry. Whether he's short, bald, fat, or ugly, help me to love his heart above all else. Help me to see him as a creation made in Your image and to love him deeply. In Jesus' name, Amen.

I know my prayer is funny, but I really did pray that many, many times! I think God appreciates honesty!

As I rewrote my list, I chose to list qualities related to the man's heart that I felt were most important. Vanity no longer had a voice on my list! I prayerfully asked God to guide me in my list-making. This is what came to mind:

God's Vision:
For God's People to be united with Him in Heaven, worshipping Him as the one true God and enjoying Him forever.

What kind of man will help me make it to the end?

God's Mission/Our Mission:
To make disciples of all nations.

What kind of man will make disciples and will support me in making disciples?

Lists may differ from person to person. I believe God wants one thing to be the same: A man who loves God—a man who believes in Jesus Christ as his Lord and Savior. 2 Corinthians 6:14 says, "Do not be unequally yoked with unbelievers. For what partnership has righteousness with lawlessness? Or what fellowship has light with darkness?" Unequally yoked is not a phrase that we often use in conversations. I hear it, and I think breakfast, especially eggs. But, seriously, it has nothing to do with how you like your eggs cooked. It has everything to do with compatibility and working together.

A yoke is a wooden bar used to keep two oxen moving together in the same direction as they pull a large weight. In order to perform the task, the oxen must be close in height and strength. If one ox is significantly weaker or shorter than the other, the load they bear will go around in circles, making the assignment impossible. Because the oxen are incompatible, they end up working against one another, unable to complete the task. The verse warns Christ-followers that they are not compatible with nonbelievers. The combination is like unequally yoked oxen.

Christ-followers are described as righteousness and light while nonbelievers are described as lawlessness and darkness. They are opposites. Partnership and fellowship are difficult to achieve with opposites, no matter how hard they try to work together. Marriage is a one-flesh connection, the closest partnership humans share. To join a Christ-follower and a nonbeliever as life partners creates an extremely difficult union because they have opposing beliefs in God and opposing visions and missions for their lives.

Here's my revised, much shorter, heart-focused husband list:

Loves God
Understands grace
Will support God's calling in my life
Will fight for me like God does
Does not have anger issues

I've included explanations of the things on my list.

Loves God

"You shall love the Lord your God with all your heart and with all your soul and with all your mind." –Matthew 22:37

"But the fruit of the Spirit is love, joy, peace, patience, kindness, goodness, faithfulness, gentleness, self-control." –Galatians 5:22-23

Understands grace

I wanted a man who not only loved Jesus as his Lord and Savior but also had a deep understanding of His grace and forgiveness. "For by grace you have been saved through faith. And this is not your own doing; it is the gift of God, not a result of works, so that no one may boast" (Ephesians 2:8-9).

I knew I wasn't perfect, and there would be times that I would need to be forgiven by my husband. I wanted a man who would be able to extend grace and forgiveness to me. Since grace is often learned through hardship, I knew a man who understands grace would probably be a man who had faced hard trials in his life. I believed that kind of man would be better equipped to deal with the ups and downs of life. "Therefore I tell you, her sins, which are many, are forgiven—for she loved much. But he who is forgiven little, loves little" (Luke 7:47).

Will support God's calling in my life

I didn't want a man to hold me back or be a hindrance from my doing what God wanted me to do. "And let us consider how to stir up one another to love and good works" (Hebrews 10:24).

Will fight for me like God does

There have been times in my life when my character was brought into question and wrongly attacked by people who were either protecting themselves, misunderstood my heart, or meant evil against me. In those times, often the best thing to do is be silent, let God defend you before others, and trust Him to fight for your heart. In every situation, God was faithful to fight for me. God knew my heart, and He delighted in the song of my heart, which meant that He knew how to fight for me. "The LORD will fight for you, and you have only to be silent" (Exodus 14:14).

I desired for my Heavenly Husband to provide an earthly husband like Him—a man who knew my heart, who appreciated its song, and who believed in me. I wanted a man who was so loyal, loving, and valiant that he would stand up for me. That kind of man is easy to trust and follow. That kind of man is a man with whom it is easy to become one flesh. "Likewise, husbands, live with your wives in an understanding way, showing honor to the woman as the weaker vessel, since they are heirs with you of the grace of life, so that your prayers may not be hindered" (1 Peter 3:7).

Does not have anger issues

After reading my stories, I'm certain you're not surprised this made the list! Proverbs 29:22 warns, "A man of wrath stirs up strife, and one given to anger causes much transgression." That verse proved to be true as I would describe my relationships with angry guys as quarrelsome, problematic, unpleasant, unsafe, discouraging, and draining. I didn't want that kind of strife in a marriage relationship because it would consume me and distract me from God and living out God's Mission. Plus, the marriage wouldn't be much of a witness, either. "Know this, my beloved brothers: let every person be quick to hear, slow to speak, slow to anger; for the anger of man does not produce the righteousness of God." – James 1:19

Think about it!

Review your husband list. It was completed as part of Reading 1.

1—Is your list short or long? Are the majority of the items heart-related or appearance-related?

2—Now that you're almost to the end of this book, does your list still reflect your true desires? Have any desires changed? Does your list need to be revised?

Are we spiritually compatible?—Questions

As I worked on my husband list, I developed some questions to aid me in discerning my spiritual compatibility with a guy. I hope you put these questions to good use!

- Is this man's presence in my life edifying me to grow closer to Jesus or farther away?

- Is my presence in this man's life edifying him to grow closer to Jesus or farther away?

- Is this a man who would support me in following God's call on my life, or would he hold me back?

- How has God called and impassioned this man to serve Him? Will I be able to help him fulfill his calling?

- Is this a man I can follow and submit to if I married him?

Pray about it!

Heavenly Husband,
You are the best husband in the world! I ask that one day, You provide me an earthly husband who is like You and who supports Your Vision and Mission. Enlighten me to know what key characteristics I should look for in an earthly husband. I pray for my future husband that You would help him grow closer in His relationship with You. Protect Him from sexual impurity. Guard His mind, heart, and body. Strengthen His identity in You. In Jesus' Name, Amen.

Once your husband list is completed, use the list to pray for your future husband on a regular basis.

48 - Boundaries

I worked at a church that had some relationship guidelines for male and female coworkers. For example, a male staff member who was married could not ride in a car or meet in a public place with only one female coworker; other staff had to be with them. If a married man held a meeting at the church with only one woman, the meeting room door had to have a window. All of the same rules applied to married women. I always wondered why there were no rules for the elevator. (Please tell me I'm not the only one who thought of that.)

Oh—there was an unspoken rule: If a married staff member hugged another coworker of the opposite sex, then they gave a side hug. If you've never seen a side hug, it's where two people stand next to each other, put one arm on the other person's back, semi-lean into each another for about a second or two. *Awkward!* Let's be honest; the side hug doesn't rightfully deserve the title "hug."

Why did the church have these relationship guidelines for its staff? These guidelines, these boundaries, promoted purity in staff relationships by helping staff members be mindful of the differences in marriage and coworker relationships and be intentional to not blur the lines. In recent readings, I encouraged you to think about boundaries that would promote emotional and physical purity in guy-girl relationships. At the end of this reading, you'll have the opportunity to define your boundaries. First, let's consider the differences in three relationships: marriage, engagement, and dating.

MARRIAGE RELATIONSHIP

Description: Marriage symbolizes Christ's relationship with His Church. When a man and woman marry, they make a promise to be faithful to each other and to God. This promise reflects God's promise to His People to rescue them from sin.
Commitment Level: High
Emotional bond: The husband is the leader in the relationship, and the wife follows the lead of her husband as he follows Christ. The husband is to love his wife like Jesus loved the church and sacrificed Himself for her, and the wife is to respect her husband.
Physical bond: One-flesh connection—sex can be enjoyed! The husband has authority over his wife's body, and the wife has authority over her husband's body.

ENGAGED TO MARRY

Description: Engagement is the middle ground between dating and marriage.

Commitment level: Medium

Emotional bond: During engagement, a man and woman begin preparing to build a life together and to live out the BIG Story together. They share their hearts on a deeper level than they did when dating.

Physical bond: Though heart-sharing increases, body ownership does not increase. The engaged man and woman do not have ownership of each other's bodies. Their bodies belong solely to God.

DATING RELATIONSHIP

Description: The dating relationship is a very basic relationship meant to edify, or encourage, the man and woman involved.

Commitment level: Low

Emotional bond: The man and woman do not have ownership of each other's hearts. Since dating is a way to test spiritual compatibility, it is good for the woman to give the man some appropriate and very basic opportunities to lead and for the woman to try to follow his lead.

Physical bond: Dating is not a one-flesh connection, so the man and woman do not have ownership of each other's bodies. Their bodies belong solely to God.

To help you determine emotional boundaries in dating and engagement, let's review the concept of a man leading and a woman responding to, or following, his lead. Man was created to display God's stronger characteristics as initiator, leader, provider, and protector. Woman was created to reflect God's softer characteristics of gentleness, graciousness, and helper.

A woman being a "helper" in a dating relationship simply means the woman has a love-your-neighbor-as-yourself kind of love for her brother in Christ. Helping her Christian brother may include praying for him. Helping him does not mean mothering him—God already gave him a momma! He deserves respect as a man who is capable of taking care of himself.

Examples of appropriate opportunities for the man take the lead (dating relationship):

- Asking the woman out on a date (initiator).
- Paying for the date (provider).
- Sharing his intentions to date the woman with the intent of pursuing marriage and asking her if she would like to do the same (leadership).
- Communicating and being careful not to play games with the woman's heart (leadership, protector).

Examples of the woman responding to the man's leadership (dating relationship):

- Thanking the man for something nice he did for her (kindness).
- Answering his questions truthfully and directly and not expecting him to read her mind (respect).

- Communicating personal boundaries to him that impact the relationship (respect).
- Recognizing that he is not perfect, giving him space to make mistakes and develop his leadership skills, and extending grace to him when he messes up (respect, graciousness, kindness, helper).
- Acknowledging when he leads well (respect, kindness, helper).
- If the man leads the woman to do something that goes against God's commands and/or makes her feel uncomfortable, she should speak up. As women, we are responsible for our own actions, and we have every right to say, "No," to a man's leading. Pushing back on an unrighteous leading of the man can be used by God to help the man remain pure in mind, heart, and body (respect, helper).

At the end of every date and every day, remember that God is your Heavenly Husband who holds ultimate authority in your life. When you date, be careful not to *act* like you're married. You are responsible for your own actions, and you have the choice and the right to say, "No," to a man's leading. A guy paying for your dinner does not give him ownership of you, your heart, nor your body. You belong to God.

1 Corinthians 6:19-20
"Do you not know that your body is a temple of the Holy Spirit within you, whom you have from God? You are not your own, for you were bought with a price. So glorify God in your body."

Proverbs 2:11-15
"Discretion will watch over you, understanding will guard you, delivering you from the way of evil, from men of perverted speech, who forsake the paths of uprightness to walk in the ways of darkness, who rejoice in doing evil and delight in the perverseness of evil, men whose paths are crooked, and who are devious in their ways."

Think about it!

For the two relationships below, write down the emotional and physical boundaries you want to adopt. To reference your thoughts/notes on emotional boundaries, go to Reading 44. To reference your thought/notes on physical boundaries, go to Readings 40-43.

ENGAGED TO MARRY

Description: Engagement is the middle ground between dating and marriage.
Commitment level: Medium
Emotional bond: During engagement, a man and woman begin preparing to build a life together and to live out the BIG Story together. They share their hearts on a deeper level than they did when dating.
Emotional boundaries:

Physical bond: Though heart-sharing increases, body ownership does not increase. The engaged man and woman do not have ownership of each other's bodies. Their bodies belong solely to God.
Physical boundaries:

DATING RELATIONSHIP

Description: The dating relationship is a very basic relationship meant to edify, or encourage, the man and woman involved.
Commitment level: Low
Emotional bond: The man and woman do not have ownership of each other's hearts. Since dating is a way to test spiritual compatibility, it is good for the woman to give the man some appropriate and very basic opportunities to lead and the woman to try to follow his lead.
Emotional boundaries:

Physical bond: Dating is not a one flesh connection, so the man and woman do not have ownership to each other's bodies. Their bodies belong solely to God.
Physical boundaries:

Pray about it!

Heavenly Husband,
Your Word says, "How can a young {woman} keep {her} way pure? By guarding it according to your word. With my whole heart I seek you; let me not wander from your commandments. {Help me to} store up your word in my heart, that I might not sin against you. Blessed are you, O Lord; teach me your statutes! With my lips {use me to} declare all the rules of your mouth. In the way of your testimonies {show me how to} delight as much as in all riches. {May I} meditate on your precepts and fix my eyes on your ways. {May I} delight in your statutes; {may I} not forget your word" {Psalm 119:9-16}. In Jesus' Name I pray, Amen.

49 - Communicating Boundaries

O ne of the most challenging aspects of seeking purity in your relationships is defining boundaries. Whether you have already determined physical and emotional boundaries or are still contemplating them, well done! What you are doing is not an easy process, and it takes character, time, and courage. My friends, you are displaying many characteristics of emotionally healthy, full cup kind of people! You're building your character in the areas of loving God and man, thinking through decisions, and applying God's Truth in your life. You're displaying the fruit of the Spirit: love, patience, goodness, faithfulness, and self-control. I'm so proud of you!

Today, we'll think through how to communicate your boundaries. Did I freak any of you out with that last sentence? Does the thought of communicating a boundary to a guy seem like an interesting challenge, a necessary part of life, or a terrifying task?

I understand that communicating a boundary is not the easiest thing to do. Choosing to be pure for the sake of God's glory is not for wimps! It takes character to create a boundary, to communicate it, and to stay committed to it. You have the character, power, and boldness needed through the Holy Spirit within you! The good news is that your whole list of boundaries won't need to be communicated to every guy you date. Some boundaries can be communicated nonverbally. Many boundaries can be communicated over time as the relationship grows.

Why share your boundaries with a guy?

Remember, a personal boundary is *your* boundary. It's your preference, backed by your conviction (and inspired by God), to guard what is special to you. The guys you date may not have the same boundary you do.

Guys can't read your mind, so you will need to communicate with them. Doing so helps a guy understand your expectations. It invites him to become a part of the process of honoring the boundary, and ultimately, honoring God in the relationship. It makes it much easier for you to uphold the boundary later.

To uphold a boundary, a man and woman who are dating must "work together." This requires a certain level of respect, agape love, and sacrifice. It presents the opportunity for them to grow in character individually and to see how well they do in pursuing goals and maneuvering through challenges together. This is good information when you are questioning if this is the person you want to marry.

God may use your words to encourage, inspire, or convict the guy in his own relationship with God. Jesus said this about the Holy Spirit: "And when he comes, he will convict the world concerning sin and righteousness and judgment" (John 16:8). Remember Troy, who adopted my "No Kissing Boundary" and later wrote me a thank you e-mail? Troy made a point to mention how God used the boundary to reveal a place in his heart that needed God's healing touch. The revelations God gave Troy about his heart were not minor and strengthened his walk with Jesus. That was SO WORTH taking a few minutes to share my boundary with him! Isn't it amazing what God did?!

According to Acts 1:1-2, Jesus communicated commands (standards) to apostles "through the Holy Spirit." After Jesus ascended into Heaven, His disciples received the promised Holy Spirit. "And divided tongues as of fire appeared to them and rested on each of them. And they were all filled with the Holy Spirit and began to speak in other tongues as the Spirit gave them utterance" (Acts 2:3-4). As the disciples went into all the world to proclaim the gospel, the Holy Spirit emboldened them and guided their words (Luke 12:11-12, Acts 4:8). The Holy Spirit anointed the disciples' words—the gospel message—and people throughout the world were saved! The same Spirit will empower you to communicate your boundaries.

As you rely on the Holy Spirit to help you communicate and uphold your boundaries, you'll learn how to live a disciplined life, worshipping God above self and selfish desires. I believe God uses everything on this side of Heaven, especially the pursuit of purity, to prepare us to worship Him throughout eternity. It's a worthy pursuit, don't you think?

When you tell a guy about your boundary, keep in mind that you may need to give the guy some time to think about how your boundary will impact him. He may react with shock, confusion, silence, curiosity, acceptance, disappointment, or even rejection. Trust me, when a guy hears the news that he won't get a kiss from you anytime soon, possibly never, he will probably be a little disappointed!

I can only imagine what thoughts ran through the heads of the late twenty-something and thirty-something guys who wanted to date me when they heard they wouldn't get a kiss from me. Though I didn't get any super negative responses, I'm sure a few guys thought I was crazy! Whatever reaction you get, my advice is: Don't take the guy's response personally. Your boundary denies the guy something he may have thought he deserved. Your boundary also requires something of him.

Will had been a good friend of mine for years. When he talked to me about dating, I shared a heart-protecting boundary that requested he meet and build relationship with a married couple who were my dating mentors. Will DID NOT like what he heard and was adamant that he would not honor my boundary. I didn't see Will's response as rejection. I saw it as a blessing! My boundary defined who I was and who I was not. Will wasn't able to accept and respect me, which revealed that we were not spiritually compatible. What a blessing that we discovered this before we ever began dating! Simply communicating the boundary protected both of us from heartache!

I think about the guys who accepted and adopted my "No Kissing Boundary" and the strength of character it took on their parts to do so. After all, a kiss isn't a bad thing, and God didn't tell us to not kiss. What humble and loving guys to give up something pleasurable for the sake of helping a woman seek purity and honor God in dating! Those guys helped me grow closer to God, and for that, I am eternally grateful!

There may be times when you backslide in keeping a boundary. Remember that you're not perfect, and you're in a very real battle between the mind and flesh. If you try to fight the battle in your own strength, you will inevitably fail. This battle is more than you can handle alone. Most importantly, remember that you are not alone. God is with you, and His Spirit lives within you! It's a God-sized battle, and it's His battle to fight. Commit your heart, mind, and body to Him, and He will rescue you. Jesus was victorious over death and sin. Because of Jesus, you can overcome anything! The Holy Spirit will empower you to leave your old self and old ways behind and to move forward in your new self and new ways.

2 Corinthians 5:17
"Therefore, if anyone is in Christ, he is a new creation. The old has passed away; behold, the new has come."

Think about it!

Using the common boundaries and scenarios below, think through how you would communicate the boundaries.

1—Boundary: Let's say you've committed to not kiss a guy until after you've had at least 3 dates with him. Scenario: Your first date comes to a close, and he walks you to the front door. What will you do if the guy leans in for a kiss?

2—Boundary: Let's say you have a boundary of not kissing until after you and the guy have agreed to go from casual dating to a dating relationship. Scenario #1: You've been on several dates with a guy whom you would like to continue dating. He has a sincere talk with you, expressing that he would like to date you with greater intention. He gives you the opportunity to share your thoughts. Do you share your boundary with him? If so, how do you tell him?

Scenario #2: You've been on 5 dates with a guy 5 weekends in a row. You really like him. He keeps asking you out and has begun to hold your hand. He hasn't talked to you about dating more seriously. Do you share your boundary with him? If so, how do you tell him?

3—Review your physical and emotional boundaries from Reading 48. Identify the boundaries that need to be communicated verbally vs. nonverbally. Think through how to communicate each boundary. For some practice, role-play with a friend, parent, mentor, or group leader.

Pray about it!

Heavenly Husband,
I praise You, for You have strong character, and You do all things with love. Your character and love, revealed through Jesus, saved me and redeemed my relationship with You. My soul is eternally grateful.

I dedicate my boundaries to You. I ask that You use my boundaries to guard our relationship from sin and hate. May my boundaries foster greater love in my heart for You. God, grant me wisdom to know when and how to communicate my boundaries to a guy. Strengthen my heart to share, and prepare my heart for whatever reaction comes from the guy.

May my boundaries help the guys I date and others to behold Your glory and encourage their hearts to seek hard after You. In Jesus' Strong and Loving Name, Amen.

50 - Social Share or Strike?

P hone calls, texts, emails, blogs, tweets, status updates, pictures, stories, and videos—there are many, many opportunities to share your heart in today's world. Oh, let's not forget an actual face-to-face conversation!

When you're having a heart-to-heart talk with someone face-to-face, how mindful are you in choosing your words wisely? When it comes to social media, are you mindful of your words? Do you guard yourself more or less than you do in a one-on-one conversation?

When you're on social media via your cell phone, iPad, or computer, it's easy to forget that virtually millions of human beings are connected to you. It's easy to become comfortable sharing your heart. As I've discipled young ladies over the years, I've discovered that one of the easiest ways to know what they are thinking and feeling and struggling with is to look at what they post on social media.

Many young women put their hearts "out there" with reckless abandon. When a piece of their heart shows up in their posts, I consider how to encourage them or pray for them, but not everyone who sees their posts cares about their hearts. Social media has opened the door for us to share our hearts with the world. How far can we go past the doorway without giving our hearts away too much?

Kate's perspective

Kate is a college student who is active on social media. When it comes to the personal information/interests sections found on many social media sites, she intentionally does not answer every question. Her reasoning behind that emotional boundary: She says, "If someone wants to know me, then that person can get to know me!" Kate has a point. If a guy is interested in dating her, he won't be able to look her up online and learn everything about her! He will need to pursue getting to know her. Kate's boundary leaves room for good conversation and mutual sharing.

Julie's perspective

Julie married Ross when she was 41. The first time she mentioned Ross on her Facebook profile and in a post was when she and Ross got engaged. Prior to Ross, Julie dated several guys. She never mentioned any of the guys on her Facebook profile or in posts, not even in the "Relationship Status" section. She didn't post pictures taken on dates.

When asked about applying discretion when using social media, Julie said, "First, when you share something personal with possibly hundreds of 'friends,' you have no control over what they do with the information. Will they misinterpret what you post and judge you incorrectly? Will they twist it into something that embarrasses you? People sometimes forget that a virtual friend isn't always a person that has your best interest at heart (a real friend).

Second, when you share personal information about a relationship on a social media site, you open yourself up to questions that aren't helpful. For example, a girl starts dating a guy and she wants everybody to know because she's so excited about him. Two months later, he dumps her, and she is devastated. She has to re-live the whole thing every time someone asks her about the relationship, and she has to tell them it didn't work out.

Third, social media sites often change privacy settings. It's difficult, if not impossible, to guarantee that someone who doesn't know you doesn't have access to your information. There are a lot of sick people who are looking for easy targets. Sharing personal information can be dangerous if the wrong person reads it. It's just better to be safe."

Ross's perspective

Ross, Julie's husband, said this: "Sharing a lot of personal information is like dressing provocatively. A person who doesn't know the boundaries of what is appropriate in the manner of clothing likely doesn't know where to draw the line with the amount of information she shares."

Julie added, "I agree with Ross. Putting it all out there, whether it's personal information or a person's body, opens a person up to judgments and assumptions that usually don't paint a person in a favorable light. Keeping private things private is wise for a lot of reasons (whether it's with clothing or with personal information)."

Matthew 7:
"Do not give dogs what is holy, and do not throw your pearls before pigs, lest they trample them underfoot and turn to attack you."

Once we post something on the internet, it's there forever (on this side of Heaven). What we post today might become big news 10 or 20 years from now. We can all think of stories that made national news about people who got fired from their jobs when something they posted on social media called their character into question.

When you post a comment, picture, video, etc., you need to keep your future in mind—your future job, future spouse, and future children. When you post, you also need to keep your relationship with God in mind and the Mission to help others know Him. If you are in Christ, you represent Him through the words you post and your actions captured in posted photos.

Think of it this way: You might become famous one day. Celebrity news shared on tv shows, radio, internet sites, and in magazines will report stories about you to viewers across the nation. Don't post anything about yourself on social media that you would regret for the whole world to know. Don't post anything that you would regret for your future husband or children to see. Don't post anything you think you might regret one day.

Our words mean something. The Bible instructs us to give thought to our words before we share them, whether they come out through the mouthpiece of our lips or our social media accounts.

Proverbs 13:3
"Whoever guards {her} mouth preserves his life; {she} who opens wide {her} lips comes to ruin."

Ecclesiastes 10:12
"The words of a wise {woman's} mouth win {her} favor, but the lips of a fool consume {her}."

Proverbs 31:26
"She opens her mouth with wisdom, and the teaching of kindness is on her tongue."

Luke 6:45
"The good person out of the good treasure of {her} heart produces good, and the evil person out of {her} evil treasure produces evil, for out of the abundance of the heart {her} mouth speaks."

What comes out of your lips and social posts reflects what is in your heart. Being mindful of your words means balancing your emotions with logic, or lining up your heart with your head. Another way to think of it is to consider what happens when you walk across a tightrope. If you've ever participated on a zipline/canopy tour, then you walked a tightrope high in the air above the trees. It's not enough to use your feet to walk the rope. You must also stretch out your hands or hold onto rails to maintain the balance needed to successfully walk across the rope. If you don't actively utilize your hands, it's inevitable that you will fall off the rope. Following your heart is like walking the tightrope without helping hands. You are destined to fall. Your mind is the helping hands that provide balance and enable you to make it safely to the other side. Who knows, you might even enjoy the beauty of the trees while you're up there!

Think about it!

1—Do you think it shares too much heart to…

…update a relationship status? And why?

…post pictures from a date? And why?

…post "I love you" to the guy or profess your adoration of him? And why?

2—List all forms of social media you use. What guard-your-heart boundaries would you like to adopt for general posts? For posting about dating relationships?

Social Strike or Share?—Questions

Before posting on social media, here are some questions to use to line up your heart with the mind:

- If I post this, am I sharing something from my heart?

- What is my motive in sharing this? (Am I venting? Am I encouraging others? Am I seeking the *Triple A's—Attention, Acceptance,* or *Adoration?*)

- What does this reveal about me? Does it reveal too much?

- Is this something I need to process before I post? (Do I need to go through the exercise of "Reading my Heart" from Readings 34 and 46)?

- Is this the right forum for sharing my heart? Would journaling or talking to my mentor, parent, or friend be a better place to express myself?

APPLICATION ACTIVITY: For the next 7 days, before you post on social media, answer the *Social Share or Strike?* Questions.

Pray about it!

Heavenly Husband,
I praise You for Your words are thoughtful, wise, purposeful, life-changing. Thank You for inviting me to talk with You and for always turning Your ear to hear me. Help me to never take for granted the gift of having a voice at Your throne and all that Jesus suffered to give me this Holy opportunity.

Father, You've given me a voice in this world. I confess that I sometimes broadcast my voice in careless, ignorant, meaningless, hurtful, and discouraging ways. Please forgive me! Father, I commit my voice to You to be used for Your glory and the building of Your Kingdom. "Set a guard, O LORD, over my mouth; keep watch over the door of my lips" (Psalm 141:3)! Keep watch, as well, over my fingers as I type my thoughts and feelings on paper, via social media, and in texts.

Make me a woman of discretion who does not blindly throw her heart out into the world to be trampled. Train me to pay attention to my heart, my wellspring of life, and to carry my raw emotions to You, for You understand and comfort me like no one else in this world. Help me identify wrong motives behind unhealthy heart-sharing and surrender those to You. Protect my mind from lies. Train me to take lies captive, casting them on the cross before they take root in my heart. Let my words flow from a mind and heart balanced with truth and bring life as Jesus' words did. In Jesus' Life-giving Name, Amen.

51 - Your Heart's Song

Apostle Paul gave this relationship advice:
"I want you to be free from anxieties. The unmarried man is anxious about the things of the Lord, how to please the Lord. But the married man is anxious about worldly things, how to please his wife, and his interests are divided. And the unmarried or betrothed woman is anxious about the things of the Lord, how to be holy in body and spirit. But the married woman is anxious about worldly things, how to please her husband. I say this for your own benefit, not to lay any restraint upon you, but to promote good order and to secure your undivided devotion to the Lord." –1 Corinthians 7:32-35

Basically, Paul is encouraging everyone to remain single and enjoy the greatest gift of singleness: the freedom to love, worship, and serve Jesus without distraction. After doing the hard work of boundary-making, not worrying about dating and marriage might sound like an Ah-MAZING option! If you are in middle school or high school or haven't started dating, this reading is definitely for you! For the rest of us, it will be a refreshing change from boundary-making and a great reminder that God loves His girls!

My relationship advice to young women who are in high school is the advice I wish someone had given me: Go on special dates, such as Homecoming and Prom, but don't get into a serious dating relationship until after high school.

I know most young women don't give my suggestion a second thought. Feelings of anxiousness and excitement about experiencing a relationship with a guy can be hard to tame. They probably think I'm crazy, and you may think I'm crazy, but it's important for them and you to know that's an option.

In general, high school guys have not yet learned how to care for their own hearts, much less the heart of a woman made in God's image. Dating relationships are new territory for these boys, and they are learning as they go. If you are one of their first girlfriends, then you are basically their guinea pig!

Think about it! Some guys aren't Christians and don't have the Holy Spirit inside them to guide them. Many guys don't have good role models or parents who take the time to teach them about relationships. The part of their brains that makes decisions is still developing! Their hormones are in high gear, elevating the battle between their flesh and spirit. No matter how good their intentions may be, someone will likely get wounded in the battle.

Why not wait to date? Why not give the guys time to make mistakes on other girls and time to learn and grow from their mistakes before you date them?

My friend, Katherine, chose not to date seriously during her high school years. Her closest friends dated, and Katherine sometimes felt like the odd woman out in conversations and during weekend activities. Her friends questioned why she didn't date. Katherine is beautiful, intelligent, fun, and a cheerleader. I'm sure she caught the attention of many guys. Katherine had a lot of guy friends at her school, but she said they weren't the kind of guys she believed she would marry. Katherine was unusual. At 16, she already had a good sense of what she wanted in a guy. Her list of what she wanted in a guy wasn't long or even superficial. She didn't expect him to be perfect. She wanted a guy who loved God, had godly character, and was growing in his relationship with God.

The summer after she graduated high school, Katherine and I met for lunch and had a great time catching up. She shared that she was glad she made the decision not to date during high school. She said she learned a lot as she watched her friends go through painful, heartbreaking things in dating and end up with broken hearts. She learned without experiencing the pain herself!

While her friends were stressing or crying over a guy, her heart was undistracted. Katherine was free to grow in her relationship with God, develop her cheerleading skills, discover new talents, pursue new hobbies, and simply enjoy being a teenager. Katherine's boundary brought freedom to get to know *herself*. Her heart was free to discover her pure PURPOSE and powerful POTENTIAL. She began discovering the gifts and talents God gave her and what He called her to do in the BIG Story.

Psalm 139:13-16
"For you formed my inward parts; you knitted me together in my mother's womb. I praise you, for I am fearfully and wonderfully made. Wonderful are your works; my soul knows it very well. My frame was not hidden from you, when I was being made in secret, intricately woven in the depths of the earth. Your eyes saw my unformed substance; in your book were written, every one of them, the days that were formed for me, when as yet there was none of them."

God knows the number of your days, and He knows what every day holds. Your days are in His book, a part of His BIG Story. Your heart holds the glorious imprint of a glorious God. Your intricate design is a fabulous mix of purpose, gifts, talents, desire, vision, dreams, and a future. God knows you inside and out. He wove you together with love. He knows how awe-inspiring wonderful you are, but do *you* know?

YOUR HEART'S SONG

God knows your heartbeat, what makes your heart sing. Do you know the song of your heart? God is the real way to know your heart! With diligence, guard your heart, and with a diligent heart, seek Him! There is no one better to give you a tour of your heart than its Creator! He can teach you how to appreciate and care for your heart as a museum curator tends to the finest artwork.

Your spiritual gifts
"Now there are varieties of gifts, but the same Spirit; and there are varieties of service, but the same Lord; and there are varieties of activities, but it is the same God who empowers

them all in everyone. To each is given the manifestation of the Spirit for the common good." —1 Corinthians 12:4-7

God has gifted all believers with at least one spiritual gift (1 Corinthians 12:7, 11 & Ephesians 4:7). A spiritual gift equips us for the purpose of building up His Church and extending His Kingdom. Discovering our spiritual gifts reveals the types of ministry through which we can best honor and serve God and make an eternal impact in the world. Spiritual gifts include: Prophecy, Serving, Teaching, Exhortation, Giving, Leadership, Mercy, Wisdom, Knowledge, Faith, Discernment, Apostleship, Administration, Evangelism, Shepherding, Hospitality, Intercession, and Music.

What are your spiritual gifts? To identify your spiritual gifts, there are spiritual gifts tests available. Check at your local church or a Christian bookstore or online Christian book distributer. Many churches offer a course on spiritual gifts.

Your natural talents
What natural abilities has God given you? What are you good at doing?

Is there something you have an interest in learning? This might include: playing an instrument, painting, cooking, learning another language, and playing a sport. Explore your interests, and see which ones you have a natural talent to do.

Your hope
"The Lord is my strength and my shield; in him my heart trusts, and I am helped; my heart exults, and with my song I give thanks to him." —Psalm 28:7

"For I know the plans I have for you, declares the LORD, plans for welfare and not for evil, to give you a future and a hope." —Jeremiah 29:11

Where do you find hope?
What makes your heart come alive? What brings your heart joy?

Your heart's desires
"Delight yourself in LORD, and he will give you the desires of your heart." —Psalm 37:4

What do you desire for your life?
What do you desire for your relationship with Jesus? And with others?

What are you thankful for?
"Rejoice always, pray without ceasing, give thanks in all circumstances; for this is the will of God in Christ Jesus for you. Do not quench the Spirit." —1 Thessalonians 5:16-19

"I will give thanks to the Lord with my whole heart; I will recount all of your wonderful deeds." —Psalm 9:1

Thankfulness is the key to being content. It takes our eyes off the things we don't have, and helps us more fully appreciate and enjoy the blessings God has given us!

Dream the dreams God has for you!

Let's say you have just been given a blank check. This check represents an unlimited amount of resources available to you. This check makes it possible for you to do whatever you want for God's glory. Nothing can hold you back from pursuing your dreams. What would you do? Write down your answer!

"For we are his workmanship, created in Christ Jesus for good works, which God prepared beforehand, that we should walk in them." –Ephesians 2:10

I hope you've had fun with today's reading! You have a beautiful heart! Keep your heart free so that you can live out your pure PURPOSE and powerful POTENTIAL and take your precious place in the BIG Story!

Think about it!

1—Read Isaiah 12:1-6.

2—Spend some time going through the *"YOUR HEART'S SONG"* section, and record what you discover!

"Express Your Heart"—A CREATIVE CHALLENGE!

If something in today's reading touched your heart, then explore it creatively. The CREATIVE part is up to you: Write. Draw. Paint. Take photographs. Dance. Act out a scene. Blog. Write a song. When sharing your creations on your social accounts, tag @AimforHimblog, and use hashtags #LovebyDesignBook and #AimforHim.

Pray about it!

Heavenly Father,
You are a caring Creator! I am happy to be Your fearfully and wonderfully-made creation! "Do not let {my} adorning be external—the braiding of hair and the putting on of gold jewelry, or the clothing {I} wear—but let {my} adorning be the hidden person of the heart with the imperishable beauty of a gentle and quiet spirit, which in {Your} sight is very precious" (1 Peter 3:3-4). Heavenly Father, help me to discover the song of my heart. In the Name of Jesus, who made my heart come alive! Amen.

52 - Eyes on Jesus

A description of dating: Run on the path God has paved for you in His BIG Story. Run that path with all of your heart, and keep your eyes on Jesus. Eventually, God will bring a guy's path side by side with your path. Don't stop! Keep running—eyes on Jesus! Both of you will learn that you have common interests. You'll begin dating, but don't start running. Keep running on your God-given path with all of your heart—eyes on Jesus! Every once and awhile, look over to see if the guy is keeping up with you! Your paths will either separate or continue in the same direction. If you have been running together in the same direction for many miles, then that might be a good indication you are spiritually compatible and would make great running partners in the BIG Story! If you marry, God will merge your paths into one path![26]

As I ran the path God paved for me, He taught me the song of my heart. I learned that my spiritual giftings are faith, exhortation, and shepherding and began exploring ways to apply them. Serving as a discipleship leader for children's and student ministries, God ignited a passion for discipling young women. My creativity was expressed through scrapbooking, stamping, card making, and writing. Invitations to share my testimony publicly and to write devotionals for women's events and magazines revealed that God was using my words to minister to hearts. Participating in mission trips to Guatemala, Portugal, and Africa stretched my faith. I returned to my love for dancing and learned to swing dance. I also developed my cooking skills.

Knowing my path was paved by Jesus, all these activities became more than good works or hobbies pursued. These were steps taken with God, experiences shared with Him. This is how I enjoyed fellowship with Him:

Creative activities connected me to God as a creator who exemplified the beauty He brought into the world. As I poured my heart into my creations just as He imprinted His likeness into us, I felt joy.

Cooking delicious meals were achievements which sparked blessings of thanks for God's provision and the abilities He gives us.

Discipling others is living out God's Mission; it's following Jesus' example! Growing up, I had very few Christian influences. Discipling young women—being the Christian mentor for them that I never had—is redemptive. One of my first discipleship groups had 3rd grade girls, and I will always remember walking down the church hall with girls on each side holding my hands and the other girls crowded so closely around me that it slowed our walk together. I imagine that's the sweet love Jesus felt as children crowded around Him, desiring to be near Him.

Mission trips carried me far from my comfortable home to unfamiliar places in the world to precious people in need of a Savior. Jesus' journey from glorious Heaven to earth's dirt roads that led to His ultimate sacrifice became far more real. God's loving heartbeat for people to know Him grew louder. His vision for people from every tribe and tongue to worship Him forever came into focus and was magnified in my heart.

Writing is a pathway to God that leads me into deep, sweet, and powerful communion with God. When I'm writing something that is Christ-centered, I often find the words flowing out of my heart so quickly that I can barely type them fast enough. God inspires my words. He feels very near to me when I write. Sometimes I wonder if that's what Paul and other writers of the Bible experienced as God inspired them to record stories about Him.

Enjoying sweet fellowship with God all along the path taught me the notes and lyrics of my heart's song. It began playing louder to me and to the world!

It was good that my song grew louder because voices of scrutiny called to me. I was leading a 3rd grade girls' discipleship group that met on Sunday mornings at the same time the singles' group met. An older lady in my church questioned, "How are you going to meet a husband when you're with kids? The singles' group at (insert name of the new, large church down the road) has a larger singles' group than we have here. Why don't you go there?" My response, which I meant with all my heart and mind: "I feel led to serve the kids and to be a part of this church. I believe God is BIG enough to provide a husband for me, even when I'm not a part of a singles' group." She didn't ask me again. Unfortunately, others did. I continued running the path—eyes on Jesus!

Philippians 3:14
"I press on toward the goal for the prize of the upward call of God in Christ Jesus."

Hebrews 12:1-2
"Therefore, since we are surrounded by so great a cloud of witnesses, let us also lay aside every weight, and sin which clings so closely, and let us run with endurance the race that is set before us, looking to Jesus, the founder and perfector of our faith, who for the joy that was set before him endured the cross, despising the shame, and is seated at the right hand of the throne of God."

Running the path, with all of its mountains and valleys, taught me a lot about Jesus and led me to the Garden of Gethsemane. Jesus entered the garden to prepare His heart for what lie ahead—betrayal, arrest, trial, beatings, and the cross where He bore the world's sins and death. The painful weight of His calling would make any of us desire to run the other way. Our Savior described the pain to His disciples, "My soul is very sorrowful, even to death; remain here, and watch with me." Matthew 26:38. He called us to stay awake, as well—to keep our eyes open to what happens around us.

Jesus wasn't excited about going to the cross to die. He didn't *feel* like enduring the emotional and physical pain of giving up His life. Luke 22:44 says, "And being in anguish, he prayed more earnestly, and his sweat was like drops of blood falling to the ground." Emotion took the lead over logic, but how do you find the logic in the innocent and Holy Son of God dying for the sins of the world? The emotionally healthy One dying for emotionally unhealthy people?

"And going a little farther he fell on his face and prayed, saying, 'My Father, if it be possible, let this cup pass from me; nevertheless, not as I will, but as you will'" (Matthew 26:39). His heart poured forth; blood dripped from His forehead, His cheeks, His chest. The disciples were so relaxed they drifted to sleep and escaped into their dreams. "Again, for the second time, he went away and prayed, 'My Father, if this cannot pass unless I drink it, your will be done'" (Matthew 26:42). Emotion still flowing forth in bloody red drops, His heart carried a heavy burden. A third time, He prayed the same words. Then He rose to run the path. His emotion balanced with His Father's love. His heart lined up with the Father's will. That was surrender compelled by love.

1 Corinthians 13:4-8
"Love is patient and kind; love does not envy or boast; it is not arrogant or rude. It does not insist on its own way; it is not irritable or resentful; it does not rejoice at wrongdoing, but rejoices with the truth. Love bears all things, believes all things, hopes all things, endures all things. Love never ends."

Jesus said, "For the Son of Man came to seek and to save the lost" (Luke 19:10). Jesus backed up His words with actions. "For one will scarcely die for a righteous person—though perhaps for a good person one would dare even to die—but God shows his love for us in that while we were still sinners, Christ died for us" (Romans 5:7-8). His commitment to us is one in which we rest secure, now and for all eternity. This is true love. This is the depth of love God wants for us. Stop and think about that.

Our paths are paved with Jesus' blood. There's nothing we earn along this perfect PATH. He did it ALL. Because of Jesus, we get it ALL.

Ephesians 2:4-9
"But God, being rich in mercy, because of the great love with which he loved us, even when we were dead in our trespasses, made us alive together with Christ—by grace you have been saved—and raised us up with him and seated us with him in the heavenly places in Christ Jesus, so that in the coming ages he might show the immeasurable riches of his grace in kindness toward us in Christ Jesus. For by grace you have been saved through faith. And this is not your own doing; it is the gift of God, not a result of works, so that no one may boast."

On my canvas of dating relationships, one image reoccurred often. It was my desire, my "stretching out after" a guy for *attention, acceptance, and adoration*. The curse placed on Mother Eve became my inheritance. "Your desire shall be for your husband, and he shall rule over you" (Genesis 3:16). The curse made its way all the way from the Garden of Eden onto my canvas. Sometimes it stood out as a bold stroke of the brush and other times as a subtle dab of the brush. I was reaching for love, and once I grasped what I thought was love, I held on too long. I behaved as if I could "help" God bring marriage my way sooner. I acted as if there was something I could do to make a man love me.

Moving forward, I didn't want to do anything that would manipulate or pressure a man to love me. I wanted a man to love me because God placed a love in his heart for me, and vice versa. I desired to put the Garden of Eden far behind me and remember what I observed in the Garden of Gethsemane. When I stretched out my arms, I wanted it to be for Jesus. I poured out my heart and prayed, "God, into your hands, I commit my dating relationships."

Think about it!

Read about Jesus' time in Gethsemane in Matthew 26:36-46 and Luke 22:39-46.

1—What does Jesus' way of surrendering His heart to the Father's will teach you about surrendering your heart to the Father's will?

2—What do you need to surrender to God (your heart, a weakness in character, a relationship, a particular situation, etc.)?

Pray about it!

Whatever you surrender to Jesus, let the verses below inspire your prayer time.

Matthew 6:33
"But seek first the kingdom of God and his righteousness, and all these things will be added to you."

Matthew 26:39
"And going a little farther he fell on his face and prayed, saying, 'My Father, if it be possible, let this cup pass from me; nevertheless, not as I will, but as you will.'"

Matthew 6:9-10
"Pray then like this: 'Our Father in heaven, hallowed be your name. Your kingdom come, your will be done, on earth as it is in heaven.'"

53 - Butterflies

Here's another story about a guy I dated and didn't kiss:
I waited nervously for him to arrive. I passed the time by journaling and praying and looking up every five minutes or so to check the clock. My mind replayed the experience of the previous two months—what a whirlwind!

We met at a party of a mutual friend. He was tall, handsome, funny, and charming. He pursued me like no other guy had before him. It was as if he was reading my mind; he did everything in a way that appropriately edified me without crossing any lines. He showered me with phone calls, messages on my voicemail, notes, and compliments. I never had to wonder what he was thinking or how he felt about me because he communicated his intentions and feelings clearly and often. I knew he was attracted to me, enjoyed my company, and appreciated God's work in my life. Because his words and actions were consistent, I found it easy to follow his lead.

Our dates were a blast! He creatively planned times together that we would enjoy. During the two months we dated, he never took me to a movie—that was much too "ordinary" for his style. For the first time in years, I really enjoyed being taken out on a date. Our talks were deep in the sense that they usually included theological discussions, which I loved because it challenged me to think about my walk with Christ.

If Cinderella were living today, and she was a Christian, I think her story would have been a lot like what I experienced during those months. It was so good that it didn't seem real. There were times when I felt like I was in a movie…the lead actress who was being swept off her feet by the leading man. Yet, this story didn't end with the characters riding off into the sunset to live "happily ever after."

I glanced at the clock…again. Only 15 more minutes before he was due to arrive. *This will be over soon,* I thought with a sigh of relief. I had to tell him that I knew we didn't need to continue dating. I knew he would take it hard, and I dreaded telling him. *If he doesn't understand my reasons,* I contemplated, *then I can't blame him.* I was struggling to understand what was happening.

I had wrestled the whole week before about whether we should continue dating. I had prayed over and over about it. Although I enjoyed his company, my heart did not feel a growing intimacy with him. If we continued dating, I would need to be more vulnerable about myself. I just didn't have a peace that God wanted me to be vulnerable in this relationship.

The decision seemed obvious, but there was one thing I couldn't rationalize. When I was around this man, I would often get butterflies—that tingly feeling in your stomach that seems to make all your other senses shut down. I asked a man who was like a brother to me if he got butterflies when he was dating his wife. He said, "Yes, all the time." His response only confused me more. I questioned, *If this is not the man for me, then why do I get butterflies when I'm with him?*

Knock. Knock.

Oh, he's here.

I jumped up to get the door.

We sat down on the couch. I saw no point in wasting time and got to the heart of the matter quickly. Our time together went pretty much as I thought. At one point in the conversation, he expressed with great emotion, "It's hard to sit in front of the most beautiful woman in the world and want to spend the rest of my life with her and you know you can't."

Then, it happened! I got butterflies in my stomach!

Eventually, our talk ended...and so did our dating relationship. But, that wasn't the end of the story. God chose to teach me more through this man's presence in my life. After he left that evening, I journaled: *There I was, sitting across from a man I knew I didn't love. He said I was the most beautiful woman in the world. And I felt butterflies! Interesting that a man I'm no longer attracted to can say those words and inspire such a response in me. Those words must touch a weak spot, a vulnerable place in me. Randy (my pastor) always says, "Love is a choice, not a feeling." Maybe there is more truth in that saying than I realize.*

The day after the "we shouldn't continue dating talk," I felt especially burdened. I spent my lunch hour in my car, reading my Bible, journaling, and praying. I prayed for my brother in Christ. I meditated on the question my mentor would pose to me whenever a man began pursuing me: "Do you like him, or do you like the *attention* he's giving you?"

Huh. (Deep breath...exhale.)
I liked the attention he gave me. Huh!!!

This man's adoring compliments, sweet notes, and unwavering pursuit of me fit my perception of what it should feel like to be loved by a soulmate. The attention he showered on me made me feel noticed, appreciated, adored...and loved. I wasn't "in love." I was allowing this man to satisfy my need for love. Greater surrender of my heart was needed to keep running the path.

Surrender

A place exists deep inside each of our hearts, a place as deep as Jesus' journey into the Garden of Gethsemane. A place as deep as Jesus' desire to commune with God that night in the garden. When we accept Jesus as our Lord and Savior, we give our hearts to Him. We surrender our lives to Him. But in that precious moment, do we truly comprehend the meaning of ultimate surrender to Him?

Mark 14:3
"And while he (Jesus) was at Bethany in the house of Simon the leper, as he was reclining at table, a woman came with an alabaster flask of ointment of pure nard, very costly, and she

broke the flask and poured it over his head."

The woman's alabaster flask (or more commonly referred to as the alabaster box) was more than a container filled with valuable ointment. The alabaster box was part of this woman's dowry. In Jesus' day, a dowry was the money, goods, clothing, and estate a woman brought to a marriage. The woman in the story had reached the age to marry and was waiting for a husband. Her family purchased the alabaster box for her and had filled it with precious ointment. The size of the box and the worth of the ointment correlated to her family's wealth. On the day that a young man asked for her to marry him, the custom of the time would lead the young woman to break the alabaster box at the young man's feet. The purpose was to anoint him and show him tremendous honor.

The woman in the Bible story found Jesus worthy of such honor that she broke her alabaster box for him. She gave up her most valuable possession to Jesus. She gave up her opportunity to break her alabaster box at an earthly bridegroom's feet in order to anoint Jesus for burial. This was a profound sacrifice on the woman's part. Jesus had not yet died for her sins. He had not yet risen from the dead. She still chose to give her all to Him. Her actions reflected a heart that loved Jesus as her Heavenly Bridegroom. Her actions revealed a heart that was surrendered Him. She loved Him above all things, above all people, above herself, above her will.

The disciples scrutinized her gift. "Why was the ointment wasted like that? For this ointment could have been sold for more than three hundred denarii and given to the poor. And they scolded her" (Mark 14:4-5). Her heart for Jesus was not always appreciated and respected in the eyes of other people, but her heart was always appreciated and respected by the One who mattered most.

Mark 14:6-3
"But Jesus said, 'Leave her alone. Why do you trouble her? She has done a beautiful thing to me. For you always have the poor with you, and whenever you want, you can do good for them. But you will not always have me. She has done what she could; she has anointed my body beforehand for burial. And truly, I say to you, wherever the gospel is proclaimed in the whole world, what she has done will be told in memory of her.'"

The woman gave Jesus her whole heart. The disciples (who were fellow Christ-followers) rebuked her adoration for Jesus. But her Heavenly Bridegroom stood up for her. He fought for her.

Think about it!

Revelation 5:11-12 describes what will happen in the end of the BIG Story:
"Then I looked, and I heard around the throne and the living creatures and the elders the voice of many angels, numbering myriads of myriads and thousands of thousands, saying with a loud voice, 'Worthy is the Lamb who was slain, to receive power and wealth and wisdom and might and honor and glory and blessing!'"

Jesus, the One worthy to receive all honor, glory, blessing—and all that we have to give—honored the woman whose heart was surrendered to Him. The story of the woman with the Alabaster Box reminds us that we hold a part in the BIG Story.

1—Are you willing to let God write your storyline, or are you still trying to write it?

2—Are you holding on to *your* plan, or are you holding on to His promise "to give you a future and a hope?"

Pray about it!

Psalm 37:4
"Delight yourself in the LORD, and he will give you the desires of your heart."

If you're ready, journey to the deepest place in your heart. Open it up. Close your eyes, and in your mind's eye, visualize that deep place opening wide. Open it up completely, and surrender that most tender part of who you are to God. Let His love spring forth to fill the emptiness. Let all of your desires for *attention, acceptance,* and *adoration* be filled by Him.

Colossians 2:9-10
"For in him the whole fullness of deity dwells bodily, and you have been filled in him, who is the head of all rule and authority."

Take a moment to listen. You just might hear the song of your heart.

54 - I Belong to Him!

M ary was a young woman who was walking the path towards marriage. She was engaged to a man named Joseph, from the lineage of David. Angel Gabriel visited Mary and affirmed she was part of the BIG Story, a very important part! "And behold, you will conceive in your womb and bear a son, and you shall call his name Jesus. He will be great and will be called the Son of the Most High. And the Lord God will give to him the throne of his father David, and he will reign over the house of Jacob forever, and of his kingdom there will be no end" (Luke 1:31-33).

Mary respectfully questioned the Plan:
"How will this be, since I am a virgin?" –Luke 1:34

Gabriel answered,
"The Holy Spirit will come upon you, and the power of the Most High will overshadow you; therefore the child to be born will be called holy—the Son of God." –Luke 1:35

God had written a storyline for Mary that was much BIGGER than the little story she had in mind. It would be a miracle many wouldn't understand. They would see a pregnant and unmarried woman and think the worst of her...and of Joseph. Her family, friends, and family members would misunderstand her, judge her, and even reject her. What about Joseph? Would he believe her and support God's calling in her life, or would he abandon her? Either way, the man she loved would suffer hardship. Embracing God's Plan would mean extreme sacrifice.

What was Mary's response?
"Behold, I am the servant of the Lord; let it be to me according to your word." –Luke 1:38

Mary could have resisted God's Plan. She could have "stretched out" her hand to hold on to Joseph, to her family, to her reputation, and to her own dreams for the future. Instead, she surrendered herself to God's Story. "I belong to Him!" she proclaimed. Mary's proclamation to follow God was more than words. It was a desire of her heart.

A surrendered heart embraces God's will with joy, no matter what the cost.

Mary's response revealed that she surrendered her heart to God. She believed in God and lived her life to please Him. She was familiar with Him and His ways. God sent the angel Gabriel to comfort her and encourage her, providing what she needed to walk by faith.

After Mary gave birth to Jesus, shepherds, notified by an angel, found Mary, Joseph and baby Jesus in a manger in the middle of nowhere…and worshipped Him. Luke 2:19 says, "Mary treasured up all these things, pondering them in her heart."

Later in Luke 2, it says Joseph and Mary were astonished when they found 12-year-old Jesus holding His own in a wisdom-filled conversation with teachers and doctors. Verse 51 says, "And his mother treasured up all these things in her heart."

God used Mary's life to radically and eternally impact the world! Through Mother Eve, sin was birthed along with a curse that fell on all future generations. Through Mary, a Savior was born who would defeat sin, set us free from the curse, and become the perfect PATH that would lead us to eternal relationship with God! One woman reached out to take hold of her own desires. The other woman surrendered her heart to God and delighted in doing His will.

Psalm 37:4
"Delight yourself in the LORD, and he will give you the desires of your heart."

Another story of surrender

The path we run is filled with opportunities to surrender our hearts to God. Like Mary, we can choose to open our hearts to God, letting go of our plans and fully embracing His plans.

Philippians 3:7-11
"But whatever gain I had, I counted as loss for the sake of Christ. Indeed, I count everything as loss because of the surpassing worth of knowing Christ Jesus my Lord. For his sake I have suffered the loss of all things and count them as rubbish, in order that I may gain Christ and be found in him, not having a righteousness of my own that comes from the law, but that which comes through faith in Christ, the righteousness from God that depends on faith—that I may know him and the power of his resurrection, and may share his sufferings, becoming like him in his death, that by any means possible I may attain the resurrection from the dead."

I prayed, "God, into Your hands, I commit my dating relationships." I opened up that deep place in my heart and surrendered it to God, and He gave me the desires of my heart. I kept running—eyes on Jesus, and this is how surrender looked farther down the path:

As I prayerfully completed homework assignments for meetings with my counselor, I discovered that I was protecting myself in dating relationships to an unhealthy degree. My behavior was influenced by a subconscious belief that no one in my life viewed me or my heart as worthy of protecting. As a result. I tried to be so emotionally strong that I was actually taking on the strength that a father would demonstrate in protecting his teenage daughter. This overdone trait was a heavy burden and caused me to attract and date several emotionally unhealthy guys.

When it came to dating and my future marriage, I wanted to be *free* to be the woman God created me to be and make a difference in the world. In my heart, I knew that I needed to stop overprotecting myself, open my heart even more to the community of believers around me, and invite others to help me where I was weak.

God gave me the idea to have dating mentors. I found a married couple who agreed to come alongside me and provide spiritual support and accountability in my dating relationships. I met Jim and Kathy when they served as volunteers for a church event I helped organize. Serving as my dating mentors basically meant that Jim and Kathy took on the protective role parents assume when their twenty-something daughter brings a guy home for them to meet. It would have been more ideal to have my parents fill this role. Unfortunately, my parents were not strong believers, and the spiritual aspect of what mentors would provide is what I needed most.

I asked for Jim and Kathy to provide advice about guys. If there was a guy I was considering dating, I wanted them to meet the guy and help me discern his character. I believed it would be especially helpful to gain the insights and wisdom of an older, Christian man. By the second date with a guy, I typically knew whether I wanted to date him or not. I decided that I would not continue dating the guy past the third date until he met Jim and Kathy AND they approved of us dating.

Jim and Kathy met with me regularly, which was an amazing commitment when you consider that they have three children of their own, two of whom were of dating age at the time. It is an incredible testimony to God's love and how He provides for our needs.

It's important to mention that when Jim and Kathy became my dating mentors, I was 29 years old! Getting dating mentors was a courageous act of surrender to God. I did have this thought, *Doing this may mean that I never marry because guys might not want to meet with my mentors.* In the same breath, I concluded, *If a guy is man enough to meet my mentors, then maybe he's man enough for me to date.*

After getting dating mentors, the first guy to come along was Will. We had been good friends for five years. In years past, we had actually been on a few dates that never led to anything more. Will and I found ourselves drawn once again to the idea of dating. Will shared that he wanted to pursue a dating relationship with me. I told him about Jim and Kathy and asked if he would meet with them. He firmly replied, "No." We never went on another date. I kept running the path—eyes on Jesus!

Think about it!

1—When it comes to surrendering your heart to God in guy-girl relationships, what is the next step?

For you, surrendering your heart to God might mean sitting down with your parents and asking them to be involved or more involved in protecting, helping, and advising you. It might mean that you only date in groups. You might decide to wait until college to date. You might need to take a step back from friends who are influencing you to move away from God. Remember, you can think out of the box—you don't have to go the way of the world, or the way of Aimee, or the way of any other person! Your goal is to go God's way!

Pray about it!

Let these verses inspire your prayer time.

Philippians 3:13-14
"But one thing I do: forgetting what lies behind and straining forward to what lies ahead, I press on toward the goal for the prize of the upward call of God in Christ Jesus."

Matthew 6:33
"But seek first the Kingdom of God and his righteousness, and all these things will be added to you."

Luke 1:38
"Behold, I am the servant of the Lord; let it be to me according to your word."

Psalm 37:4
"Delight yourself in the LORD, and he will give you the desires of your heart."

Luke 2:19
"Mary treasured up all these things, pondering them in her heart."

55 - Heart Treasures

P hilippians 3:8-11
"Indeed, I count everything as loss because of the surpassing worth of knowing Christ Jesus my Lord. For his sake I have suffered the loss of all things and count them as rubbish, in order that I may gain Christ and be found in him, not having a righteousness of my own that comes from the law, but that which comes through faith in Christ, the righteousness from God that depends on faith—that I may know him and the power of his resurrection, and may share his sufferings, becoming like him in his death, that by any means possible I may attain the resurrection from the dead."

As a 15-year-old girl, dating was a new, white canvas ready for me to record on it the multi-colored pursuits of life, love, and happiness. I anxiously awaited an opportunity to dab my paintbrush in the palette of many colors and begin filling that canvas. What vibrant, joyfully intricate designs would find a place on my canvas? What sorrowful brushstrokes would fill pure, white spaces with darkness?

I could have never anticipated the joys and sorrows that would fill my canvas.

As a 29-year-old woman, the most spectacular design took form on my canvas. I just stood there, eyes glued to the canvas, marveling at the sight before me. It started with one radical red stroke of the brush, which curved around to the left and swooped down, then rising up on the right, and curving downward to meet its beginning...a heart. And faithfully, day after day, spirals of brilliant color danced out from that first mark...

Swirls of LOVE in hues of magenta...
Royal blue twists of GRACE...
Lavender loops of FORGIVENESS ...
Sea green waves of REDEMPTION flowing forth.

Beautiful buds popped up, complementing the impressive weave of swirls, twists, loops, and waves. There were...

JOY buds colored lemon yellow...
Kiwi green blossoms of KINDNESS...

Blooms of SELF-CONTROL in golden peach…
Plum-painted PEACE buds…
Berry blue blossoms of GENTLENESS…
Strawberry red LOVE buds…
PATIENCE blooms in pineapple yellow…
GOODNESS buds brushed in grape green…
FAITHFULNESS florets formed in vivid tangerine.

As I admired this gorgeous bouquet bursting across my canvas, I was pleasantly surprised when pretty petals of pure PURPOSE and powerful POTENTIAL opened up!

All of the bright petals, buds, spirals, loops, waves, twists, and swirls originated from that first stroke of red that formed a heart. I leaned in to take a closer look.

It was a heart that symbolized the heart of the Savior surrendered in the Garden of Gethsemane. The heart that beat for us to know the glory of the Father. The heart that bled for us on the cross. The heart that paved the perfect PATH for us to enjoy relationship with God forever.

It was symbolic of the heart that believed in Jesus. The heart that became ONE with Him. The heart that found its Heavenly Husband, surrendered all to Him, was made complete in Him, and sprung forth with the colors of new life.

Then, I smelled the sweetest scent! "But thanks be to God, who in Christ always leads us in triumphal procession, and through us spreads the fragrance of the knowledge of him everywhere. For we are the aroma of Christ to God among those who are being saved and among those who are perishing" (2 Corinthians 2:14-15).

Like Mary, I treasured up all these things!

On the path

After Jim and Kathy became my dating members, the first guy to come along didn't want to meet them and ran the other way. Steve was the next guy to come along. When I asked him if he would meet with my dating mentors, he was more than willing. Steve and I had been friends a while. In fact, months before when I shared with him that I was looking for dating mentors, he prayed for God to help me in my search! Steve was the first guy to meet Jim and Kathy…and the last guy I brought to them!

Over the next few months, another image found its place on my canvas. It was the outline of a man and woman, holding hands, and running to the heart. They were helping each other make it to the end!

Like Mary, I treasured up all these things!

Perspective

Fifteen-year-old me waited just short of fifteen years for God to provide an earthly husband. God graciously blessed me with a loving *and* loveable husband and a very sweet, loving marriage. I consider both a gift from God. I also consider all of those years of singleness a gift. I enjoy being married far more than I enjoyed being single. Yet, if you asked me which one was the GREATEST gift—singleness or marriage—I couldn't choose one over the other. God uniquely used singleness to point me to Jesus. Now, He uniquely uses marriage to point me to Jesus. You see, Jesus is the true gift.

The journey, with all of its ups and downs, is worth it as long as Jesus becomes your perfect PATH. Jesus is the GREATEST gift.

Think about it!

My friend, your canvas was meant to be a breathtaking work of art, painted by a God who loves and delights in you. Let Him paint your canvas. Surrender your heart to Him— the One who gave His ALL to You, and wait with eager anticipation!

1 Corinthians 2:9
"But, as it is written, 'What no eye has seen, nor ear heard, nor the heart of man imagined, what God has prepared for those who love him.'"

My prayer for you!

Heavenly Father,
I pray for the woman reading this prayer right now. Help her to know that she is loved, deeply and completely loved. Show her how wide and long and high and deep is the love of Jesus for her (Ephesians 3:18). Build her relationship with You. Make it sweet, strong, and delightful.

Break the curse passed down to her from Mother Eve; do not allow it to have a stronghold on her heart and life. If there is another sin that is holding her back from drawing near to You, give her the faith to claim the forgiveness offered to her through the shed blood of Christ on the cross. Sin has no power over her. "It is finished" (John 19:30).

Guard her mind. When she starts to become too focused on the situations and challenges of the day, remind her that she is part of a BIGGER Story. Don't allow her to settle for living her little story. Guard her mind from believing lies from the evil one. Teach her to dream the dreams You have for her. Guard her heart from impure situations and unrighteous people. Keep her from seeking attention, acceptance, and adoration from others. Give her the faith to trust You as I AM, the One who satisfies her heart and fills her cup to overflowing!

Develop in Your beloved daughter the "imperishable beauty of a gentle and quiet spirit which in Your sight is precious," and form her into the woman of excellence you created her to be (1 Peter 3:4). Grant her tremendous desire to seek out Your truth, profound understanding of it, and a deep love for Your Word. Empower her to apply truth in her life.

Let her heart beat for You and for Your glory. Reveal her role in the BIG Story, and anoint her to live out your HIGHER Vision and Mission. May the fruit of Your Spirit—love, joy, peace, patience, kindness, goodness, faithfulness, gentleness, and self-control— overflow into all of her life and relationships. May she be the "pleasing aroma of Christ among those who are being saved and those who are perishing" (2 Corinthians 2:14-16). In the Precious Name of Jesus, Amen.

"Love by Design"—A CREATIVE CHALLENGE!
If you feel inspired to design a new canvas, then go for it! I can't wait to see your creative work on social!

Afterword:

The couple on the canvas

For those who would like to know a little more about the love story God wrote for me, here you go!

How we met

Steve and I met at Perimeter Church, where we were both on staff. He joined staff a year after me. Around that time, my roommate unexpectedly decided to move home and save money to get married with about a month left on our apartment lease. I wasn't able to find a roommate and a place to live that quickly, so I moved back home with my parents temporarily. They lived an hour and a half from my work. Steve lived in the same town as my parents, so we decided to carpool. We carpooled until I found a place to live, which was about three weeks.

Through our conversations in the car, I got to know him. I thought Steve was a great guy. I was in the aftermath of a breakup, had no interest in dating, and didn't think twice of Steve as a potential date. He didn't view me like that, either. We would occasionally run into each other at work and would stop and chat for a few minutes.

Two years later

I moved out of my apartment and into a friend's townhome. Steve was one of three guys who helped me move. At one point in the moving process, I was with my dad and the guys. Steve and I were the main ones talking when I suddenly noticed my dad giving me a funny look. I realized that I was grinning like a Cheshire cat as I talked with Steve! This was the first time I thought I might like him as more than a friend! It was like blinders were falling off my eyes.

A month later

Steve was eating lunch with his friend, Jerry, and told him that he was spending time with a friend (i.e. me) that night. Jerry asked where he was taking me. Steve replied, "Dante's Down the Hatch" (a very nice restaurant). Jerry retorted, "Dude, that's a date!" At that moment, Steve realized it was a date, and he became nervous! He left lunch early to prepare for the date. Because he had decided that he would only date to marry, he wanted to discern quickly if there should be a second date. He came up with questions to ask me on the date—enough questions to fill two letter size pages!

BTW, I knew all along it was a date!

When Steve came to my door, he looked so handsome! He was a gentleman and opened the car door for me. When he got in, I could tell he was nervous. He shared, "I don't know how you are viewing this. For me, this is a date. I want you to know that is my intention. I'm telling you this in hopes that I can be somewhat normal during this date."

I loved his honesty! I was so tired of guys playing games with me, and Steve's honesty and leadership were so refreshing. I think he won a little of my heart in that moment!

Dinner was wonderful, and Steve's company was even better! We laughed a lot, and he asked me a LOT of questions on a variety of topics from life, love, and other mysteries to theology. During the date, I had no idea he had a list of questions! I loved that he asked me all those questions. I had gone out with so many guys who talked about themselves and had big egos. I appreciated that Steve drew out my heart and honestly shared his own heart. The questions were appropriate, and I felt safe with him.

The day after the date

My friend, McKenzie asked me, "On a scale of 1 to 10, how was the date?" I thought for a minute and enthusiastically replied, "It was a perfect 10!" It was my first perfect 10 date.

More questions

This incredible man who gave me a perfect 10 date left me with a difficult question to consider. Remember the story of staff prayer where two unmarried coworkers confessed to having sex that resulted in a pregnancy? I said the guy's name was Brad, but his name was actually Steve. Now, you see where I'm going with this.

For dessert, Steve took me to the Cheesecake Factory where he communicated that he wanted to date me to pursue marriage. He made sure I understood that marrying him would mean I would take on a stepchild, child support for almost two decades, would probably need to work to offset child support, and other things that come with that type of situation. I appreciated his honesty, but WOW! I felt overwhelmed and scared!

After our date, I distanced myself from Steve for a while to think through all he had shared. He believed that was the end of our story.

I shared my thoughts and feelings with a mentor. As you know, my mentor had supported me through some unhealthy dating relationships and was concerned that Steve might be an emotionally-empty-cup kind of guy. She asked, "Why are you attracted to a man like that?"

I seriously considered her question. "Why am I attracted to a guy like that?" As I analyzed Steve's character, I came up with a list of godly qualities. When I heard Steve confess in staff prayer, I believe God was giving me a unique opportunity to observe Steve's character. At the time, I had no idea God's Plan would have us marry one day. I saw a brother in Christ who was going through one of the hardest trials of his life, and he was sincerely repentant. In the days that followed, Steve displayed much character in seeking God and submitting to accountability partners and church elders. Though that was NOT AT ALL how I *wished* for my future husband's character to be revealed to me, I had *prayed* for a man with that depth of character. (A man who loves God—#1 on my wish list for a man!)

As I pondered my mentor's question, I tried hard to come up with character flaws in Steve that would keep me from dating him, but none came to mind. I then asked myself, *Why wouldn't I be attracted to a man like that?!!*

Though I encountered many people who judged Steve for having a child outside of marriage, I believe God allowed me to see Steve as God sees him—a man full of purpose, character, and potential. A man who has been forgiven. Every child is a God-given gift, and God used the circumstances surrounding the child to shape Steve into a man after His own heart (like God did for David in the Bible.) If I married Steve, I knew I *would not* get a husband who was a virgin or had a clean slate. I *would* get a husband who had experienced

God's forgiveness and grace in a deep, deep way and who would extend grace to me. (A man who understands grace—#2 on my list!)

It took about a month of praying and pondering before I was confident God wanted me to date Steve and explore the idea of marrying him. At that point, the ball was in my court to communicate that to Steve.

We went on a second date, and it was another perfect 10 date! The next step was for him to meet my dating mentors, Jim and Kathy. I wasn't the only one who had accountability in the area of dating. Steve had determined that he wouldn't enter a dating relationship unless his dad, two mentors, and the head of our Human Resources department at work gave him approval. (The HR department had made a policy stating staff members couldn't date.) EVERYONE gave us their full blessing—evidence God was in it!

Let the dating begin!

We began dating when I was 29 years old, and Steve was 27. Our mentors continued to play a key role in our lives and dating relationship.

Two months into dating, Steve became extremely sick and had to be hospitalized. I went to the hospital every day. He was very open to me caring for him, which came as a surprise to his mom because he was a very independent son. The fact that he was comfortable with me helping him was big.

Steve continued to get worse, and it looked like he was going to die. I remember walking into work, my mind focused on the reality that Steve might die. I felt incredible sadness at the thought of losing him. I tearfully prayed, *God, I don't want to lose him. But if I do, thank You for giving me the time I've had with him.*

A few days later, Steve took a miraculous turn and recovered! To this day, we don't know for certain what made him sick. That experience made me realize how much I loved him.

Several months later, I spoke twice on the topic of *"Dating"* to girls in the high school ministry. Steve prayed for me and was super supportive. If you remember, I wanted a guy who would support me in what God called me to do. (A man who will support God's calling in my life—#3 on my list!)

Fast forward a few more months. Someone close to me betrayed me and attacked my character in hopes of ending my relationship with Steve. It was an especially troubling situation for me. I trusted God to fight for me. Not only did God fight for me, but He also had Steve fight for me! If you remember, I wanted a man who would fight for me like God did. (A man who will fight for me like God does—#4 on my list!)

As I dated Steve, I observed a lot about his character. He was a strong leader with a servant's heart, humble, and easygoing. His character was always consistent. (A man who does not have anger issues—#5 on my list!) It became clear that I loved Steve and that he would make a great husband for me. I wasn't sure if I was ready to become an instant mom; I also didn't know exactly how that would look. As you and I have learned from my friends who shared their stories for this book, each situation is unique and holds uncertainty.

During the eight months Steve and I dated (before getting engaged), we faced a variety of intense trials. No matter what we faced, we communicated well and resolved conflict well. As we persevered through challenges together, we emerged stronger as a couple and in our relationships with God. I realized the conflict we encountered was always with others outside of our relationship, and Steve and I were truly a team. God gave me confidence that Steve and I could do anything with His help. God gave me unexplainable peace and faith to move forward.

Some "Firsts"

My first "I love you" with Steve was special. I knew I was saying I love you to my future husband. My first kiss with Steve was special, too. It meant, "I love you." It had been more than five years since I had kissed a guy. When God says He makes us new creations, He really means it!

Yes!

We went through a premarital course at our church, and Jim and Kathy were our course mentors! After dating eight months, Steve and I got engaged! Three months later, we married! I was 30 years old. Three months later, I turned 31 years old.

Community

Steve and I considered eloping because we didn't have much money to put towards the wedding. The only thing that made us question the idea of eloping was our community of friends and family. So many people, including mentors and friends, had loved us through the ups and downs of our lives. God used them to help us become better people, and we wanted to celebrate our marriage with them.

While Steve and I prayed about whether to elope, we didn't let on to friends. Out of nowhere and before we were engaged, several friends started telling us they wanted to contribute to our wedding! Friends offered to design and pay for our wedding invitations, address our wedding invitations, pay for the stamps, make wedding decorations, design the printed program, cater food for the reception, set-up special lighting, etc.. Moms of the young girls I discipled bought my wedding cake, helped me shop for wedding supplies, and threw me bridal showers!

Steve and I decided to marry at our church, surrounded by our community. The girls who were in my discipleship group were my junior bridesmaids! They were 11 years old at the time! I chose to ditch the traditional bouquet toss. Every woman who was single received a red rose at our wedding along with an encouraging poem to remind them of God's love for them.

Acknowledgments

God—I'll always be Your girl. Thank You for redeeming my soul through Jesus! Thank You for continually healing my heart and taking the awful mess that was my love life and redeeming it into a beautiful story that honors You and helps others grow closer to You. Thank You for making writing times some of the sweetest experiences on earth. This is Your book, and it's a book of grace. May You be glorified through every word.

Steve Simmons—You were worth the wait! Thank you for loving me well and always supporting me in whatever God has called me to do. Thank you for believing God could do great things through me, for praying for me/the book/the readers, for encouraging me to trust God in His timing, being my theological proofreader, for always keeping my coffee mug and water cup filled through countless hours of writing, and for building my website! For God to give me a husband who loves me so deeply—who gave of himself throughout the writing of the book and has helped me grow closer to God—is a profound gift. I love you more than words and my catchy and slightly off-key songs about you could ever express!

Carolyn Bahr—my first spiritual mentor! Thank you for helping me survive the roller coasters of dating and singleness. Thank you for praying HARD for me, loving me well, and allowing God to use you as an instrument of healing. I feel this book reveals the beauty of your investment in my life!

Jim and Kathy Stewart—my dating mentors! Thank you for sacrificially sharing your time, love, and wisdom to support a young woman who desired to honor God in her dating relationships. Thank you for loving Steve, too, and going above and beyond *again* to walk alongside us as marriage mentors. Thank you for loving God so deeply and for impacting my life so profoundly. The world needs more people like you!

Carolyn Bahr, Cheryl Flanagan, Linda Lee, Mary Ann Taylor—the Fantastic Four and first prayer warriors for the book! Your prayers were woven into the pages of this book and carried my heart to God over and over again. I'm certain your prayers will continue to carry readers to Him.

Randy Pope—a man after God's own heart and my pastor through the writing of this book! Thank you for valuing God's Word above your own words, boldly teaching what it means to have a right view of God, of self, and fellow man. You've taught me much about grace. You have always cared FAR more about lifting up Jesus than lifting up your own name, and your example has impacted my heart in profoundly wonderful ways.

Carol Pope—a woman more precious than jewels who opens her mouth with wisdom and teaches kindness (Proverbs 31:10, 26)! Thank you for loving God, often sacrificially. In loving God, you have modeled for me what it means to be a godly woman, wife, and mother.

Alice Arraez, Kim DeGuido, Julie Dudley, Julie Grant, Mallori Hamilton, Kelley Hardy, Lisa Jones, Katherine Keller, Barbara Mansfield, Leslie Mansfield—Proverbs 31 Women! Thank you for your passion for God, your desire to see young women know they are loved and valued by God, and your belief in this book. Your love, prayers, and support made the book even more beautiful!

Judith McNeely, Olivia Siniard, Kaitlin Fowler—cherished sisters in Christ! Thank you for sharing your inspiring stories of adoption and entrusting me to carry them well in the book. May God use your stories to touch longing hearts and save the lives of babies who don't yet have a voice.

Laura Dudman, Jordyn Fulbright, Katie Henrich, Ciara Loperano, and Whitney Schremmer—the first group to go through the book! Thank you for your excitement to be a part of the group, honest sharing, for getting mad when I was treated badly in a story (so sweet!), and for your feedback, which led to an extensive edit that made the book more impactful.

Abby Fisher—May you "act justly, love mercy, and walk humbly with your God," experiencing the awe and adventure of a love story written by the Author of love (Micah 6:8).

Bill Wood—the definition of book lover and encourager! Thank you for your willingness to read the book and provide valued feedback and for always encouraging me to write.

Tina Riemer—editor extraordinaire! Thank you for editing the first version of the book, your generosity, and friendship!

Mallori Hamilton—devoted and talented friend! Thank you for designing the book's beautiful cover! The image bears the mark of a God who brings hearts alive, makes colors more vivid, love songs sweeter, and words on a page inspired. It also bears the mark of your sweet relationship with Him!

Ben May—creative, encouraging friend! Thank you for helping me wrap up the paperback (literally) with a fully designed cover that inspires such joy when I see it!

All of the amazing women I've discipled—You've helped me see Jesus more clearly, experience His love more deeply, and helped me develop my voice in sharing His Truth. Always *Aim for Him* first, and keep developing your voices and God-given talents. The world needs to hear and see what your hearts treasure!

Notes

[1] "content." Def. 1. Dictionary.com Unabridged. Random House, Inc. 04 Apr. 2014. <Dictionary.com http://dictionary.reference.com/browse/content>.

[2] Quote taken from Passion and Purity: Learning to Bring Your Love Life Under Christ's Control by Elisabeth Elliot. Copyright © 1984, © 2002 by Fleming H. Revell, a division of Baker Book House Company. www.bakerbookhouse.com

[3] "purity." Def. 1, 4, 5. Dictionary.com Unabridged. Random House, Inc. 04 Apr. 2014. <Dictionary.com http://dictionary.reference.com/browse/purity>.

[4] "attention." Def. 5. Dictionary.com Unabridged. Random House, Inc. 04 Apr. 2014. <Dictionary.com http://dictionary.reference.com/browse/attention>.

[5] "acceptance." Def. 2. Dictionary.com Unabridged. Random House, Inc. 04 Apr. 2014 . <Dictionary.com http://dictionary.reference.com/browse/acceptance>.

[6] "adoration." Def. 1, 3. Dictionary.com Unabridged. Random House, Inc. 04 Apr. 2014. <Dictionary.com http://dictionary.reference.com/browse/adoration>.

[7] "perspective." Def. 1. Collins English Dictionary - Complete & Unabridged 10th Edition . HarperCollins Publishers. 04 Apr. 2014. <Dictionary.com http://dictionary.reference.com/browse/perspective>.

[8] "glorify." Def. 2. Dictionary.com Unabridged. Random House, Inc. 04 Apr. 2014. <Dictionary.com http://dictionary.reference.com/browse/glorify>.

[9] Idea taken from Matthew Henry's Commentary on the Whole Bible by Matthew Henry. Copyright © 1991 Henrickson Publishers, Inc.

[10} Idea taken from Matthew Henry's Commentary on the Whole Bible by Matthew Henry. Copyright © 1991 Henrickson Publishers, Inc.

[11} Idea taken from Matthew Henry's Commentary on the Whole Bible by Matthew Henry. Copyright © 1991 Henrickson Publishers, Inc.

[12] Quote taken from Sermon by Randy Pope, Perimeter Church, Johns Creek, GA. www.perimeter.org/messages

[13] "desire." Definition from The Complete Word Study Dictionary. Copyright © 1992 AMG International, Inc. Revised 1993.

[14] Quote taken from Boundaries: When to Say YES, When to Say No, To Take Control of Your Life by Dr. Henry Cloud and Dr. John Townsend. Copyright © 1992 by Henry Cloud and John Townsend. www.zondervan.com

[15] Idea taken from Matthew Henry's Commentary on the Whole Bible by Matthew Henry. Copyright © 1991 Henrickson Publishers, Inc.

[16] Quote taken from Silence of Adam: Becoming Men of Courage in a World of Chaos by Dr. Larry Crabb with Don Hudson and Al Andrews. Copyright © 1995 by Dr. Lawrence J. Crabb, Jr., Ph.D., P.A., dba, Institute of Biblical Counseling. www.zondervan.com

[17] Quote taken from Boundaries: When to Say YES, When to Say No, To Take Control of Your Life by Dr. Henry Cloud and Dr. John Townsend. Copyright © 1992 by Henry Cloud and John Townsend. www.zondervan.com

[18] Quote taken from Let Me Be a Woman by Elisabeth Elliot. Copyright © 1976 by Tyndale House Publishers. www.tyndale.com

[19] Quote taken from The Answer: Putting an End to the Search for Life Significance by Randy Pope. Copyright © 2005, © 2007 by Life-on-Life Resources, a Division of Life-on-Life Ministries. www.perimeter.org/lifeonlife

[20] "cast." Def. 1. Dictionary.com Unabridged. Random House, Inc. 04 Apr. 2014. <Dictionary.com http://dictionary.reference.com/browse/glorify>.

[21} "cast." Definition from The Complete Word Study Dictionary. Copyright © 1992 AMG International, Inc. Revised 1993.

[22] "share." Def. 7. Dictionary.com Unabridged. Random House, Inc. 04 Apr. 2014. <Dictionary.com http://dictionary.reference.com/browse/glorify>.

[23] Idea taken from Matthew Henry's Commentary on the Whole Bible by Matthew Henry. Copyright © 1991 Henrickson Publishers, Inc.

[24] Quote taken from Sermon by Randy Pope, Perimeter Church, Johns Creek, GA. www.perimeter.org/messages

[25] Idea taken from Matthew Henry's Commentary on the Whole Bible by Matthew Henry. Copyright © 1991 Henrickson Publishers, Inc.

[26] Idea taken from The Book of Romance by Tommy Nelson. Copyright © 1998 by Thomas Nelson, Inc. www.thomasnelson.com

About Aimee

Aimee is an author, speaker, discipler of young women, and the creator of *Aim for Him* blog at *AimeeSimmons.com*. She disciples and encourages young women to aim for Him first, embrace abundant life with Jesus, and share Him with others. She and her husband, Steve, live in Atlanta, Georgia.

Aimee works at Ravi Zacharias International Ministries and has over 20 years of ministry experience working in church and parachurch organizations in the areas of discipleship for children and teens, marketing, and communications.

As a staff member at one of the largest churches in Atlanta, Perimeter Church, she received training in Life-on-Life Missional Discipleship, a ministry of global impact. At Perimeter, she created curricula for children and students, recruited and trained group leaders, discipled young women and girls, served as a speaker, and came alongside families in crisis situations.

The topics she writes about are often inspired by the questions of the young women she disciples. Her creative, honest, and often humorous storytelling and scripture-filled writing style help readers feel like they are sitting across the table with a friend and mentor, enjoying conversation about God, life, love, purpose, potential, and their greatest dreams! Her writing is an arrow that points to God, equipping readers to aim for Him in their daily lives and prayers, and developing a love for His Word along the way!

Her discipleship-focused writings also serve as helpful resources and discussion starters for young women's mentors, small group leaders, discipleship leaders, church and campus ministry staff, and parents.

Website: AimeeSimmons.com
Follow @aimforhimblog on Instagram, Facebook, and Pinterest.

To contact Aimee about writing or speaking: email aimforhim@aimeesimmons.com.

Made in the USA
Monee, IL
02 March 2020